Creating
from the
Spirit

By Dan Wakefield:

NONFICTION

Creating from the Spirit: Living Each Day as a Creative Act

Expect a Miracle: The Miraculous Things
That Happen to Ordinary People

New York in the Fifties

The Story of Your Life: Writing a Spiritual Autobiography

Returning: A Spiritual Journey

All Her Children: The Making of a Soap Opera

Supernation at Peace and War

Between the Lines: A Reporter's Personal Journey

The Addict: An Anthology

Revolt in the South

Island in the City: The World of Spanish Harlem

FICTION

Selling Out

Under the Apple Tree

Home Free

Starting Over

Going All the Way

Creating from the Spirit

LIVING EACH DAY AS A CREATIVE ACT

Dan Wakefield

BALLANTINE BOOKS
NEW YORK

http://www.randomhouse.com

Library of Congress Cataloging-in-Publication Data
Wakefield, Dan.
Creating from the spirit : living each day as a creative act /
Dan Wakefield. — 1st ed.
p.   cm.
Includes index.
ISBN 0-345-37430-4
1. Creative thinking.   2. Creative ability.   I. Title.
BF408.W24   1996
153.3'5—dc20   96-5533

Text design by Holly Johnson

Manufactured in the United States of America

First Edition: June 1996

10 9 8 7 6 5 4 3 2 1

To the memory of my parents,
Brucie Ridge Wakefield and
Benjamin Harbison Wakefield,
who created me, and created a place for me to grow.

And to my wise, kind, and dedicated teachers at wondrous Public School #80 in Indianapolis (like the era itself, the school is no longer extant, the building now a condominium): Roxie Lingle Day, Leta C. Shute, Jane Seal, Grace Grimes, Louise McCarthy, Louise C. Wheeler, and principals Fern Hall and Wallace Montague; and the librarians at the Broad Ripple Branch Library, Miss Hodapp and Mrs. Logan.

With love to them all, and their counterparts today and tomorrow—the parents, librarians, and public school teachers who create the creators—this book is dedicated.

Acknowledgments

First and foremost I thank Cheryl Woodruff, the editor of this book, who pushed me far beyond its original conception; whose greater vision led me to many creative revisions and resulted in a far richer, more useful book than I had originally imagined, and which I am especially proud to send out into the world.

Thanks to Clare Ferraro, for important encouragement, communication, and moral support.

To Rev. Carl Scovel, of King's Chapel in Boston, who taught me how to teach as well as how to keep the faith.

To the people who have enabled me to offer and develop the workshop on creativity in their own institutions: Rev. Florence Pert and Rev. Ann Benefield of Marble Collegiate Church in New York City; Rev. Roger Cowan of the First Unitarian Church of Palm Beach, Florida; Rev. William Tulley of St. Bartholomew's Church in New York City; Rev. Forrest Church of All Souls Unitarian Church in New York City; Paul Valenti of the Omega Institute; Nancy Lunney of the Esalen Institute; Roger Paine of Interface; Rev. John Buchanan of the Fourth Presbyterian Church in Chicago; Robert Reber, dean of Auburn Theological Seminary; Phyllis Pilgrim and Victoria Larrea of Rancho La Puerta, in Tecate, Mexico; as well as those others who have graciously hosted my workshops, in Spiritual Autobiography and

Expecting Miracles throughout the country, in Belfast, Northern Ireland, and at Sing Sing Prison.

To Les Standiford, and my colleagues and students at Florida International University in Miami, for giving me a base and a home.

To Lynn Nesbit, most creative agent and friend, and Tina Bennett, whose creativity and spirit brought me into the "audio" world for the first time.

To my old and always growing circle of friends, who are family.

Contents

Part One

Creation: Works in Progress

Chapter 1

CREATING OUR
DAILY LIVES

Not only are we all created, we all create. We create our lives, and then create stories to explain them, make art and music and drama to make sense of our experience and our world. In our creating, we ask questions, pose answers, and celebrate our humanity. We often forget that every day is a creation—not only for us but by us. We wake to it, step into it, and take our part in creating it by what we think and say and do. We don't regard our daily activities as "creation" or "being creative," it's just "what we do," it's just "life." We take our days for granted, as if they were not moment-by-moment miracles.

To enhance our lives, to give them meaning and color, rhythm and narrative, form and beauty, we engage in activities we call creative—writing, painting, singing, dancing, playing a musical instrument—and we seal them up in a special compartment and keep them isolated from the rest of our experience. We're not alone. Even though professional writers, artists, and musicians think of their work as creative, they usually view that work as a separate realm of doing and being apart from their daily, or "real" lives; so do many creative people in business and medicine, science and technology.

Do you gulp down good food while you talk, read the paper, or watch television without even noticing the taste of what you're eating? Do you "go on automatic," move in a kind of waking coma through the rituals of the day? I know how easy it is to fall into these routinized bad habits because I do it myself, unless I pay attention, bring myself back to wakefulness. Most of us dismiss as boring the nitty-gritty of waking, eating, washing the dishes, carrying on relationships with loved ones, paying the bills, answering the phone, solving problems, mowing the grass, tending the garden, feeding the cat, walking the dog, going to bed and to sleep again, waking anew each morning.

Seeing these ordinary activities as part of our creative lives, related to everything else we do, and seeing all we do as *creation* infuses us with power. If we realize that we create our very reality, then we have a new relationship to it, and we can take more control of our lives. We can alter them and refine them as we would a work of art, like adding more color to a painting, or adding more characters to a story, or changing the end, or perhaps the setting, singing a song in a new key, doing a dance with a different rhythm.

UNLOCKING CREATIVITY

Just as we sometimes feel blocked, and shut off from the flow or animating principal in our "officially" creative activities, we also sometimes get "stuck" in our lives, our relationships. We seem stale, in a rut, burned out, locked up. When it comes to "artistic" creative activities, we know techniques to help us loosen up, refresh, and unblock, but we seldom think to apply those methods to other parts of our experience. Looking upon the whole of our experience as creative frees us from such restrictive, compartmentalized thinking. If we see our lives as art, as story, as dance, and as song, we can apply the techniques of the creative arts to make all our activities more creative, more enlivened by our own spirit—that force which animates each of us and makes us vital.

When we recognize that all aspects of our lives are open to creation, the creative spirit is no longer confined, and is free to flow into new and unexpected areas, bringing change, making us aware, waking us from the numbing sleep of rote behavior, the mechanism of addiction.

"The whole secret of the spiritual life," wrote the English author Gerald Heard, "is just this painful struggle to come awake, to become really conscious. And, conversely, the whole process and technique of evil is to do just the reverse to us; to lull us to sleep, to distract us."

This book is based on that premise, that coming awake is a necessary and essential human struggle. Life is filled with spiritually sleep-inducing distractions and diversions. They account for our sometimes frustrating inattentiveness and impatience; they may lead some of us into a reliance on drugs and alcohol, sexual promiscuity, overeating, anorexia, bulimia, and other attitudes and behaviors that deaden our senses and stifle our spirit, the source of our creativity.

MAKING CREATIVE CHOICES

Every act is a choice, and our choices determine the path we take. I used to scoff at the warning that "soft" drugs like marijuana lead to hard drugs like cocaine or heroin, laughing it off with my friends (we thought we were hip) as "square" propaganda put out by the Establishment. I'd forgotten that back in college I'd quickly progressed from beer to bourbon. It did not dawn on me for a long time that after a while one form of stimulation grew stale and I was ready for bigger, more dangerous nirvanas. One thing really does lead to another; none of our decisions is an isolated act, enclosed in some airtight chamber.

I'm a slow learner. Even after I finally recognized the truth of my experience with steps that led me progressively downward, I didn't see that the same principle operates in the other direction. Just as marijuana may lead to the search for a new high with cocaine or heroin, and beer may be the prelude to bourbon or vodka, so a little exercise leads to a desire for greater use of the body. Once I started using an Exercycle, I found myself getting interested in tai chi and yoga. After attending church for a while, I wanted to go on a retreat for prayer and meditation. A little exercise may lead to one of the martial arts, or running so many miles a day; a little prayer naturally leads to a thirst for deeper spiritual exploration, or involvement in a faith community. Once we get a taste of something powerful, we want more. Just as some paths lead to oblivion, other paths lead to an awakened spirit. That is the way of creativity.

All of us are endowed with spirit—which means that all of us are naturally creative. Yet, you've heard people say, with frustration or despair, sometimes with perverse pride, or in other cases false modesty, "Oh, I'm not creative." That's like proclaiming, "Oh, I'm really not human—I may *look* human, but it's just a costume."

A woman in one of my workshops in Spiritual Autobiography sat with her hands folded in her lap while everyone else was busy with crayons drawing a picture of a room from their childhood home. I went over to her and asked if there was some reason that she couldn't or didn't want to draw.

"Oh," she said, "I'm not visual."

At first I thought she meant something was wrong with her eyesight, but that was not the case. Her *eyesight* was fine, her *I sight*, the vision she had constructed of herself needed refocusing. Maybe someone long ago had told her she was "not visual," or maybe someone had criticized a childhood drawing, so she had decided she couldn't—wouldn't—try to draw anything ever again. She decided she lacked "visual-ness."

What a waste to construct, or let others construct, blocks in our lives that really don't exist until we accept them and live by them. It's not uncommon. In one of my interviews with creators, singer Judy Collins recalls how a high school teacher's accusation of plagiarism froze her from writing her marvelous songs for many years. A priest I met at a workshop in Ireland told me how a grade school teacher advised him he wasn't "college material," and it put a damper on his academic work, delayed his education, and siphoned his creative energy into anger.

When I was starting out as a writer, the publisher who brought out my first book—a nonfiction work—read fifty pages of my first attempt at a novel and told me over a lavish lunch (designed to console me), "You're not a novelist." It was like a sentence from a literary court of law—a death sentence to a dream—and for a while I accepted it. But I happily began writing fiction again, finishing and publishing my first novel a decade later, followed by four others (with more to come).

When people say they are not creative, it may mean someone has branded them with that mistaken opinion. Or it may simply mean they don't know how to access their creativity.

FINDING NEW WAYS

To get hold of something that seems to be eluding us, we first need to know what it is. I like my new *Random House Unabridged Dictionary* definition: Creativity is "the ability to transcend traditional ideas, rules, patterns, relationships, or the like, and to create meaningful new ideas, forms, methods, interpretations, etc." Looking at how professional creators do this in their work gives us clues about viewing freshly our own issues, our own behavior. We often search for ways to change our circumstances, ways to jump from the worn grooves of life's daily record. Similarly, creative artists search for ways to break through "the way it's always been" in their own work, to shatter some of those "set in stone" rules.

Someone who transcended traditional rules in our recent cultural history is Tom Wolfe. He helped create the "new journalism."

Wolfe said he was bored by writing what he called "totem journalism," which was standard procedure for daily newspapers, the plain, dry, "just the facts, ma'am" tradition of newsroom "objectivity," which purposely omitted irony, humor, and the personal vision and style of the reporter. Talk about style! He even changed the use of punctuation, employing lots of exclamation points !!! to indicate special excitement or surprise, and lots of colons :::::::::: to suggest pauses in the interior thoughts of his subjects. Wolfe used punctuation in a whole new way, and expressed new moods and feelings with methods that had never been tried in traditional journalism.

Around the same time, Joan Didion made another significant breakaway from "totem journalism" by using her personal feelings and impressions to illuminate the lives of runaway kids in Haight Ashbury during the "Summer of Love" (*Slouching Towards Bethlehem*), the passions of murder and lust in middle-class California ("Some Dreamers of the Golden Dream"), and proving in subsequent reportage into the '90s that journalistic "objectivity" was a mask for distortion. She demonstrated that the first-person style, so scorned in traditional journalism, could provide authenticity and truth when practiced by an artist. She opened the way for a whole new way of seeing and describing the news of the day.

Both of these breakthroughs took courage as well as talent and vision. Meeker souls might well have feared that styles and methods that broke the old rules would be rejected. They might have felt trapped inside the image of themselves they and others had created. They would have held back, not wanting to alienate editors, even though they saw a different, fresher way of doing things. Courage is always an essential element of change—in art, as in life.

The abstract expressionist painters whose work brought the capital of art from Paris to New York devised new ways of using paint, and even used new tools as they "approached the canvas head-on, in direct, unpremeditated confrontation, and left it strewn with drips and splatters, accidental gestures and studio debris." Art historian April Kingsley, conveying in *The Turning Point* the fresh excitement of these innovators' work, goes on to explain that "chance, gravity, and paint viscosity were, for the first time in the history of art, important factors in making a painting. New techniques of applying paint were exploited—dripping, throwing, squirting, squeegeeing and spattering—using crude, untraditional tools like unwieldy housepainters' brushes, sticks, basting syringes, and trowels. Cheap enamels substituted for tube colors. Yankee ingenuity replaced standard textbook studio practice for painter and sculptor alike." Besides seeing themselves and their roles in new ways, creators employ old and new methods in startling combinations.

In mid career, tenor saxophonist John Coltrane took up the soprano sax, a smaller instrument that hadn't been used in jazz since the '30s and '40s. Encouraged by Miles Davis, Coltrane found that by playing this new "old" instrument, "A new shape came out of the thing and patterns . . ." Mastering the soprano sax helped him develop his individual style, which became part of the New Thing movement that energized jazz in the '60s.

New eras, with new ways of living, call forth new ways of seeing and representing the world, through words, paint, music, film. Creators in every field find means of freshly communicating new experience, using what's never been used before, challenging taboos, boldly experimenting to break the old molds, giving us new ways to see, hear, and experience.

ART IS NOT LIMITED TO A FEW

Professional artistic creators like musicians, painters, and writers are not the only ones who find new ways to refresh their work. Their innovations should not intimidate us, but remind us that creativity is available to all of us, whatever we do.

Dr. Dean Ornish overcame skepticism and denial from his own profession in order to create a new and successful approach to reversing heart disease without using drugs or surgery. He was rejected for funding by major foundations and medical institutions, as well as the National Institutes of Health, when he first applied for grants to study the effects of diet, exercise, and meditation on heart patients.

"It was discouraging," Ornish wrote in his bestselling book *Dr. Dean Ornish's Program for Reversing Heart Disease.* He was told by medical authorities that "It's impossible to reverse heart disease," and besides, "people won't change their lifestyles to that degree anyway." Dr. Ornish was asked by a leading cardiologist why he wanted to try something so "radical" as lifestyle changes, rather than "something more conventional," such as bypass surgery.

Ornish finally got the necessary funding to begin his study from Gerald D. Hines, a Houston real-estate developer, who helped raise financial support from Houston-based individuals, corporations, and small foundations. (So much for the myth that businessmen are "not creative.") The results have been revolutionary, showing that heart disease can in fact be reversed by basic lifestyle changes, without resorting to drugs or surgery.

Yoga teacher Danielle Levi-Alvares broke out of what had become a stale routine by taking one of her classes outside to do a Zen walking meditation in a muddy yard. It awakened everyone. Danielle believes that "creativity is to take a fresh look at life, play with it."

The American painter and inspired art teacher Robert Henri believed that art "is simply a question of doing things, anything, well. It is not an outside, extra thing." In his wonderful book, *The Art Spirit,* Henri proclaims, "Art when really understood is the province of every human being."

The appreciation of art, and the creation of art, are not limited to a special few, an elite touched by a magic wand. They are part of the splendor of being human, part of our common heritage, regardless of race, gender, color, background, language; regardless even of mental or physical handicaps.

All of us are endowed with spirit—which means that all of us are naturally creative. We wouldn't exist without the creative force, whose power is acknowledged and dramatized by the first story in the Bible, the creation story. These are the first words of the sacred texts of Judaism and Christianity: "In the beginning, God created the heavens and the earth."

In the story that follows, God creates humans, and these humans are also creators; in fact, their ability to create makes them human, distinguishes them from the animals. Animals may create—or, more strictly speaking, *construct*—nests or dams or hills or holes—but they are locked into their instinctual programming. They cannot think and act beyond that, cannot transcend their animalness, their sparrow- or hound- or horse-ness that restricts their movements, their communication, and confines them to their biological and geographic place in the universal order.

Humans have no such restrictions. We create stories and songs, pictures and sculptures, rockets that fly to the moon and beyond, machines and medicines that help to heal the human body and mind, networks of instant communication and information that link the diverse people of the whole planet. Humans create new forms of society and economy and ways of being and living on the earth. We have free will, the power to create our own destiny, the very pattern and course of our lives. Such godlike powers are not dispensed to just a few geniuses and seers, but to all of us.

We fail to use our powers when we fail to think of our lives and our work, whatever it is, as creative—as potential art, or "life art." I don't mean this abstractly; I've seen people do it in all different kinds of situations. When a telephone operator sings her greeting as she answers the phone, that is art. When a chef adds the right ingredient to a soup at the crucial moment, that, too, is art. The masseuse's pressure on the right point in the shoulder, the businessman's observation of a child's shoe, the yoga teacher's guided meditation—all that is art and creation as much as the painter's brush stroke, the writer's choice of words, the sculptor's shaping of the clay, or the actor's intonation of a phrase.

One of the most awakening experiences for me in writing this book was to interview people from a wide variety of fields to learn how they used creativity in their own work. These are not just famous people, like singer and songwriter Judy Collins, or financially successful people, like businessman and benefactor Arnold Hiatt; nor are they only writers like Marcie Hershman and Gish Jen, or religious thinkers like Rabbi Harold Kushner and theologian Elaine Pagels; I learned about creativity in body work from masseuse Elizabeth Valentine, in cooking from chef Odette Bery, and in yoga from Danielle Levi-Alvares.

Creators see art not only in their professions, but also in the creation of daily life activity. There is art in the lighting of candles at breakfast. There is art in being mindful of the food we eat, in remembering to honor the light or soul or God within ourselves and every person we come in contact with throughout the day, whether friend, lover, family member, fellow worker, waiter, meter maid, or stranger passing in the street. There is art in taking time to appreciate the clean wash of the mind's silence.

One of the major blocks to experiencing creativity and creating experiences is the myth that we can enhance our creativity through the use of artificial stimulants, the ingestion of drugs and alcohol. I am not speaking as a moralist in exposing this myth, but as a truth-seeker. As we'll see over and over again from the experiences of artists and creators, the magic idea of a muse inside a bottle of booze, or a puff or sniff or injection of drugs, is a deadly delusion. Rather than enhancing our creative ability, these substances suppress and distort them, and can, eventually, end not only our creativity but our lives.

I have written about this myth extensively because as a writer I was under its spell for a long time, as were many of my generation, and as many continue to be in new generations—from Dylan Thomas to Kurt Cobain, from Jim Morrison to River Phoenix. There are always new brands of booze and drugs that promise different magic transformations, new variations of the genie in the bottle. Old genies like LSD are revived, repackaged, and reglamorized for a fresh crop of exploring, curious, talented young people who are all too often captured by the myth that we can enhance our creativity by altering our state of consciousness. That myth, and others like it, are simply not true.

YOU DON'T HAVE TO BE MYSTIC

Clarity of mind, body, and spirit is the key to creativity, to finding and producing the art in our work and our lives. No matter how deeply we may have sunk to some numbing addiction that stifles the creative spirit—whether drugs, alcohol, overindulgence in food, sleep, television, or simply depression and malaise—there is always a road to recovery of our natural clarity.

I associate clarity with "spirit," in the broadest sense of the term, as defined by the *Oxford English Dictionary*: "The vital or animating principal in humans and animals; that which gives life; the breath of life." For some this may be a religious principle, for others it is best signified by the broader term of "spirituality," others may have another word for it.

You don't have to be a mystic, or be struck by a lightning bolt from the heavens, or hear supernatural voices to tap into what I mean by spirit. You only have to be clear, that is, unencumbered by rigid preconceptions, unbound from the chains of repeated patterns of negative behavior, unafraid of taking risks.

Robert Henri expresses my findings and my feelings in *The Art Spirit*: "When the artist is alive in any person, whatever his kind of work may be, he becomes an inventive, searching, daring, self-expressing creature. He becomes interesting to other people. He disturbs, upsets, enlightens, and he opens the way for a better understanding. Where those who are not artists are trying to close the book, he opens it, shows there are still more pages possible. . . . He does not have to be a painter or sculptor to be an artist. He can work in any medium. He simply has to find the gain in the work itself, not outside it."

Something in the world wants to destroy our hard-won clarity, some anti-spirit that tells us creation and art lead to madness and death. Those who promote the mythical glamour of the "doomed artist," psychoanalyzing art into an expression of neurosis, seldom if ever mention the central aspect of the creative experience: the incomparable joy of it—not the illusory bubble of fame, but what Robert Henri calls "the happiness that is in the making." As Molly Bloom puts it in the final, life-affirming lines of James Joyce's *Ulysses*: "And yes I said yes I will Yes. . . ."

Life is a lot more fun and fulfilling when you see it as creation, and yourself as a cocreator of it (rather than a victim or passive passenger)—along with God, or fate, or the universe, however you understand the force that turns the world. True creativity never leads to despair; creativity leads out of despair.

If there is one word that embodies the true path to creativity, that serves as a key to the full use of our creative powers, it is *clarity*. To aid you in reaching an understanding of it, in a way that will enable you to use and enjoy both the idea and the condition of clarity, I have set up a kind of model of successive stages in this book, called "Breaking the Myth," "Emptying," "Filling," and "Creating." To achieve clarity you need only be in awe of the mystery of the universe, the life force and its power, and be willing to open to it.

On this journey, my model will serve as a road map for this fresh exploration of creation. We'll use exercises with drawing, listening to music, writing, and looking at nature to explore and unlock our own creative powers. We'll look at ways to use those powers to shape our daily lives, to give our moment-by-moment experience (which is where we always live) the grace and pleasure of art. This is what I mean by creating from the spirit.

Chapter 2

THE CREATIVE SPIRIT

"The consolation, the dignity, the joy of life are that discouragements and lapses, depressions and darknesses, come to one only as one stands *without*—I mean without the luminous paradise of art. As soon as I really re-enter it—cross the loved threshold—stand in the high chamber, and the gardens divine—the whole realm widens out again before me and around me—the air of life fills my lungs—the light of achievement flushes over all the place, and I believe, I see, I *do*."

A novelist wrote those uplifting words at a difficult time in his life and career, when even greater professional discouragement was just around the corner. With his novels selling poorly, the author was working on a play with all his might in hopes of restoring his financial as well as literary fortune, both of which were in decline. The play on which he pinned his hopes turned out to be such a flop the audience hurled vegetables onto the London stage at the opening night performance. Undaunted, the author wrote in his journal the next morning in exhortation to himself: "Produce; produce again; produce again better than ever and all will be well."

We usually don't associate Henry James—known as "The Master" of language and story—with failure, yet he suffered it as painfully as any other artist whose work is scorned. Since James is sometimes denigrated today as a privileged member of the literary and social elite of his time, it's enlightening (perhaps even inspiring) to note that he, too, suffered defeat, indifference, and hostility. He was pained by bad reviews (they don't get any worse than vegetables hurled on the stage!) and struggled to make enough money from his work to be able to live and continue writing. He once wrote that each of us, no matter what our situation or station in the world, had to deal with "the terrible algebra of your own existence." His fight against defeat, and his compassion for his characters, as well as the lyric power of his prose, have continued to inspire writers as diverse as James Baldwin and Cynthia Ozick.

The poet and teacher Martha Collins recently recalled, "I fell in love with literature because of reading *Portrait of a Lady*, a novel about a woman's mind, a woman's thinking, and James 'got it right.' Isabel Archer faced different problems than women do today, but the basic dilemma of her humanity is our own stuff, too." Collins, whose most recent book of poetry is *A History of Small Life on a Windy Planet*, said, "What I owe most to Henry James is he taught me I wanted to be a writer."

Perhaps James inspires so many because, for him, creating his novels, stories, and plays was an act of faith, a testimony to his belief in the achievement that brought a "flush of light" to his inner vista: "I believe, I see, I *do*." The world of his art is a "paradise," its gardens "divine," flushed by that light—all elements of the sort of transcendent experience his brother William wrote about in his own psychological masterpiece, *The Varieties of Religious Experience*.

The act of creation is one of the most powerful of those "varieties of religious experience," even for people like Henry James, who are not formally religious. For some artists the religious nature of their work is a given factor, the heart of the matter, even though the art itself may not overtly deal with religious themes. The painter and sculptor Norma Lewis, a member of the Unitarian Universalist Church of the Monterey Peninsula in Carmel, California, told the denomination's magazine, *The World*, "I see creativity as the ultimate religious act. My art and my religion are not only very connected; they are one and the same."

The sixty-four-year-old Russian composer Sofia Gubaidulina told a *New York Times* interviewer that she writes music to serve God. "I can't think of any way to explain the existence of art other than as a means to express something greater than ourselves," she said. "I can't reach a single musical decision except with the goal of making a connection to God. If I separated the religious goal from the musical one, music would have no meaning for me."

MUSICIANS ON A QUEST

Playing and composing his innovative music became a religious quest for the great jazz saxophone player and composer John Coltrane. He had a spiritual revelation while kicking his drug habit in 1957 and said years later, "My goal is to live the truly religious life, and express it through my music. If you live it, when you play there's no problem because the music is part of the whole thing. . . . My music is the spiritual expression of what I am, my faith, my knowledge, my being."

Ridiculed by some critics for his innovative sounds, and for his search for God through his music, Coltrane was even blasted in an obituary by the English poet and sometime jazz critic Philip Larkin, who called Coltrane's music "enormously boring" and said his death "leaves in jazz a vast, blessed silence."

Coltrane himself addressed such harsh—and inevitable—criticism in a letter to a friend: "It seems history shows (and it's the same way today) that the innovator is more often than not met with some degree of condemnation; usually according to the degree of departure from the prevailing modes of expression or what have you. Change is always so hard to accept. We also see that these innovators always seek to revitalize, extend, and reconstruct the status quo in their given fields, whatever is needed. Quite often they are the rejects, outcasts, subcitizens, etc., of the very societies to which they bring so much sustenance. Often they are people who endure great personal tragedy in their lives. Whatever the case, whether accepted or rejected, rich or poor, they are forever guided by that great and eternal constant—the creative urge. Let us cherish it and give all praise to God."

In his sensitive book *ascension: John Coltrane and His Quest*, Eric Nisenson, jazz editor and author of *'Round About Midnight*, writes that Coltrane's remarkable composition "A Love Supreme" has been described as a prayer, a work of devotion, and a psalm, but in fact is more than that: "a searingly confessional, frankly personal piece based on Coltrane's quest to reach and find God through seeking within." A few years before his death from cancer at age forty-one, Coltrane said he wanted to "become a saint."

His vision has been realized in the St. John's African Orthodox Church in San Francisco, a storefront proclaiming "St. John Will-I-Am Coltrane" as its own patron saint. The church plays his music for an hour of inspired improvisational jazz at every Sunday service, and provides hot meals and clothes to the homeless, as well as free counseling services and even music lessons!

I felt the living legacy of Coltrane as I joined one Sunday morning with the worshipers—old and young, black and white, male and female, some in clerical robes and others in T-shirts, some playing their own musical instruments along with the regular jazz group of tenor and soprano sax, guitars, drums, and piano, others just singing or swaying to the music, everyone welcome and welcoming, joined in spirit. All of us were there out of respect for Coltrane's music, faith, and vision.

After his religious conversion, Coltrane thought of his music as prayer—which it continues to be for the parishioners of the church he inspired, and for listeners around the world. Coltrane saw the inseparability—the unity—of his creativity and his religious faith.

Duke Ellington is another jazz great who turned to religion in the later part of his career, blending belief with music as he created "Sacred Concerts," which Eric Nisenson described as "large-scale efforts to explore the idea of God through jazz."

In a new generation, Fleetwood Mac guitarist Lindsey Buckingham told an interviewer that creativity serves the same purpose for him as attending religious services: "One of the reasons I enjoy working alone—and that's when things will often come out well—is because it's very much akin to a religious [experience.] There is some tie between religion and art; I think there's a lot of crossover."

Jenny Boyd, a psychologist and lecturer who got to know the music scene as the ex-wife of Mick Fleetwood, interviewed Buckingham and seventy-four other contemporary musicians about the creative process for an absorbing book she coauthored with Holly George-Warren, *Musicians in Tune*. They learned that for a number of well-known rock and pop musical artists "the act of creating often verges on the spiritual." Ravi Shankar told Boyd that performing music was part of his own spiritual practice. Bass player Robert Warren said, "I believe there is a transcendent power, and you can get to it through the creative act."

In his own book, *Drumming at the Edge of Magic*, Mickey Hart of the Grateful Dead speaks of "the spirit side of the drum," and how the drum took him "on a mythic quest."

Spiritual inspiration came to the rap group Run DMC after the veteran rappers Joseph Simmons, Darryl McDaniels, and Jason Mizzell, who were childhood friends in Hollis, Queens, returned to church and overcame drug and alcohol problems. Their comeback album *Down with the King* refers to their own religious reawakening. In a *New York Times* story of their recovery and subsequent comeback on the charts, "Run" told reporter Amy Linden that when people asked him how he could be a born-again Christian and a rapper, "That's like asking how can you be a singer and a Christian. I'm only using my mouth to talk. It's not that rap stands for violence; it doesn't stand for anything. It's poetry. It's an art form."

WE ALL HAVE A POEM

The iconoclastic comic Bill Hicks told an interviewer: "We are facilitators of our creative evolution. We can ignite our brains with light." Hicks is an African American born in Texas who has found an enthusiastic following in London, where he draws record-breaking crowds for what a critic described as "acid home truths about the U.S.A." (Hicks calls it "the United States of Advertising.") A high school friend says Hicks was the first person he'd ever met whose goal was enlightenment.

Theater critic John Lahr wrote in *The New Yorker* that Hicks's comedy "takes an audience on a journey to places in the heart where it can't or won't go without him. Through laughter, Hicks makes unacceptable ideas irresistible. He is particularly lethal because he persuades not with reason but with joy."

When Hicks left Lahr's house after an interview he turned and said in parting, "I believe everyone has this fuckin' poem in his heart."

However stated in this most cynically sophisticated era, this belief in the "poem in the heart"—another way of describing spirit—keeps popping up from the new creators and artists, even those angry at the Establishment.

In that defiant, iconoclastic spirit of laughter at self and society to get to the heart of things, actress Claudia Shear created the one-woman show *Blown Sideways Through Life*, which opened in a small off-Broadway theater to rave reviews. It's the drama of her own "failure"—the plight of an overweight, no-longer-young woman trying to survive in New York in the '90s, having left or been fired from forty-five jobs, ranging from short-order cook to receptionist at a midtown house of prostitution.

Out of this dismal, all-too-familiar saga of rejection and discrimination, Ms. Shear created a funny, wise, provocative satire capped with a joyous, triumphant dance that brings a surge of new life and hope to the audience. At least it did to me, and from the faces I saw around me that night and the ovation I joined, I was not alone. I was delighted to learn that the show moved on to a larger stage, and its creator-performer was invited to Robert Redford's Sundance Film Institute to develop her material for a motion picture.

There is no doubt that Claudia Shear has that poem in the heart—the spirit, the breath of life that brings meaning to existence and enables us to create.

UNEXPECTED SPIRIT

For some that "poem" comes out literally as poetry, for others as a dance or play or comedy routine; still others manifest it in work that we often fail to appreciate as creative because it doesn't fit the usual categories. Yet, it calls on that same spirit, no matter what labor or activity is involved, from salesmanship to surgery.

Even science. A cliche that persists is that of the scientist as anti-religious and anti-artistic, enemy of spiritual truth and beauty. The Nobel Prize physicist Richard Feynman challenged that view in his memoir *What Do You Care What Other People Think?*, disputing the argument of a painter friend who held up a flower and said that he as an artist could appreciate its beauty, "but you, as a scientist, take it all apart and it becomes dull."

Feynman responded that the fascination arising from a knowledge of science "only adds to the excitement and mystery and awe of a flower. It only adds. I don't understand how it subtracts." Feynman recalls standing at the seashore and looking at the ocean as a scientist, and being inspired to write a free-verse poem about the wonder of the universe, and himself in it, all made up of atoms. He adds that "the same thrill, the same awe and mystery, comes again and again when we look at any question deeply enough." He describes that feeling of awe and mystery as "a religious experience."

FAITH IN POETRY

You don't have to be formally religious to have a peak experience while creating. When the Pulitzer Prize–winning poet Maxine Kumin was asked in an interview if her poetry was in some way "a fulfillment of some sort of spiritual need," she answered, "I call myself an agnostic. I do not really have any faith, any coherent religious faith, and yet the one thing in my life that I feel passionate and evangelical about is poetry. I want to contribute to its well-being and to its future. And I suppose that speaking about the way poems occur is, if you read William James, something like the quality of a religious experience for me."

Her words reminded me of an experience in my own early struggle to write, when I was not simply an agnostic who didn't know if there was a God, but a newly minted Columbia College *atheist*, emboldened by discovering Neitszche, Freud, and Hemingway's "nada," or nothingness. I knew there was *not* a God, and was proudly condescending to those who still believed, like my parents and most of my friends back home in Indiana.

In this smugly enlightened state I returned to my dorm room one evening to struggle with a short story I was trying to write. A few hours after I had plunged into it again the story seemed to come alive, to take over, with a force of its own, carrying me along as page after page came out of my typewriter, scenes and dialogue and descriptions proceeding in some natural way, as if I were simply transcribing them. I lost all sense of time. When I finally came to the end of the story I looked up and saw that it was light outside. I felt tears welling up in my eyes, not of sadness but joy, and without thinking, but following some natural impulse, I sank to the floor on my knees and uttered a prayer of thanks for having finally "created" what seemed like a real story—or, as it felt like, for having been the transcriber, the vessel through which the story came.

To whom did I offer this prayer of thanks? The God I no longer believed in? I didn't know or care; the impulse was deeper than intellect, beyond reason or argument.

Not just writers experience the spiritual nature of creation. The ceiling of the Sistine Chapel, with Michelangelo's unforgettable depiction of the finger of God reaching out to man—one of the basic images of Western culture and civilization—is perhaps the most eloquent testimony we have of the painter as transmitter of the sacred. It's a tradition that began with the earliest drawings in caves, flowered in the inspired paintings of Biblical scenes and figures by the masters, and continues in the painting of contemporary artists like Agnes Martin, whose luminous new works have been likened to prayer by the art and literary historian Benita Eisler.

Creative artists in many fields find inspiration in one another's works, an interaction vividly described by the nineteenth-century French poet Charles Baudelaire, who found "new energies" from looking at paintings. Baudelaire believed that all the arts inspire one another; that a piece of music as well as a painting or a poem "throws open immense vistas to the most adventurous imaginations." So passionately did Baudelaire relate to painting that he began to write about it, and became one of the leading art critics of his time.

Rembrandt's classic painting of the Prodigal Son inspired a recent devotional book by the writer-priest Father Henri Nouwen. Jazz musician John Coltrane wrote to a friend, "I was reading a book on the life of Van Gogh today, and I had to pause and think of that wonderful and persistent force—the creative urge. The creative urge was in this man who found himself so much at odds with the world he lived in, and in spite of all the adversity, frustrations, rejections, and so forth—beautiful and living art came forth abundantly."

TEACHERS AS GUIDES

We learn and are inspired—*awakened*—by the other arts and sciences through the grace and wisdom of teachers. In my Spiritual Autobiography workshop, there is an exercise in which people write about a friend, mentor, or guide who has helped them move forward on their own journey. The people most often remembered in this honored category are schoolteachers.

I can't imagine my own life journey without them—I don't mean just for the facts and dates and numbers they taught me, I mean for the richness of spirit they evoked in me, opened to me, through gentle and wise introductions to the work of great creators. I remember sitting spellbound in a classroom at Shortridge High School listening to a scratchy record player render the voice of Carl Sandburg reading his poem "The People, Yes." I went home to read more of those American Midwestern poems about Chicago, and Lincoln, and the longings of the heart, and something stirred in me, deeply.

It wasn't a poetry class but a history class, and Sandburg wasn't part of the curriculum, but was added to enrich our understanding and appreciation by the teacher—not a poet or literary person, but the freshman track, football, and basketball coach, Roy V. "Abie" Aberson, one of the many dedicated teachers who blessed my life and nurtured as well as educated me—along with several other generations of fortunate students.

The most undervalued and underpaid professionals in our society, who not only create but give us our own basic tools for creating, are teachers. Teachers must not only know their subject, but constantly keep pace with the rapidly changing world in order to help their students understand it. How creatively they do that was illustrated when the Department of Education brought two hundred outstanding teachers to Washington to give their views on education reform. One of those, voted Teacher of the Year in her state, was Vicki Matthews Burwell of Caldwell, Iowa. She wrote of what goes on in her classroom at the New Plymouth Elementary School:

"Today our fifth-grade class stood on a model of a Tenochtitlán causeway and fended off the enemy, we touched three-million-year-old stromatolites and mammoth-toothed fossils and we composed e-mail for a school in Pennsylvania. Through videos, we visited the Anasazi ruins in Chaco Canyon, had the magicians Penn and Teller introduce us to David Hockney's surreal look at a chair and were mesmerized by Gary Paulsen's passionate writing about the Alaskan Iditarod.

"We fell through the day like Alice in Wonderland, soaking up ideas, experimenting with and stretching our talents. We were civil engineers, archaeologists, detectives, paleontologists, art critics, computer nerds, teachers and community planners. We used technology, bright construction paper, dog-eared books, parents. We used our imagination, our background knowledge, and our intuition. We went home exhausted and satisfied. Tomorrow we'll be back for print making and teamwork in long division. And Corey says he has a few card tricks to show us. Steven Spielberg never had it so good."

IS THERE SPIRIT IN SELLING COSMETICS?

Well, of course teaching is creative, but what about business? Isn't that the last endeavor we associate with creativity, much less spirituality? Business still carries the old '50s stigma of "the rat race," the "Organization Man," the "Hucksters"—updated by even more crass and cutthroat practices and anti-ethics that made the '80s a byword for greed and corruption. Certainly, many businesses still operate in that paradigm, but it doesn't have to be that way. The possibilities of business being created from the spirit open wide when listening to Anita Roddick, founder (*creator*) of The Body Shop, an international naturalcosmetics firm with more than nine hundred shops trading in nineteen different languages in forty-two countries around the world, from the Arctic Circle to Bondi Beach.

"I see business as a Renaissance concept, where the human spirit comes into play," Ms. Roddick says in her book *Body and Soul*. "It does not have to be drudgery; it does not have to be the science of making money. It can be something that people genuinely feel good about, but only if it remains a human enterprise.

"How do you ennoble the spirit when you are selling something as inconsequential as a cosmetic cream? You do it by creating a sense of holism, of spiritual development, of feeling connected to the workplace, the environment and relationships with one another. It's how to make Monday to Friday a sense of being alive rather than a slow death. How do you give people a chance to do a good job? By making them feel good about what they are doing. The spirit soars when you are satisfying your own basic material needs in such a way that you are also serving the needs of others honorably and humanely. Under these circumstances, I can even feel good about a moisturizer."

The idea of work as spiritual experience comes up in places we don't expect it—because we've narrowed our view of the concept, trying to domesticate spirituality by restricting it to places of formal religious worship. Deanna Teifenthal, who took one of my workshops,

wrote me later about her unexpected discovery of creativity and spirituality on a tour of the Skydome, the baseball stadium of the Toronto
Blue Jays.

"Before we started, they showed us a wonderful video on the building of the dome and its retractable roof. If you expected to hear about
the mechanics of how it worked, you were disappointed. What it was,
was a smattering of the spiritual journeys the workers and architects
had! Guiding the steel beams into place with just a touch of the hand.
Carefully choosing a partner you could trust your life with high above
ground. Struggling to feel with your frozen fingers when the bolts
slipped into place to join the beams. Soaring through the air at the
end of a rising beam. Feeling the wind in your ears while working high
in the air. Being one of a team of 5000 to dust the seats and spruce up
the Skydome before the first game.

"The architect defined creativity as 'just discovering what's already
there,' as he got the idea for the retractable dome roof from observing
among other things a lobster shell."

NAVAJO HEALING

The idea of work as a holistic endeavor rather than an isolated part of
life, walled off from any spiritual source or practice, is rarely associated
with mainstream, AMA-based American medicine. It is present,
though, in the world and work of Dr. Lori Cupp, a staff general surgeon at the Indian Medical Center of Gallup, New Mexico. The first
Navajo woman to become a surgeon, she views surgery as a powerful,
spiritual experience.

"In the Navajo religion and culture, there is an emphasis on how
you relate to everything around you," Dr. Cupp explained in an interview with Elizabeth Cohen of the *New York Times*. "Everything has to
be measured, weighed, and harmonious. We call it *nizhoni*—walking in
beauty—and I believe what I do as a surgeon fits into this philosophy. I
know my actions directly alter the course of people's lives."

Dr. Cupp has drawn on her own heritage to creatively devise
methods of making her Navajo patients feel more comfortable: "Now I
know how to gauge a person's discomfort by asking a few questions at a
time and asking them to only uncover that part of their body I need to
see." She has proposed that the hospital use a medicine man for heal-

ing ceremonies, and has requested that when a new medical center is built, it include a traditional Navajo round room for such ceremonies, called "sings."

Dr. Cupp said that for many illnesses a ceremonial sing may be the best treatment—depression, for instance. "But if I had a breast mass, I would want it surgically removed for a biopsy," she added.

"What an amazing and rare thing it is to actually work inside another human being," Dr. Cupp said. "At the time, I may be stressed or scared, but I also feel an unbelievable link to something larger—call it God or whatever, a universal spiritual connectedness."

THE BREATH OF LIFE

Whether we are surgeons or stand-up comics, Pulitzer Prize poets or "Sunday painters," jazz musicians or business leaders, for most of us the process of creation is—if not specifically religious (which implies a specific creed or denomination)—a *spiritual* experience in the broad sense of the term. I use the *Oxford English Dictionary* definition of *spirit*: "The animating or vital principle in humans (and animals); that which gives life to the physical organism, in contrast to its purely material elements; the breath of life."

Henry James echoes this definition of spirit when he writes that while in the realm of his art, "the air of life fills my lungs." Dylan Thomas described it in his poetry: "The force that through the green fuse drives the flower/Drives my green age."

Spirit is "something larger than the self," writes the author, critic, and Harvard lecturer Lewis Hyde in "Alcohol and Poetry"; it has "the power to change you. It alters your Gestalt, your whole mode of perception and action. Both alcohol and the Holy Ghost can do this. But a spirit does more than just give you new eyes: it is the mover. . . . Spiritual thirst is the thirst of the self to feel that it is part of something large, and in its positive aspect, it is the thirst to grow, to ripen." As King Lear put it, "Ripeness is all."

To reach a ripeness in our personal growth, to tap into our inherent creativity and spirit, we need to dispel some popular illusions. By confining creativity to fenced-off, predefined areas, our society has tamed its power; our accumulated cultural myths have limited and sometimes hidden our access to this power. A good way to break through to a new understanding of creativity and find ways of claiming it for ourselves, is to expose some of the mythology that has grown up around the subject like crabgrass, obscuring it from view, choking off our access to it, keeping us distanced from its full use and enjoyment.

Let's look at some of the myths about creativity that are commonly accepted in our own culture.

Part Two

"Creation Myths"

Chapter 3

MYTHS OF CREATIVITY

MYTH NUMBER 1
CREATIVITY IS ONLY FOR THE ARTISTIC ELITE

This myth tells us that a few special people have been blessed with the mysterious gift of creativity, and everyone else was passed over when God was giving out these valuable prizes! While everyone may not be a master or a Pulitzer Prize winner, everyone does possess creative power, a force that may be articulated in many different ways, from cooking and gardening to painting and writing.

Another part of the myth is that creativity is only for the social and financial elite, a frivolous pastime. Ann Morrissey, a participant in a workshop I gave at the Unitarian Universalist Conference Center at Ferry Beach, Maine, wrote, "Creativity isn't a big topic in a working-class neighborhood—if anything it was laughed at. I think that the assumption was that creativity was for people who didn't have to work for a living. The sons and daughters of the rich could afford the luxury of spending years exploring their creativity.

"By definition, therefore, anything done well by neighbors or family members was a skill. Baking well, sewing well, singing, etc., were skills where practice was needed. I don't remember them being seen as creative."

In my definition, those skills are no less creative than composing music, painting a picture, or writing a novel. Many creative artists come from working class neighborhoods; some left those neighborhoods because their creative work was laughed at there.

Creative ability comes in all sections of the country and the globe, without regard to race, color, religion, background, age, or wealth. Talent isn't for sale—except through development of skills by love and work.

Being creative is part of being human, and one of the key elements of humanity is the creative gift of storytelling. It is basic. Joan Didion wrote, "We tell stories in order to live." My great-grandmother, who never finished high school, and sold women's corsets door-to-door during the Depression to feed her family, told me marvelous stories of growing up in Georgia, of seeing the flames of Sherman's march to the sea when she was six years old. When I was a child my mother created stories for me of animals' picnics, using all the elements I most loved— bears, deviled eggs, and trains. My pharmacist father told me stories of Kentucky, his birthplace, and pioneers like my ancestor Daniel Boone, chopping their way through the wilderness. I gulped these stories like lemonade, and was thrilled to be able to tell them myself.

Whatever our work or talents or inclinations, we all possess, I believe, a gift of storytelling. Sometimes it is untapped or untried because we have been told, or have come to assume, that if we aren't professionals we aren't gifted with the capacity to express ourselves in this way. After leading workshops in Spiritual Autobiography for five years at churches and adult education centers across the country, I've had firsthand confirmation of the natural ability of people of different ages, backgrounds, and occupations to create fascinating stories from their own experience.

THE DEMOCRATIZATION OF WRITING

The playwright and journalist Barbara Graham came to one of my workshops to write an article on it for the magazine *New Choices*, published by *Reader's Digest*, and she made the insightful observation that this sort of activity represented a new phenomenon. She called it "the democratization of writing"—the recent popularity of opportunities for "ordinary people" (those who are not professionals)—to enjoy the creative pleasures of writing.

The upsurge of this democratization has also led to a kind of backlash among professional writers themselves, some of whom scorn any processes that provide such openings to "amateurs." I heard about one such literary pro who expressed this disdain with the comment, "Everything that's wrong with contemporary society can be summed up in one word: 'workshop.' " I think there's a protective response among some of the pros who fear their thunder will be stolen by these upstart amateurs! The mere notion that any literate but untrained and unpublished neophyte can spend a weekend writing stories that please and enlighten and entertain not only the authors but their fellow participants—that writing stories of our lives is available to most of us— seems to demystify and thus somehow lessen the godlike aura of the professional storytellers.

I don't mean to suggest that anyone who takes a weekend workshop and writes entertaining stories can then quit her job and become the next Toni Morrison or Kurt Vonnegut. What I mean is that people who can write their names and high school theme papers can also tap into a creative source that enables them to tell their own stories, through drawing as well as writing.

No one was more shocked and pleased than I, who always considered myself "artistically illiterate" because I couldn't draw a human shape (today it might be called "pictorially challenged") to find that through a simple exercise with crayons I was able to portray a part of my past. I was even able to draw a shape and form that resembled a human being, beyond my usual rendering of a stick figure, and this primitive crayon sketch seemed such a miracle to me I had it framed and hung it above my writing desk. Pleased as I was by my crayon pictures, I did not harbor any illusions that I could whip up some pastels or portraits to show and sell at a New York art gallery, or rival the work of Franz Kline or Willem de Kooning! I was simply enjoying my own ability to use a dormant part of my creative powers for my own pleasure and enlightenment.

Commitment to a *professional* path in the arts is a whole other order of experience than learning to call up and exercise one's creative powers for personal pleasure and insight. The discipline (much less, extraordinary talent) required for that kind of work— what Henry James called "steadily driving the pen"—is enormous, rigorous, and psychically as well as mentally challenging. That doesn't mean you shouldn't try it, but be aware of the wholly different demands of this path.

MYTH NUMBER 2
YOU HAVE TO SUFFER TO BE CREATIVE

The world seems to love the story of the suffering artist. Is it some kind of revenge on those who are artistic, that in popular mythology one of the components of successful creativity is personal agony and pain? The American writer who has had the most books written about his life is Edgar Allan Poe. Yes, he was a creative genius, and yes, he did suffer the torments of alcohol and drug addiction. The irony is, though, that he is almost alone among the great American writers of the nineteenth century who fell prey to those diseases! The giants of our literature in that century—Hawthorne, Melville, Thoreau, Emerson, Dickinson, Whitman, Twain—were not alcoholics or drug addicts, nor was their human suffering probably any more or less severe than that of the mass of men and women of their time. But it is Poe, the doomed, whose life remains the most popular story.

We love the image of the artist as wild and kooky, but as Robert Henri writes, "Art tends toward balance, order, judgment of relative values, the laws of growth, the economy of living—very good things for anyone to be interested in." This is the testimony of most working artists, as opposed to psychologists or sociologists generalizing about them. The prize-winning novelist Reynolds Price notes that "most productive writers live calmer lives than winkles."

That will never sell. Despite our society's outward changes in attitude about the destructive nature of alcohol and drugs, the phoney glamour of the stoned, smashed, self-destructive artist still has tremendous appeal. Witness the astounding fact that among current American writers one of the most common subjects of biography is none other than Hunter S. Thompson, the self-proclaimed "gonzo journalist" whose "fame attended his decline as a writer," as Christopher Lehmann-Haupt noted in reviewing *Hunter: The Strange and Savage Life of Hunter S. Thompson* by E. Jean Carroll in the *New York Times*. Two other biographies of this author, who has become more famous for his "out of control, drug-abusing self" than his writing, were soon to come: *When the Going Gets Weird: The Twisted Life and Times of Hunter S. Thompson*, by Peter O. Whitmer, and *Fear and Loathing* by Paul Perry.

This American folk hero, who earns a good part of his living now speaking to college audiences while he glugs from a bottle of bourbon, began by working hard at reading and writing, producing his first and best book, *Hell's Angels*, in 1966, and then, as Lehmann-Haupt reports, "dissipated himself once his career began to gather steam. This hurt his marriage, which was never idyllic to begin with: Mr. Thompson seems to have believed that while it was all right for him to sleep around, any suspected disloyalty on his wife's part deserved a beating. So the great scourge of public hypocrisy turns out to be something of a hypocrite in private. His intemperance also seems to have hurt his writing, as many of his editors can and do tell."

THE DOWNHILL PATH

It is true that many creative people drink too much, just as it's true that many creative people suffer from anxiety and depression. It is also true that people from all segments of the population suffer from a variety of neurotic disorders and drink too much! It does not follow, however—as the myth would have us believe—that suffering and/or drinking are necessary for creativity. Rather, as in the case of Mr. Thompson and almost every other artist who hits the booze and drugs trail, that path leads them and their work downhill, on a journey of diminishing health and creative production.

The recent book *Touched with Fire* dusts off some of the old clichés about writers and suffering, buttressing them with new statistics. Yet the author, Kay Redfield Jamison, a psychologist at the Johns Hopkins University School of Medicine, explained to an interviewer, "It's very safe to say there is a greatly increased rate of depression and manic depression in artists and writers but that's not the same as saying you have to have depression or manic depression to *be* an artist or writer."

In fact, a number of writers and artists interviewed by *Newsday* reporter Fred Bruning challenged even the first premise of Jamison's theory about the "greatly increased" rate of depression and mental illness among creators. Author Geoffrey Wolff scoffed at the notion that excellence results from instability and chaos: "The idea of driving yourself nuts to be a good writer is crazy and adolescent," he said. "There's a snobbishness about it—that people who have lives of equilibrium can't be interesting. That is a child's notion of art. . . . Writing isn't like other work, but it isn't more dangerous or more painful. I'd be the last to cry, 'Woe is me, how hard for the writer.' Some do, and I always nod off."

An eloquent response to Jamison's premise came from Erica Jong, author of *Fear of Flying*, who said, "As a young person I suffered over tiny things and then found ways to use the hypersensitivity in my work. I could take the pain and put it somewhere. We heal ourselves by writing and, at the highest level, we heal other people too."

Novelist and newspaper columnist Pete Hamill, whose recent memoir, *A Drinking Life*, won critical praise (he gave up the booze twenty years ago), said, "I don't buy the whole line that somehow art comes from neurosis and you should do nothing or you'll damage the art. My sense is you have to remain healthy physically and mentally. That doesn't mean surrendering knowledge of the darker impulses, just understanding them better."

The most succinct refutation of the Jamison theory (how glamorous it sounds, to be "touched with fire"!) is the insight of Oregon University professor Robert Grudin, who writes on the subject of artistic suffering in his brilliant book *The Grace of Great Things: Creativity and Innovation*:

"The Romantics saw the creative individual as a kind of Faust or an aesthetic Flying Dutchman, doomed by talent to torment and alienation. A more modern version of this myth, common among recent generations, is that inspiration lies somewhere between intoxication and psychosis, that it can result only from some physiological or psychological distortion of one's humanity. While these theories have some value in consoling the uninspired, they do not hold up in history. Creative individuals, even those whom society misprizes, do not necessarily face mental disorders or other woes.

"They more generally *do*, however, face temporary but severe pains in the nature of their work. Their pains are symptomatic of many typical phases in the creative process: the failure of experiments, the refutation of hypotheses, the shock of criticism, the endurance of contradictions or anomalies, the reorganization or trashing of one's own material, and the mere awareness that such experiences necessarily await one."

Another misconception about creativity is that it is dangerous, that it may undo you, lead to your mental imbalance, drive you to kill yourself. The suicides of many creators are cited as proof of this damaging effect of creation. More often, the mental disturbances and suicides of creators have been stoked by alcohol and drugs, while creative acts have sustained them, kept them alive much longer than they might have lived without that positive force.

Anne Sexton was a friend of mine, and I say it was booze, not poetry, that deepened her depressions and hastened her death. She began writing poetry at the suggestion of her psychiatrist, who felt it would be therapeutic for a bored suburban housewife in the '50s suffering from anxiety and depression. Anne took a poetry course at the Boston Center for Adult Education, where she met and befriended other budding poets like Maxine Kumin and George Starbuck. Her work was almost immediately recognized as powerful and unique. Her first book, *To Bedlam and Part Way Back*, established her at once as a major poet with a fresh, new voice. Her poetry was called "confessional"; yet, I felt it "confessed" for all of us, by bringing out the dark thoughts of the psyche we're afraid to confront and holding them up to the light. Her poetry sometimes laughed, sometimes cried—it was a cathartic experience for me as a reader, and I think for most of her many devoted fans.

Anne continued to write and work despite periods in mental hospitals, and attempted suicides. When she finally died from an overdose of pills at the age of forty-two, her death was ascribed by some to poetry, as a manifestation of madness. Yet, Anne told friends in talks and in letters, "the poetry keeps me alive." For many artists, creation is salvation. To create is to live, and to want to live. The alcohol, I believe, killed her.

PUBLIC DEFEAT

I've never seen mentioned another important element that helps explain in a very mundane, practical way the mood swings of writers and artists. I once had lunch with a writer friend in my neighborhood when a local politician who had just lost an election came in. We expressed our sympathy, saying we had voted for him. My writer friend observed that perhaps politicians were the only people who went through the same kinds of public defeats that we endured as authors. When you get a bad review in the hometown paper or the *New York Times* or a national magazine, all the neighbors know. The world knows. Our equivalent experience with the politician who lost an election was getting a bad review and having the neighbors come up and sympathize, saying they had bought your book anyway (a way of "voting" for you). And, like the politician's, our defeat would not merely be a blow to the ego, as in a popularity contest, but also to the income, as in paying the rent and putting food on the table.

If a doctor loses a patient, or a lawyer loses an important case, it's usually known only in their professional circles; rarely do friends and neighbors hear about it, much less read about it in the Sunday paper! Yet no writer with a new book, or artist with a new show, is immune to public disdain and ridicule. Reviewers of both art and literature can be vicious. I once had an otherwise successful novel (*Starting Over*, which later became a movie starring Burt Reynolds and Candice Bergen) described in a review in the *Washington Post* as "despicable." It went downhill from there. My friends in D.C. called to express their condolences. It felt as if I'd died, as least in D.C.; in fact, my book did, killed by that review, though it did well almost everywhere else. Not even the most successful, garlanded writers are immune to such put-downs; John Updike's latest novel was demeaned by one reviewer as "ugly."

Powerful art raises passions, from love to outrage, and in a sense the reviewer is expressing the public's emotional as well as intellectual response to the work. The anger stirred by innovative plays, symphonies, paintings, and sculpture has even caused audience rebellions and governmental bannings.

Then there are the times when reviews glow but sales falter. One talented writer friend seemed to never recover from having his first novel highly praised, shipped by the publisher with a good advance order that indicated a modest success, only to be told a few months later that half the books had been returned, unbought, and he would not even earn back his modest advance against royalties. The double demons of money and artistic standing (which rises and falls like the stock market gone mad) remain a constant concern in the career of every writer, actor, painter, musician, director. As they say in Hollywood, the bottom line is, you're only as good as your last picture. That pressure alone is enough to drive anyone to dramatic swings of mood.

Looked at from this perspective, one could argue that creative artists must be mentally and emotionally tougher than people in most other professions—especially those who earn a steady income. Virginia Woolf called for "a room of one's own" and a small monthly stipend for women writers in the early part of the century. Most writers I know today, of all genders, races, and creeds, long for the basic physical and financial security of that modest underpinning. Except for screenwriters, who are members of the Writers Guild of America, writers do not receive the "benefits" common to most Americans, such as health care and retirement funds. Is it any wonder writers get anxious or depressed? Sweating over the rent, or worrying about how to pay the doctor or hospital bill, are not stimulants to creativity.

Yet such practical, down-to-earth pressures are rarely mentioned in discussions of the psychology of writers; they are not glamorous enough to suit the myth. More popular is the topic of a conference held at the 92nd Street Y in New York City in 1994 called "Wanting to Die: Suicide and American Literature." The *New York Times* reported that the daylong conference "explored the links between depression, creativity, and suicide."

One of the famous writers discussed at the conference was Ernest Hemingway, who committed suicide after a lifetime of alcohol abuse had led to failing health and paranoid delusions. Was it the alcohol, or the creativity, that led to his suicide? Or was it genetics, or environment? Those are especially pertinent questions in the case of Hemingway, whose father, brother, and sister also committed suicide, though not one of them was a writer. His father was a doctor.

Have you heard about any conferences on the links between practicing medicine and committing suicide? As far as I know, this is not generally acknowledged as a dangerous phenomenon; but perhaps it should be. Dr. Dean Ornish, the heart specialist and best-selling author, pointed out in *Reversing Heart Disease* that "As a profession, we [doctors] have among the highest rates of drug addiction and divorce of any identifiable group, and the average physician dies ten years prematurely. Each year, enough physicians commit suicide to equal a large medical school's entire graduating class. And that's just the known suicides."

What about the links between law enforcement officers and suicide? In a recent year, twelve New York City policemen committed
suicide. I don't believe as many writers in New York City committed
suicide in any recent year, despite bad reviews, manuscript rejections,
lowering income, lack of health plan or pension benefits, or any other
stress-related circumstance common to the life of the writer.

My favorite story to counter the suffering-is-necessary-to-create
myth is the true-life experience of the great English novelist George
Eliot. Eliot was a plain and rather miserable young woman grinding
out reviews for an intellectual magazine until she met a man she fell
madly in love with. He was married to a woman who had continually
betrayed him and even bore the child of his best friend, but in the
England of that day he was unable to divorce her. In love with Eliot,
he went off with her to the Continent, where they lived happily "in
sin," as some of their old friends back home in England huffed at them
across the channel in pious recrimination. George's friends even wrote
her to break it off and come back, claiming they were worried about
her welfare. She wrote back, asking why they hadn't been worried
about her when she was lonely and miserable!

Love was a creative potion for George Eliot, who started writing
the novels that would make her world famous (*Silas Marner*, *The Mill
on the Floss*, *Middlemarch*) when she found domestic happiness. As a
lonely person longing for love, she felt lucky to eke out a living with
her reviews of other people's creative works; as a woman living with the
man she loved, she created great works of fiction that live today.

TESTIMONY OF A HAPPY NOVELIST

Novelist and poet Rosellen Brown, author of the highly praised bestseller *Before and After*, is a contemporary writer who doesn't buy the
myth that you have to suffer and lead a miserable life to be creative. "I
had a happy childhood, loved my parents and my two brothers, who
I'm still very close to," she told me recently. "I don't think you have to
be unhappy to create. John Irving said having a happy childhood
was *good* for him as a writer because he had no axes to grind, and I feel
the same.

"I've been married to the same man for thirty-one years, and he's
more delightful every day, and we have two terrific daughters. I've had

the most ordinary life—boring, no great traumas. When people ask me where I get these painful stories for my books I say that's not my experience, those are my nightmares—I put them on the page to work them out. I do think most of us artists and writers have at some time or other felt like outsiders—but I don't think you have to suffer personally to write or paint, you just have to keep your eyes open, look around you."

So much for the idea that suffering is necessary to create.

MYTH NUMBER 3
ONLY THE ARTS ARE CREATIVE

Some people throughout history who have proved this rule wrong are: Marie Curie, Wilbur and Orville Wright, Joan of Arc, Albert Einstein, Jonas Salk, Eleanor and Franklin D. Roosevelt, Bill and Hillary Rodham Clinton, Mahatma Gandhi, Winston Churchill, Golda Meir, Martin Luther King, Jr.—to name but a few.

According to this well-worn myth, sometimes science qualifies as creative (surely Einstein can be counted!), but business is still often regarded as plodding, pedestrian, unimaginative—even running a profit-making corporation. When I called Arnold Hiatt, the innovative entrepreneur who pioneered some of the most advanced employee and community relations in recent American business, as head of the Stride Rite corporation and now director of its Foundation, he said he'd be glad to talk with me about creativity but explained he was not himself "a creative person."

I disagreed. Hadn't he created a day care center, a non-smoking workplace, and a gym for employees, and captured new markets for his company when he anticipated the changing taste of consumers? Wasn't all *that* creative? Not by our usual definitions.

LOOKING FOR DETAIL

I learned in talking to Hiatt that his observing of detail, like that of a novelist, led to some of his greatest business successes. As treasurer of the Eugene McCarthy campaign in '68, he noticed the college kids were wearing work boots, and he bought a company that produced them. In the next decade he noticed Harvard students wearing boat shoes that could only be purchased in marinas, and he bought a company that made them, and put them on the national market.

Business people often use their creative imaginations to turn obstacles into assets. California restaurateur Larry Mindel told Bill Citara, an interviewer for *Bay Food* magazine, how two of his successful San Francisco restaurants benefited when he saw a problem in a different light, and turned it to an advantage. "Ciao did exhibition pasta because it was such a tiny restaurant we didn't have enough room in the kitchen to make pasta. So I said, let's make it out here, what's the difference? The same thing happened at Prego on Union Street. In the middle of the bar area was a fireplace. And we didn't have any place to make pizza. So, I said, why don't we make pizza where the fireplace is? Then we don't have to put in another flue. So we did the first exhibition pizza thing at Prego."

Like The Body Shop founder Anita Roddick, Mindel emphasizes the importance of creating a good working atmosphere, being in business with people you like, and loving what you do. For his popular Il Fornaio restaurants he uses all Italian ingredients and recipes, and hires Italian chefs "who do it out of love, not just for a job."

My old friend and mentor, the Reverend Norman Eddy, began his creative ministry with the East Harlem Protestant Parish and still works and counsels in that neighborhood where he has lived for more than forty years, making tremendous contributions in political action, aid for narcotics addicts, and ownership of housing by neighborhood residents. He gained a new understanding of creativity when he was a young man searching for his own spiritual path. He went to "a theosophist who read auras," he recalled, and what she told him "shook him up."

"She said I was an administrator, an activist. This hadn't crossed my mind. When she said it, I saw I'd often taken a leadership role in situations, although I thought of myself as sensitive, shy, and intuitive—an 'artistic' type. Yet these qualities were leading me to a life of action!"

Norm's career has proved that being an administrator and activist can be highly creative. Wasn't Martin Luther King, Jr., a creative person, and his own idol, Gandhi? King and Ghandi may not have written any novels or painted any pictures, but look how they have re-created the society and world we live in today!

"ZENNING OUT" WITH THE KIDS

Like many women, April Smith has managed to juggle motherhood and family life with a career—in her case, a highly prolific and successful writing career, primarily in network television. It's the toughest market there is, one in which writers (like me) are traditionally ground up and spit out like cannon fodder. April has carved out a distinguished record. She came to Hollywood to write a script for the series I created, "James at 15," moved on to become a staff writer and producer for "Lou Grant," and then wrote and produced high quality television movies, picking up three Emmy nominations along the way. What is even more remarkable, she has pulled off what every TV writer swears they intend to do but so rarely do: she took a year off from the big bucks of TV to gamble on writing a novel.

April won the bet with her fast-moving, incisive tale of the social strata of L.A., *North of Montana*, bought by Knopf for an advance of $750,000 and tagged as a major book for its list. She rents an office in the business section of her neighborhood, not far from her house, and goes there every morning to do her writing, whether it is of scripts or a novel. She has a household helper during the day, and her husband also takes part in the child-rearing. Still, I wondered how she did it— the professional writing combined with being a wife and a mother of an eight-year-old boy and a two-year-old girl.

April said parenting was not only a help to her creativity as a writer, but also a creative act in itself. "Part of the creativity of being a parent," she said, "is being able to live in the moment, because the children's whole lives are in the present. Watching the way they grow is miraculous, the way they learn and change. It's awesome, and it makes you value the moment, when you see how it passes so quickly. It makes you grateful in a spiritual way. They really add a spiritual aspect to my life.

"You're always problem-solving with kids, and often the solution is to create a distraction. If the kid is upset you want to get them out of their own distress. Rather than have a deep encounter with their subconscious it's better to get out the Barney coloring book, or make an origami airplane.

"You have to be creative about sibling rivalry. When I'm alone with the kids they fight—my solution is to do a project together. Yesterday we cooked together—it wasn't anything great, just the old tuna-noodle casserole, but Emma got to stir and Ben got to chop, so they were busy doing something and forgot to hate each other.

"What you do doesn't have to be glamorous. I think a lot of women feel intimidated if they're not being creative like the magazines tell you to do, whipping up cookies or art projects, but sometimes you just stall out and let them watch TV. Sometimes you can really 'Zen out.' Yesterday morning it was raining and the three of us did watercolors together, I was just pulling the brush across the page. It was almost like meditation, you can just *be*. It doesn't have to be work."

April says, "Luckily, the writing I do during the day uses a different part of the brain—I'm intellectual during the day, then I come home, and with kids it's all on the gut level. It does deplete your energy, but you get a lot back. The kids help the creativity I need in my work—absorbing their spontaneity, seeing the way they think is refreshing. It loosens up a lot of structures that are calcified."

Many male writers also find creativity in their role as fathers. Novelist Ivan Gold says, "Raising a son is the most creative thing I've ever done—in the back of my mind, of course, it's always a possible subject for fiction."

Rosellen Brown, a writing wife and mother who also teaches creative writing at the University of Houston, agrees that "raising children takes great creativity and I think it feeds into your work. There are many women writers today who have children, and their writing benefits from it—Margaret Drabble, Alice Hoffman, Anne Tyler. Tyler said her children dragged the world of pop culture over the doorstep into the house, or she never would have known about it. I could say the same.

"I believe people raising children a⁻ doing the most creative activity possible. You're keeping them ealthy, fed, getting them to school—it's very much in bits and pieces, a mosaic of little acts of loving kindness, and it seems mundane but it's not. When you pull back and look at it, you see it's extraordinary."

It's extraordinary, too, how mothers can foster—and even shape—

the creative spirit of their children. When master architect Frank Lloyd Wright was a baby, his mother Anna hung prints of Gothic cathedrals around his crib, according to Meryle Secrest, author of *Frank Lloyd Wright: A Biography*. Wright's mother believed (and obviously helped to determine) that he would grow up to become a great architect.

Rosellen Brown's "mosaic" of small acts made me think of a story I heard from Alice Olsen Mann, the head of the appeals department of a major law firm in Boston and a nationally known expert in her legal field. She mentioned once that when raising her son she developed different strategies for getting him to eat his vegetables, making broccoli more alluring by telling him the broccoli stalks were like "little trees." It was much more fun to eat "little trees" than plain old boring broccoli. (Maybe if George Bush's mother had been as creative, he wouldn't have grown up to be such a broccoli hater.)

Mrs. Mann's story reminded me of how my own mother got me to eat brussels sprouts by calling them "little boy cabbages." The formerly dull vegetables took on a new meaning and interest—they were specially made for me, it seemed! Knowing that, they didn't taste so bad after all.

Isn't the ability to see broccoli as "little trees," or to rename brussels sprouts in a way that is appealing to a little boy, the same sort of creative activity as finding the right metaphor for a poem? That kind of creativity is part of the daily work of any mother. Who can doubt the creative imagination and energy it takes to be a wife and mother— or for that matter, a *single* mother, one without any outside assistance from family or hired helpers.

Journalist Jill Nelson was twenty years old and single when her daughter was born, and she had to figure out a way to write and take care of her baby at the same time. She learned to sit on the floor with her typewriter on top of a box, while a toddler crawled nearby, and then a two-year-old ran around. "I was creating what you do in that situation," she told me. A twenty-four-hour record of any such role would surely involve as much creativity as Van Gogh put into a day at the easel or Henry James used when "steadily driving" his pen.

Still, in some circles of our society, women are called upon to defend or justify their roles as wives and mothers. According to an article in the *New York Times*, when poet and musician Patti Smith transformed herself "from the belligerent Bohemian punk poet of the '70s who galvanized the New York underground to the loving wife and mother of the '80s," she "shocked her fans by disappearing to the Detroit suburb of St. Clair Shores." When Smith returned to the concert circuit on a tour with Bob Dylan at the end of 1995, some of her fans "snidely" said that she "withdrew from the music world in order to be a housewife," the *Times* reported.

Ms. Smith responded that "there's no job harder than being a wife and a mother. It's a position that should be respected and honored, not looked upon as some sappy alternative. It's much more demanding, and required much more nobility than the other work that I did. Hopefully, I can inject some of the things that I learned from that experience into the work that I'm doing now."

MYTH NUMBER 4
CREATIVITY IS NOT MANLY

When I was a freshman in college at Bloomington, Indiana, one of my jock fraternity brothers spotted me carrying a novel by F. Scott Fitzgerald—a book that was not a requirement for any class—and plucked it from my hand. He held it up with a grimace, as if examining a dirty sock.

"You like this stuff?" he asked, not so much with curiosity as contempt.

"Yeah," I said, in my best mock-thug voice. I was trying to sound macho, for I knew what was being questioned was not my literary taste but my manliness. It was understood, like an unwritten rule of life, at least in the American Midwest in the mid '50s, that real men don't read novels—or write poems; paint (or look at) pictures; play or listen to classical music; write, act in, or go to the theater (with the possible exception of a college variety show sponsored by the right fraternity); or show any sort of interest in or appreciation of the arts, which included anything that might be called creative, a word which in that time and place carried a nuance of femininity or at least un-masculinity.

Nor was this attitude just a phenomenon of the heartland; Reverend Norman Eddy found it in New York City, in the mean streets of East Harlem, among the young gang members and those who fell prey to the lure of dope.

"On the street, to be creative is not macho," Norm reflected recently, "so there's no outlet for creativity, except in athletics, with the body.

"My eyes opened when I saw heroin addicts who were unable to express their creativity, and when I visited Riverside Hospital to see them in recovery I discovered that many of those young addicts had poems tucked under their pillow. I asked if they had shown them to their therapist and they said of course not—they wouldn't dare show them to anyone. I was an exception because I was a minister, so I was supposed to understand such things.

"Even today, the body is the only accepted way—or macho way—of being creative, on the street," Norm explained. "That's a perfectly fine way, of course, but it's a shame to think of it as the *only* one. The body, mind, soul, feelings are all areas in which we can be creative. When Jesus says to worship him with all your heart, mind, soul and strength that's what he means. All of us are part of creation—one of our deepest desires is to create the beautiful.

"And, of course, everyone really *is* creative," Norm added with a smile. "Even the nineteenth-century robber barons who created the railroads and shipping lines had a kind of creative zeal."

Yes! But of course we don't think of them that way. They are seen as macho or practical or hardheaded—which in our culture are thought of almost in opposition to creativity.

Our society is more sophisticated now; yet, those old strictures still hold to our thinking. Such obsolete concepts are probably among the factors behind the national ratio of 70 percent women to 30 percent men taking adult education courses. That is also the usual ratio for the workshops I lead in creativity or Spiritual Autobiography; yet, the men who do participate enjoy and benefit from the experience as fully and actively as the women. They, in fact, show signs of being just as creative as their wives and sisters!

A NEW MESSENGER ARRIVES

Perhaps the greatest breakthrough in attitudes in our time is the acknowledgment of gay men and lesbians as major cultural contributors who need not hide their sexual orientation. Despite the prejudice that still exists in the society at large, at least in the arts the old stigma and fear of homosexuality has been largely replaced by gay pride. Where once a man's "artistic leanings" were regarded as a shameful indication of homosexuality (hence the effort to prove oneself super-macho), our respected male novelists now include openly gay authors writing frankly on homosexual themes, like David Leavitt, Armistead Maupin (both of whom have had their work dramatized for PBS miniseries), Paul Monette, and Edmund White.

The most exciting and significant theatrical event of the decade is the winner of the 1993 Pulitzer Prize for Drama, *Angels in America*, subtitled *A Gay Fantasia on American Themes*. Rather than hopelessly lamenting the victims of AIDS, the scourge of our time, *Angels*, by playwright Tony Kushner, builds to a stunning finale of courage and mystical power, with an angel descending to the hospital room of Prior Walter, the AIDS-afflicted patient, announcing:

"The great work begins. The messenger arrives."

Rarely has art in our time created—by an act of imaginative will—such a life-affirming message of hope from the very theme and throes of death.

MYTH NUMBER 5
WOMEN'S WORK IS NOT AS
CREATIVE AS MEN'S

Women's struggle for equal pay and opportunity in the business world is necessary in the world of the arts as well. Example: A painting by Jasper Johns recently sold for $17.7 million. For that same amount of money, you could buy "an anthology of all the women artists in history"—a piece by about fifty women artists—including work by such luminaries as Georgia O'Keeffe and Frida Kahlo.

This eye-opening (and hopefully mind-opening) information comes from the "Guerrilla Girls," an anonymous group of activist women artists formed in 1984 to combat "the underrepresentation of women in the arts." The inequality was made glaringly obvious when the Museum of Modern Art opened that year with an international painting and sculpture show of work by 166 people, and only sixteen were women—slightly less than 10 percent.

Both older and younger feminists combined to form the group that spells its name "guerrilla" like the freedom fighters, but whose members wear gorilla masks in public appearances and on posters as an image of their anger. Romaine Brooks, an identified member of the Guerrilla Girls, said in an interview with author Suzi Gablik in *Art in America* magazine:

"Today, when we visited the Roanoke [Virginia] Museum, there was a painting by Thomas Eakins's wife. I guess the only reason her painting was in the museum is that her family comes from around here—that's what we were told. It reminded me of a show of . . . artist wives of famous artists, and they were all extremely gifted and talented. In one case, the woman had destroyed most of her work at the end of her life because she felt it would be a burden to her children—nobody paid any attention to her the whole time she was making the work, so only a few pieces were left. Milton Avery's wife, Sally Avery, was in the show. It turned out she'd supported him for 25 years, and when the woman curator went over there to get a few pieces for the show, all of Milton Avery's work was on the walls, and her work was in a pile on the floor. So the curator said, 'Why is your work on the floor?' And she answered, 'Well, Milton gets the walls and I get the floor.' And that is a crippling attitude. And even though it's now 1993 and things should be different, I think it's still an attitude that one encounters."

Things are different in some ways, however, at least partly due to the protests of the Guerrilla Girls.

Romaine Brooks explained in the same interview, "We did a critique of the Whitney Biennial a number of years ago, at the Clocktower in New York, where we gave all these statistics revealing how sexist and racist all the Whitney Biennials have been. Well, the most recent Whitney Biennial is forty percent women, and it's probably thirty-five percent artists of color, and I'd say we really take full credit for this. Things that we've been pounding on and talking about for years are finally bearing some fruit."

I saw a documentary movie on the life and work of New York painter Joan Mitchell, who tells of going to a gallery owner in the '50s who looked at her paintings and declined to take her on. He shook his head, saying wistfully he loved her work and knew it would sell, "if you were only male, French—and dead."

MEN EARN TWICE AS MUCH

Rebecca Blunk, director of performing arts for the New England Foundation for the Arts, told me that in arts management "very few women in the presenting field [professional impresario] make over $50,000, but many men do. Art is generally undervalued in our society, so it is safe to put women in charge of it at paltry salaries. Once an organization requires big budgets and new buildings, salaries go up and men are more likely to be in the top spots. A 1994 survey in the TAB newspapers in Boston listed the top ten salaries for people in management positions in culture and the arts in the city; the only woman on the list was Ann Hawley, director of the Isabella Stewart Gardner Museum, and she was at the bottom, or tenth place, with an annual salary of $104,865. Number one on the list was Kenneth Haas, general manager of the Boston Symphony, at $275,600."

Ms. Blunk also pointed out that many women are still regarded as earning a secondary household income, and many start out in the arts as volunteers and cannot overcome that image.

I know of a case in which a married woman and a single man formed a company in the entertainment field in the '60s, and he told her she should take a lesser salary because she was married and had a second income, while he did not. She accepted this, although she did at least an equal part of the work. This was typical for that time, and probably occurs today; though, surely it is no longer taken for granted, as it was so recently.

In the world of writing and publishing, women are faring much better. Two of the biggest advances for first novels in recent years went to works by women. When I started out as a writer there were no women working as editors in chief or heads of publishing houses except for the remarkable Helen Meyer, head of Dell, who was one of the giants of the industry. Now there are women in both positions throughout publishing.

MYTH NUMBER 6
You Have to Live in an Ivory Tower or by a Pond to Create

Many talented writers of the '50s were scorned by critics for going into academic life—"retreating to the ivory tower" it was called—yet, some of our finest novelists of the era, like Saul Bellow, Bernard Malamud, Mary McCarthy, Harvey Swados, and Herbert Gold, supplemented their writing with teaching at universities, as did even more of the poets, including Maxine Kumin, Anne Sexton, Richard Wilbur, W. D. Snodgrass, and Robert Lowell, to name but a few who found nourishment for the muse as well as financial stability in college classroom teaching.

The "ivory tower" stigma largely has dissipated. Many of the new generation of writers come out of graduate writing programs, like two of my former students from the Iowa Writers Workshop—Tracy Kidder, whose *Soul of a New Machine* won a Pulitzer Prize for nonfiction, and Thom Jones, whose collection of stories, *The Pugilist at Rest*, was nominated for the National Book Award for Fiction in '93. Many graduate writing programs around the country have working writers on the faculty, from short-story writer Deborah Eisenberg and novelist Frank Conroy at Iowa, to novelist John Edgar Wideman at the University of Massachusetts and novelists Eileen Pollack and Jenefer Shute at Emerson.

On the other hand, many writers have found not only their subject matter but their creative spirit from living very much in—and as part of—the world. Louis Auchincloss worked at the prestigious New York law firm of Sullivan and Cromwell (one of its senior partners, John Foster Dulles, complained that the younger men in the office "wrote novels") while writing distinguished novels of New York society life in the tradition of Henry James and Edith Wharton. When one of his works, *The Rector of Justin*, became a critical success and a bestseller, Auchincloss left the law firm to devote himself full-time to writing. He soon found that without that structure of his other career, he couldn't write, so he formed his own law firm, working half-time on legal matters and devoting the rest of his time to writing (without any senior partners to complain.)

The bestselling Icelandic novelist Olaf Olafsson is also president of the Sony Electronic Publishing Company, a leading producer of video games like "Bram Stoker's Dracula," "Cliffhanger," and "Sewer Shark." Running a business that racked up $150 million in sales in 1993 did not keep Olafsson from writing four hours every night during the week and six hours a day on weekends in his Upper East Side Manhattan apartment. An English translation of his latest novel, *Absolution*, was published in the U.S. in '94. Olafsson was described as "the most respected novelist in the most literate country in the world" by *New York* magazine, but his literary success didn't tempt him to leave his full-time job in the business world.

"So far, it has not been a hindrance to my writing," he told reporter Dinitia Smith, "though I've had less time in the past two years than I wanted to. When I'm so busy that I can't write, I do get frustrated."

But that frustration is balanced for Olafsson by the fact that, as he says, "When I write, I don't have to please anybody but myself. I don't have to write a particular story to pay the phone bills."

Writers who seem to find creative energy in the world include novelist Joan Didion, who loves to explore, in her role as reporter, new scenes and subjects. William F. Buckley, who hosts the TV show "Firing Line," turns out a syndicated newspaper column, and lectures and debates around the country and the world, told me, "I write my novels every afternoon between the hours of four and seven."

Anne Sexton formed a rock group, Anne Sexton and Her Kind, in the early '70s to back up her poetry readings—much to her own delight, but to the chagrin of the poetry establishment. Norman Mailer has always thrived on mixing it up out there in debates, boxing rings, prisons, and politics, not only covering elections as a journalist-observer but once jumping into the fray himself by running for mayor of New York (as did his longtime debating foe, Bill Buckley). The end of the Cold War even saw the emergence of the writer as national leader in the person of playwright Vaclav Havel, who rose from political prisoner to president of Czechoslovakia.

Artists and writers also find fulfillment in working for political causes. The San Francisco painter Mayumi Oda recently took a year off from her art to devote her efforts full-time to a project for pressuring governments around the world to destroy their stores of plutonium. She feels the cause is worth the sacrifice of a year of her own work, since plutonium weapons can destroy our civilization; no more people, no more art.

Creative people have traditionally given time to causes they believe in, joining in community action on behalf of oppressed peoples, human rights, animal rights, the preservation of the earth. James Baldwin devoted great energy and time to civil rights causes, as did his friend Kay Boyle, who never in her ninety-one years was without a cause for the betterment of the world and its inhabitants. Both drew sustenance from such activities, as demonstrated by their productivity as well as the high quality of their work (they both achieved the goal of what Baldwin called creating "a shelf of books" by the end of their lives). The musicians who put on Live Aid and Farm Aid, the activist actors who are often scoffed at for their genuine dedication and beliefs, are typical of the connection between creativity and contribution to the human community. Robert Redford has not only become involved in ecology, but also given back to young people the support of a mentor with his extensive programs for development of films at the Sundance Institute. Paul Newman's foundation sponsors camps for disabled children and gives grants to community programs like Vera Gold's 96 Bay State Road writers group and magazine in Boston.

THOREAU'S DINNER AT HOME

Experiences as diverse as those just mentioned disprove the isolation myth, but I want to point out an infrequently mentioned aspect of the "lonely creation" phenomenon. Famous "loner" artists, like Thoreau, had significant and regular friends and colleagues in their lives. Thoreau helped perpetuate the isolation myth when he romanticized his own life at Walden Pond, but omitted the crucial information that he went home for dinner every week and dropped in to talk with his friend and neighbor Mr. Emerson.

Thomas Merton felt pulled from his lone outpost at the hermitage on the grounds of Gethsemane, and yearned to be at worldwide conferences of religious leaders in Europe and Asia. It was at such a meeting of Christian and Buddhist leaders and thinkers in Bangkok that he met his accidental death in 1969. I don't mean to dismiss or discredit either of these two great creators, Thoreau or Merton, yet their lives offer dramatic and even poignant illustration of the need to be nourished by community.

THE POWER OF GROUP ENERGY

I would have sworn as recently as five years ago that, at least in the actual act of writing, one has to be alone. *That* surely has nothing to do with community, and can only be stymied by it. Yet, in leading my workshops I have seen people stimulated by community while writing in the same room with the others. Participants report a kind of group energy that raises the level of their own creativity as they come to know one another through their mutual stories. I have felt it and recognized it in the course of leading these exercises in creativity. Writing in a room while other people are writing, then reading what you have written aloud to the group, raises the level of the writing and stimulates release of the story within. The community experience of sharing gives it a new resonance, increasing the richness of the creative act.

Writers, painters, and musicians love to socialize, as well as work at artist colonies like Yaddo in Saratoga Springs, New York, and Mac-Dowell in Peterborough, New Hampshire. A group of abstract expressionist painters of New York formed the Artists Club in a loft on Eighth Street in Greenwich Village for fellow painters, sculptors, and art dealers. The painter Jack Tworkov explained the club's appeal in his journal:

"I'm consciously happy when I'm there. I enjoy the talk, the enthusiasm, the laughter. . . . There is a strong sense of identification. I say to myself these are the people I love, that I love to be with. Here I understand everybody, however inarticulate they are. Here I forgive everyone their vices, and I'm learning to admire their virtues."

Maybe those in the creative arts were the first to discover the richness and support of community that is now sweeping the nation. In *Sharing the Journey: Support Groups and America's New Quest for Community*, Princeton sociologist Robert Wuthnow found that 40 percent of nearly two thousand randomly selected Americans participated in support groups—these were not Twelve Step or therapy groups but Bible study, prayer, adult Sunday School, or adult education groups.

Participants said the groups made them feel they were not alone, and supplied encouragement and support when they were feeling down.

Even groups that form for weekend workshops create such bonds. People who take my Spiritual Autobiography seminars sometimes exchange addresses and continue to meet on their own for months or years. The most frequent response of one such group, when asked what was most important to them in the course, was that they learned they weren't the only ones who went through "the dark side" on their journey. The valuable message, not just in words but in shared experience was: *You are not alone*.

There are, however, times when you may *want* to be alone—not in the context of your life, but for a circumscribed period. Sometimes we feel an overload of social interaction, no matter how fulfilling and creative it may be, and we long for solitude. Canadian singer and songwriter Sarah McLachlan spent fourteen months touring, and then she visited impoverished areas of Thailand and Cambodia with the World Vision Charity. Afterward, she rented a secluded home in the woods outside Montreal.

"I stayed there for seven months by myself, except for my cats," she told *New York Times* reporter Sheila Rule. "I'd been on the road living in a bus with 13 people. I had no sense of privacy or sense of self. I was in hibernation the first couple of months, but when spring came everything blossomed and opened up. My spirit decided to be set free and I started writing."

McLachlan, whose album written during that time was *Fumbling Towards Ecstasy*, said that her creativity "has been aided by solitude."

Everyone must go by their own instinct in such matters, deciding what is right for their own spirit, without making a mythic "must" of any single choice.

MYTH NUMBER 7
CREATIVITY IS A FULL-TIME JOB

Examples of people who have proved this rule wrong: Insurance executive and poet Wallace Stevens ("Money is a kind of poetry," he wrote); Sony Electronics Publishing president and novelist Olaf Olafsson; banker and poet T. S. Eliot; family doctor and poet Dr. William Carlos

Williams; novelist, wife, and mother Sue Miller; novelist, wife, and mother Gish Jen; poet, housewife, mother, teacher, farmer, and horsewoman Maxine Kumin; novelist, journalist, wife, and mother Joan Didion; novelist, wife, mother, and teacher Lynn Sharon Schwartz; novelist, wife, and mother Jayne Ann Phillips; and every woman writer who is also a wife and mother, as well as those who are single mothers.

Women who are married with children or are single mothers simply have no choice but to find a time and place and way to do their writing. Those I've cited are only a few examples of the many who manage to do it all with no harm or loss to their creative work, and often feel that work is fed and nourished by their other roles. April Smith says, "Having children gives me perspective, it grounds me."

Rosellen Brown believes that "raising kids keeps you in the mainstream, the world you write out of. I feel like I'm writing out of my experience of ordinary American life, though it's slightly different to be a mother who's a writer. I'm not quite as available, but neither would a woman lawyer be available to drive the car pool in the afternoon. You have to protect that time if you work at home. But it's a great and useful thing to me as a writer to go sit at an elementary school band concert, or a high school wrestling match. Children remind you that you live in the world and that world is what you want in your writing."

Many women take on these demanding multiple roles and find creative ways to make them all work. Historically it is mainly men who have moaned and whined over having other obligations that "interfere" with their creative activity, and even in our more liberated era, some men are keeping the tradition alive. Raymond Carver complained that having to share the duties of household and child-raising forced him to be a short-story writer, since taking time out for chores like going to the Laundromat precluded his sustaining the longer work of a novel. (He should have asked writers like Rosellen Brown, Alice Hoffman, and dozens of others how they managed to do it.)

Despite the dramatic gains by women toward equality as creators in the literary marketplace, it still seems surprisingly common for men to ask the women they live with as wives or lovers to support their creative habit, so that they—these sensitive men—can remain "pure" in their creativity, courting their elusive muse with full attention while the woman attends to such mundane matters as paying the rent or mortgage, taking care of the kids, and not only "bringing home the bacon" but cooking it up, and washing the greasy skillet afterward.

MYTH NUMBER 8
CREATIVE PEOPLE DON'T HAVE GOOD RELATIONSHIPS

This is often a cop-out used by creative people themselves. I know, because I've used it myself as an excuse for my own poor record of broken relationships, and even conned myself into believing it for a while. It's similar to saying, "I'm creative, so I have to drink a lot." You may not maintain relationships, and you may drink, but the same is true of many people whose work has nothing to do with the arts or creativity. Throwing in creativity as an excuse for other unsatisfactory behavior is simply a way of avoiding—for yourself as well as the world—the real issues.

According to this myth, all of one's emotion goes into creative work, so nothing is left over. Hemingway even believed that this applied to sex—that creative energy was the same stuff, or came from the same source, as sexual energy. He thought that when he was really working hard on his writing, any sexual activity would drain his creative energy. This is the male artist's version of "I can't tonight, dear, I have a headache!"

This is one of the Hemingway myths I had bought myself, largely abstaining from sex in the final creative burst that comes in the last few months of finishing a book. Then one summer I went off to the seashore with a wonderful woman I was living with, assuming that the concentrated writing I would have to do to finish the book would sap my sexual energies. My lovely lover showed me what a sap I was! Having not read or paid much heed to Hemingway's weirdo-macho philosophy, she simply proceeded on her own desires and assumptions, taking me with her, and I had the most fulfilling summer of my life as I finished writing the novel *Home Free*.

Creativity never necessarily needs to take anything away from you. Odds are, it will only expand your experience.

MYTH NUMBER 9
CREATIVE PEOPLE ARE CHILDREN
AND AREN'T RESPONSIBLE

This is a favorite of landlords who don't want to rent to writers and artists, parents who don't want their daughters or sons to marry one, and personnel executives who don't want to hire one. It's also used by some creators who like to perpetuate the myth as an excuse for their own irresponsibility: "I can't help it, I'm too sensitive and artistic to (a) pay the rent, (b) show up on time, (c) clean the apartment, (d) go grocery shopping, cook, or wash the dishes, (e) _____ through (z) _____;" you can fill in the blanks yourself!

I asked people in my workshop to write down what they had heard growing up about creative artists. These are some typical responses, which I think reflect the general attitude of our society: "aimless, shiftless, and poor," "radicals, hippies, beyond the pale," "into deviant lifestyles," "usually people with sad hearts."

Creative workers sometimes bring an image of irresponsibility on themselves, a glaring example being the refusal of some writers to join organizations acting on their behalf, such as the National Writers Union. They argue that creative people are somehow harmed by being in groups. According to this myth, their delicate sensibility is mysteriously upset by acting in concert with their fellow artists; and to think about such mundane issues as money, rights, benefits, and fair contractual agreements for all is somehow crass. This is indeed a childish opinion. Publishers are adults who correctly act in their own best interests; writers must have the maturity to do the same. In the movie industry they have done it, and members of the Writers Guild of America enjoy health insurance and retirement benefits as a result.

MYTH NUMBER 10
THE OLDER YOU GET, THE LESS
CREATIVE YOU BECOME

Oh, really? How about Marc Chagall painting in his nineties, Graham Greene turning out fine novels in his eighties, Katharine Hepburn acting on television at eighty-eight, Jason Robards performing in a Pinter play on Broadway at seventy-one, Martha Graham choreographing at ninety, Hume Cronin and Jessica Tandy performing on stage and screen in their eighties, May Sarton bringing out her collected works and writing new ones at eighty-two, Georgia O'Keeffe painting in her eighties, George Burns flicking his cigar as he celebrated his ninety-ninth birthday, Edward L. Bernays, the "Father of Public Relations," lecturing and writing two years past his hundredth birthday, Lena Horne singing in her seventies, *New York Times* reporter Harrison Salisbury retracing The Long March of Mao Tse-tung to write a new book about it at eighty-five, Elizabeth Layton of Wellington, Kansas, learning to draw in her seventies and exhibiting at the Smithsonian in her eighties, dancer-choreographer Katherine Dunham at eighty-five going on a hunger strike to call attention to the plight of the Haitian refugees.

Now that the baby boomers are getting gray, there are many signs that aging is becoming hip, and the accomplishments of older citizens are being recognized and even—gasp—discovered! A front-page headline in the *New York Times* toward the end of 1995 proclaimed "Older Writers Budding, Blossoming." The article reported that Bessie R. Doenges, who came to New York City at age nineteen to be a writer, had finally landed her first literary agent at age ninety-four.

Ms. Doenges writes, at thirty dollars apiece, a column for two small weekly newspapers. It was read with pleasure by novelist Mary Morris, who recommended the author to her own agent, Timothy Seldes. Mr. Seldes said he was struck by "the amazing vitality and originality of the voice," and was enthusiastically submitting a book of "Bessie Writes" columns to publishers. Larry O'Connor, a Manhattanite who edits the *Chelsea News* and the *Westsider*, said of Ms. Doenges, "She's a classic case of a talent being discovered." That it happened when she was ninety-four, O'Connor said, only makes it "more dramatic." (That same week, *The New Yorker* "discovered" a woman poet in her eighties.)

A photograph, which shows Bessie lying on her living room couch as she writes, reminded me of the famous photo of the youthful Truman Capote lying on a hammock when his first book was published. Maybe now that old age is becoming fashionable, the work of people in their eighties and nineties will become as "hot" as the products of teenagers. That is good news for writers' groups like the one at the West Side YMCA in New York, where writers aged sixty-six to eighty-one gather weekday afternoons to read works in progress they hope to get published.

A woman in one of my Spiritual Autobiography workshops read a piece to the group about how she wanted to be a painter but her husband didn't like her taking time out from the house and children. After the children got out of college she got divorced in her fifties, and started to paint full-time. "But I didn't really get my life together until I was seventy-five," she reported; it was after that age that she found her real style as an artist and began doing her best work, some of which now hangs in museums in New York and Boston. When she finished reading, the workshop participants broke into spontaneous applause. A doctor in his forties told her, "You've given us all hope—that there's still time to 'get it together'!"

Indeed. Having recently crossed the line of sixty—an age that once seemed to me beyond imagination, a Methuselah-like period of life—I'm amazed at how different it is (thankfully!) from what I'd been led to believe by the myths of our culture. My own experience seems in some degree a reverse of the predicted path. I feel much better today at sixty-three than I did at thirty-five because I don't wake up with a hangover anymore. I gave up drinking and took up the Exercycle, followed by tai chi and then yoga a decade ago. That was the first physical exercise I'd done since Boy Scout Camp in Indianapolis. Since '85 I've gone every year to Rancho La Puerta, a health spa in Mexico just below the border, for an all-around, weeklong workout that begins every day with a mountain hike at six-thirty in the morning. It feels great, and so do I.

In the past decade I've written a novel, a TV movie, three nonfiction books, dozens of magazine articles, taught college and graduate courses, lectured, and created and led workshops in Spiritual Autobiography and creativity in churches, adult ed centers, and prisons throughout the country. I look forward to doing more, as much as I can, as long as I can. I feel lucky to be a writer, since I can't imagine ever not wanting to write. Nor is this unusual.

When novelist Irwin Shaw was asked by a reporter on his eighty-fifth birthday when he planned to retire, he looked shocked, then answered, "Writers don't retire!" The same is true for musicians, actors, directors, painters—any creative people. Marc Chagall was painting in his nineties. The writers of my own generation, now in our sixties, continue to produce new and good work, and I can't imagine any of them stopping as long as they're breathing. Most of them have gray hair, as I do, and few are mistaken for graduate students; but none of them acts or thinks or works like the "old codgers" we were taught to believe was the norm for the sixth decade. Of course, we're blessed to be living at a time when life expectancy is longer than ever in history, and more is known about how to keep healthy.

Another happy revelation: What you heard about sex and aging is a myth, too.

Living healthy, without booze, it's better than ever.

WHAT IS YOUR CREATIVE MYTH?

Examine your reason for not creating what you want to create, and see if it's a myth you have bought or constructed for yourself. What would it mean if you saw it as myth, rather than fact? What could you create? When can you start? (*Now?*)

OLD *MYTHS* OF CREATIVITY:	NEW *TRUTHS* OF CREATING FROM THE SPIRIT:
To be creative you must *be*:	Creative people *do*:
1. A member of an elite group	1. Come from every walk of life and work in every field and occupation
2. Born with an artistic gift	2. Lead rich lives and share themselves with others
3. Neurotic, bordering on suicidal	3. Find nourishment in community
4. A lonely introvert	4. Cultivate their natural senses to stimulate their creativity
5. Effeminate or female	5. Develop clarity as the source of creativity
6. A man	6. Take responsibility for their lives and work
7. A full-time artist	7. Use their creative gifts in all areas of their lives
8. A big boozer	8. Regard age as an opportunity to apply the wisdom of experience to their art, and share it with others

9. Stoned on drugs

9. See obstacles as an opportunity to create new solutions, techniques, and skills

10. Immature and irresponsible

10. Recognize the body/mind/spirit connection

11. Young

11. Find surprising new ways to perform routine tasks

12. Single and childless, living alone in a garret, cave, or mountaintop

12. Use their dreams as a source of ideas and knowledge

13. Self-absorbed

13. Feel connected to the whole of humanity and the universe

14. Born wealthy, or doomed to poverty and deprivation

14. Practice silence and make room for it in their daily lives

15. Reckless and neglectful of your physical well-being

15. Appreciate their time on the planet and express their gratitude for it

Chapter 4

THE BIGGEST MYTH
OF ALL: BOOZE
AND THE MUSE

The deadly idea of alcohol and drugs as glamorous keys to creativity runs through our whole society, affecting people not only in literature and the arts, but in all fields, from business and industry to science and sports.

The myth serves as a paradigm for all the ways we deceive ourselves about the way to access our creative power. At the same time, a hard look at the mythology points in another direction, to the real key for unlocking and using creative energy.

In reality, alcohol and drugs are destructive not only to creativity, but to health, well-being, and successful functioning. Alcohol is more popular than drugs because it's legal and socially approved—and as if that weren't enough, it's given an extra boost with millions of dollars of creative, psychologically researched advertising.

On a deeper level than hype, however, there's a genuine reason for the confusion about alcohol and creativity: the craving for bottled spirits can mask the need for *spirit*, the real source of creation. When an alcoholic from America went to Jung for help in 1931, the psychiatric insights of the treatment did not affect the patient's drinking, and Jung finally told the man his only hope was in some kind of powerful spiritual experience or conversion. Jung wrote that "the craving for alcohol was the equivalent, on a low level, of the spiritual thirst of our being for wholeness . . . the union with God."

That is something I've experienced personally. When I began to turn away from alcohol toward a spiritual search in the early 1980s, I joined King's Chapel in Boston. I wrote to Rev. Carl Scovel, my minister, that I found myself attending his evening classes in Bible study and religious education as eagerly as I once would have hurried to a free martini party. I had not then read Jung or anyone else on the relationship of alcoholic thirst to spiritual thirst; I was simply using the only language I knew to explain what I was experiencing.

Jung went on to say, in the letter quoted above, "You see, 'alcohol' in Latin is *spiritus*, and one uses the same word for the highest religious experience as well as for the most depraving poison. The helpful formula therefore is: *spiritus contra spiritum*."

Spirits against spirit.

The confusion of alcoholic spirits with the creative force has been perpetrated in the work as well as the lives of many of our famous musical, theatrical, visual, and literary artists. Carson McCullers, author of *The Heart Is a Lonely Hunter*, a haunting and powerful first novel that was one of the bibles of my generation, abused her body and her talent with alcohol and wrote of it rapturously. In a letter to a friend she said that the wine she drank early in the morning warmed her in "a special way," and she compared it to the radiance that the stained-glass windows of a church gave to worshipers within. In "The Ballad of the Sad Café," she described a liquor that had "a special quality of its own" that glowed inside for a long time, and likened it to the "fire" that brings out the truth "known only in the soul."

Spirits confused with spirit.

Perhaps because they have not only been prey to alcohol but write about it, sometimes almost as defenders and promoters, writers have come to represent in the public mind the myth of alcohol as a necessary handmaiden of creativity. This myth of booze and the muse, which took hold in America in the '20s, was enshrined as an article of artistic faith by the '50s. Norman Podhoretz, the literary critic and editor of *Commentary* magazine, observed of that era in New York in his autobiographical *Breaking Ranks*: "A writer was expected to drink and suspected if he didn't; and far from being frowned on, drinking heavily was admired as a sign of manliness, and of that refusal of respectability that seemed necessary to creative work."

THE MYTH CONTINUES TODAY

That myth of creativity continues to hold on and influence new generations, despite the accumulation of evidence against it and a cultural, even artistic, awareness of its fallacy. Corrine Fonger, a high school teacher in Michigan who took one of my workshops, told me that as a college student in the '70s she took a writing course which the instructor convened at a bar so the class could drink beer and critique one another's works at the same time. As Corrine pointed out, it would have seemed odd for any other kind of class to meet at a bar—say, a chemistry or a history course—but it was understood that drinking and writing went together, as did drinking and all the creative arts. It was accepted as only natural for the college writing class to meet in the bar. Corrine said that myth is still operating for many of her high school students today.

I was invited to speak to students at Plainsboro–West Windsor High School in New Jersey in '94 by a parent who had heard me talk about the mythology of alcohol and drugs in one of my workshops. This mother told me she wanted her son and his class to hear the true stories I told about the destructive effects of alcohol on writers like Kerouac and Hemingway. She assured me those myths of the glamour and creative power of alcohol—as well as drugs—were alive and well among today's young people. An English teacher who asked me to her class said the same thing. No matter how much more information we have about the medical effects of drugs and alcohol, the mythology still persists, with both old and new role models.

Even with Twelve Step Programs and messages from athletes and movie stars to "Just Say No," younger and younger kids are drinking. The pressures of daily life are greater now than ever, and begin at an earlier age. The social and psychological lure of drinking as fun, creative, and inspiring is as seductive today as always.

People in their forties and older often tell me that the enlightened young people of today know better than to believe the myths of alcohol and drugs as glamorous and creative. I am assured that such appeal went out of fashion with my own ancient generation of the '50s, and is as dead as the Hula Hoop craze and "We Like Ike" buttons. It's a nice fantasy. My journey with booze may have different names and places but the plotline is still the same. I know the power of the myth, for I lived it. Luckily, I also lived to tell the tale.

DEATH BEFORE FORTY

A few months after I finished college in 1955, a fellow student who was also an aspiring writer took me to one of the hallowed literary shrines of New York, the White Horse Tavern in Greenwich Village. One of the veteran habitués of "The Horse" showed us to the holy of holies, the very table where the great Welsh poet Dylan Thomas had his last drink. (The current White Horse Tavern menu boasts of its famous patron that "his collapse came a few staggering steps from the front door.") Our volunteer guide pointed out the window to St. Vincent's Hospital, down the street, where the poet was taken to die, at age thirty-nine, of alcoholism.

I was thrilled.

Maybe I, too, could someday be a great writer and a romantic figure, like Dylan Thomas, and die of alcoholism before reaching the rotting age of forty! In fact, I began by faithfully following in his "staggering steps." When I suddenly arrived at age forty, though, death did not seem so romantic. But it wasn't until I was just past fifty that I cut down and then stopped altogether the regular alcohol consumption that was leading me toward a similar (if somewhat delayed) end as my early hero.

Dylan Thomas was, of course, not the only alcoholic role model I was given as an aspiring young writer in the 1950s. America's brightest literary lights—Hemingway, Fitzgerald, and Faulkner—were held up as inspirational examples whose literary muses were allegedly dependent on their steady, gargantuan intake of booze.

PAINTERS WHO DROWN IN THE BOTTLE

Aspiring painters had their own alcoholic role models in Jackson Pollock and the abstract expressionists who drank at the Cedar Bar in the Village in the '50s. In *The Turning Point: The Abstract Expressionists* and the Transformation of American Art, April Kingsley confirms that "modern American artists, particularly the Abstract Expressionists," followed the alcoholic patterns of their literary counterparts.

"Even as early as the end of the fifties, [Willem] de Kooning's drinking problem had become so serious that he began suffering blackout spells. Only a small amount of alcohol made him drunk to the point of illness. Elaine [de Kooning, his wife] convinced him to join Alcoholics Anonymous, but it was already too late to stop his memory loss."

Jackson Pollock, the most famous of the group, was the star of the Cedar Bar, as Dylan Thomas was the star of the White Horse, at least until his last years, when Kingsley recounts that "he was often banned from the place and would stand outside with his bloated face pressed beseechingly against the tiny glass window in the front door, begging for permission to reenter."

Kingsley tells us of Pollock's alcoholism that "with increasingly rare exceptions, after 1951 he was simply a drunk. Photographs mercilessly record his physical decline. They are excruciating to view, as painful as being close to him in those years must have been. . . . New friends were made among the adoring young writers and painters who flocked to the Cedar Bar to see the famous artist." Ms. Kingsley notes, "Mythic heroes are sacrificed while they are still young, and Pollock complied by driving himself drunkenly to his death in 1956 at the age of forty-four."

ALCOHOLIC ROLE MODELS

The fascination with artists self-damned and doomed with alcohol and/or drugs continues. Author John Cheever, who broke the cycle of alcoholic addiction, wrote: "If you are an artist, self-destruction is quite expected of you. . . . The thrill of staring into the abyss is exciting."

John Berryman, the poet who died an alcoholic suicide, wrote of the autobiographical poet in his novel Recovery that he "really thought, off and on for twenty years, that it was his duty to drink, namely to sacrifice himself."

In no other professions aside from the arts are drunkards and drug addicts held up to young people starting out as heroes or role models. Imagine a young intern being told nostalgic tales about great drunken doctors, or a first-year law student regaled with stories of alcoholic lawyers whose "collapse came a few staggering steps" from the front door of the courthouse!

DRINKING LESSONS FROM PAPA

I'm using writers as prime examples because by the nature of their work they leave tracks for us to follow. They write about their experience, not only in memoirs, but in stories and novels. They bring to their fiction their own attitudes about life and how to live it, projecting their own myths into the minds of readers. Writers are, for better and worse, teachers as well as chroniclers.

The literary gurus of the '20s taught succeeding generations about the "benefits" of booze, and made hard drinking—even drunkenness—a sign of merit and sophistication.

My college friends and I called Hemingway "Papa." He was our generational guru, not only for literature but for the way to conduct ourselves in the world. One of the means of doing that, according to the Hemingway code of macho honor, was to drink, and he told us how and why.

Malcolm Cowley, whose *Exile's Return* chronicled the lives of the "Lost Generation" of the '20s, described the common trait of Hemingway's heroes: "They drink early and late; they consume enough beer, wine, anise, grappa, and Fundador to put them all into alcoholic wards, if they were ordinary mortals; but drinking seems to have the effect upon them of a magic potion."

Drinking is the strong, manly thing to do in *The Sun Also Rises*, the bible of the Lost Generation. No wonder they were lost—they were too drunk to find their way home! Drinking is described in the novel as "direct action," it "beats legislation," keeps you warm, and even helps your memory! "Take that drink and remember," one Hemingway character advises another.

There are, of course, no footnotes in Hemingway's books that describe the alcohol-induced accidents, illnesses, broken marriages, depression, and paranoia of a life ending in suicide—as his own life ended. Perhaps the most eloquent footnote is the testimony of his granddaughter Lorian, who wrote in a powerful essay called "Help Me" in *Washington: The Evergreen State Magazine* in 1989 that when she "became physically addicted" to alcohol around 1980, "I told myself that drinking was necessary for creative existence. I was also told, by quite a few people, that I drank because I was a Hemingway. What better way to live out the world script of a poisoned legacy? I took this grand excuse and ran with it, believing that I, as one of the chosen few, was exempt from the finality of alcoholism."

After bottoming out, and barely hanging on to her life, she entered a hospital in 1988 and in 1989 was breathing "the rare and exotic air of an alcohol-free existence. . . . I think, often, in this new-found sobriety, of my grandfather, and I dearly wish I could have offered him the knowledge that he could live beyond his disease. I am bound to him by the common pain we suffered, and I know now the adventurous life, so carefully planned, was in part a sham. I grieve at his death, but there are no second chances. Alcoholism is progressive and takes little chunks of the soul and body until there is not much left to bargain with."

THE GLAMOROUS BINGE

The experience of binges as charming and fun—even leading to wisdom (the old *in vino veritas* theme, taken to extreme) is played out in that other landmark first novel that defined the '20s decade and the attitudes of generations to come, F. Scott Fitzgerald's *This Side of Paradise*. (Lorian Hemingway refers to Fitzgerald as "the ever-present dead cheerleader of my disease.")

When disappointed in love, rejected by Rosalind, his first great girlfriend, the character Amory Blaine goes on a three-week drunk, in the finest bars and hotels of New York City. At the bar of the Knickerbocker, Amory finds "his head spinning gorgeously, layer upon layer of soft satisfaction setting over the bruised spots of his spirit. . . ." We're told that his binge as a cure for disappointment in love was successful: "he found in the end that it had done its business; he was over the first flush of pain."

When my own "Rosalind" broke off my first great romance, I followed in my hero Amory/Scott's footsteps, even going to some of the same bars they frequented (my college friends and I used to meet under the clock at the Biltmore and proceeded to the hotel's bar in emulation of Fitzgerald's characters), drinking myself into a stupor. It was my first prolonged drinking binge, and although it didn't act as a cure for me as it did for the fictional Amory, it got me into the habit. From then on, regular heavy drinking was a part of my life.

I'm not saying poor Fitzgerald is responsible for my boozing, but certainly my friends and I admired and emulated the habits and attitudes about booze described in his novels and those of "Papa" Hemingway. They were our guides to a style, romance, and humor that was based on drinking, and their novels were handbooks on how and why to do it and what to think and say about it.

The tragedy is that these writers literally didn't know any better. Hemingway really believed he could "sweat out" the booze he drank, that by physical exercise he could rid his body of the alcohol he'd consumed. There was little medical knowledge then of its effects, and even less public awareness of alcoholism.

Prohibition made drinking an act of rebellion for the '20s generation, and when they were let in to speakeasies to drink they felt they were being "let in" on the rites of adulthood and sophistication. There were no Twelve Step programs or media awareness of the devastating effects of alcohol that we take for granted today. Drinking was chic, glamorous—and, oh my, literary, even political, as an act of rebellion.

The rationale of drinking as political protest was passed on to succeeding generations. The New York columnist and novelist Pete Hamill explains in A Drinking Life that as a young man he "discovered Hemingway, Fitzgerald, and the myth of the Lost Generation." From their work he "learned that drinking could be something more than mere fuel for a wild night out. It could be a huge Fuck You to Authority."

A political act! Those Prohibition-defying heroes of ours were rebels, and so were we in the '50s, as Hamill explains: "Drinking became the medium of my revolt against the era of Eisenhower. Drinking was a refusal to play the conformist game, a denial of the stupid rules of a bloodless national ethos." We exalted and excused our boozing as a protest against the middle-of-the-road politics of the time. Some of us literally went *off* the road, propelled by drink, like painter Jackson Pollock did in 1956 when he drunkenly drove himself to his death at age forty-four; like a friend from my high school did when he drunkenly smashed his car into a tree one morning after the bars closed in Indianapolis.

DOROTHY PARKER'S SCOTCH MIST

Many of our female literary idols suffered from the same disease of alcoholism as the male version; if macho Hemingway and romantic Fitzgerald were the principle literary salesmen of alcohol as a way of life, the top women writers of the time were hardly immune to the message. Edna St. Vincent Millay, the great lyric poet of the era, wrote of burning her candle at both ends, and part of that hard-living lifestyle was alcohol; fellow writer and critic Max Eastman was among Millay's friends who believed that "chemical stimulation blunted the edge of Edna's otherwise so carefully cherished genius."

Playwright and memoirist Lillian Hellman saw "hate, alcohol, and meanness" as her own failings, according to biographer William Wright in *Lillian Hellman: The Image, the Woman*. She realized that too much of her time and energy was spent in getting drunk with her alcoholic companion, mystery novelist Dashiell Hammett. They consumed pre-breakfast martinis, ran up huge hotel bills in drinks, and though Hellman had been a drinker before she met him, she believed she became an alcoholic in their early days together.

Dorothy Parker, the sharpest wit of the famous Algonquin Round Table and *The New Yorker*'s caustically brilliant theater critic at age twenty-four, was diagnosed as a "pathological drinker" at thirty-three. She lived the greater part of her life in what one biographer called a "Scotch mist" that dimmed and obscured her talent and drove her to numerous suicide attempts: slashing her wrists, swallowing sleeping pills, and drinking a bottle of shoe polish that made her deathly ill but didn't kill her. In the hospital after one such attempt she was terrified she couldn't get a drink, and persuaded a visitor to give her some gin from his flask; still, she was not convinced she was an alcoholic.

WOULD BOURBON BRING US THE NOBEL PRIZE?

I laughed with other friends who were fresh out of college in the '50s when we read a widely published article reporting that, of the seven Americans who had won the Nobel Prize for Literature, five were alcoholics, one "drank heavily," and the other was Pearl Buck. Against the evidence, we thought that women writers weren't drunks, so that explained Pearl Buck. As for the others, we thought it amusing—an occasion for humor, on the level of college fraternity pranks—because writers being alcoholics seemed a matter of pride. "All good writers are drunks," Ernest Hemingway assured F. Scott Fitzgerald.

There was also a deeply romantic aspect to the drunken author image, a belief in the "danger" of being a writer, based on the assumption that alcoholism was an occupational hazard of the literary life, like Black Lung for coal miners. Just as those daring young men in World War II movies of RAF pilots scrambled for their fighter planes, or race-car drivers strapped on their helmets before hurtling on to the death-defying curves of the Indianapolis 500, so we aspiring authors seated ourselves before the old Smith-Corona, ready to risk life, limb, and liver in the mission that might require such consumption of liquor as to render us physically ill, depressed, shaky, or in need of electroshock therapy, like Faulkner, prey to an early death, like Fitzgerald, or ending in suicide by shotgun, like Hemingway.

Ivan Gold, who dramatizes the destructive effects of the alcohol-creativity myth in his novel *Sams in a Dry Season*, says of his alcoholic author-narrator Jason Sams: ". . . he had become as smashed as Papa ever got, in Cuba or the Keys, as creatively looped as Faulkner ever got in his own barn, ah now, *that* bastard, I devoured him."

If Faulkner drank all the time, and wrote those great novels, wouldn't it help us to drink, too? Many of us felt, as author Donald Newlove did, that the southern bard's bourbon was part of his inspiration, and we looked to the bottle for our own. Newlove, like my friends and I, had read an article in *Life* magazine reporting that Faulkner "mixed whiskey and writing." Newlove reacted as we did to the information, as he explains in his tough-minded memoir *Those Drinking Days*: "I drank up this fact, hopeful that alcohol would give me access to Faulkner's auroras. I drove home ringing with dreams."

The fact is, Faulkner became so sick from the alcohol that he decided to conduct his own experiment to see if it was possible for him to write a novel without drinking. He did write a novel while dry, *Light in August*, recognized as one of his great ones. It proved he didn't need alcohol as a muse. He started drinking again just because he liked it, because he was hooked on it and didn't want to give it up. Tragically, countless aspiring writers have used his steady intake of alcoholic spirits as justification for their own imbibing, believing it would help make their own writing as great as Faulkner's.

DISCOVERING GREAT SOBER WRITERS

At a conference sponsored by the National Council on Alcoholism on the subject of Alcohol in Literature, I once found myself immersed in a deep discussion of alcohol as a stimulus to creativity, as if it were an established fact. People were even talking about genetics, and right-brain/left-brain functioning that showed how alcohol stoked creativity, something writers supposedly had known through the centuries. That's a message we've been getting at least since the time of Horace, who declared (sounding like a Roman Hemingway), "No poems can please for long or live that are written by water drinkers."

Suddenly I recalled my disappointment when during my heavy drinking days I had learned that my hero Dostoyevsky was *not* a rummy! It occurred to me that neither was Tolstoy a big drinker, nor Chekhov, nor Turgenev. So why, I asked, could the great Russian writers manage to create without depending on alcohol, when they lived in a society famous for its overindulgence in vodka?

Someone in the audience said that, now that he thought of it, the great English writers weren't alcoholics, either: Dickens, Trollope, Thackeray, Austen, Eliot. And how about the Germans, someone else asked, citing Goethe, Thomas Mann, Kafka. This was getting weird. Here were all these great writers from all over the world who weren't alcoholics—I wondered if perhaps only American writers had fallen prey to this disease. Was there something in the New World climate that affected our genes in some mysterious manner?

Then someone else volunteered that our own great nineteenth-century writers—Hawthorne, Melville, Whitman, Dickinson, Emerson, and Thoreau—were not alcoholics. In fact, the only alcoholic in the rich pantheon of nineteenth-century American literature was Edgar Allan Poe—and, not by accident, he is the subject of more biographies than any other American writer. He satisfies our attraction to the story of the doomed creator. As Donald Goodwin observed in *Alcohol and the Writer*, "Wholesome geniuses are not much in demand."

Ironically, Poe was the exception among writers in a country otherwise so tipsy that European literary visitors in the nineteenth century were shocked by the amount of drinking they saw—deTocqueville dubbed America "the Alcoholic Republic." Yet, our literary giants of the time were not big drinkers. Even Mark Twain, who began as a roustabout journalist getting drunk with the boys, later restrained himself from such displays; it might have made him a hit in the mining camps, but it only earned disapproval from his literary peers, and brought him not popularity but embarrassment. Twain wrote a friend in 1860 that he didn't want to get drunk in public because, "It sets back a man in the esteem of those whose opinions are worth having." What a far cry from the literary outlook of the Roaring Twenties!

More powerfully moving as a critique of the damaging effects of alcohol on creativity than the judgment of any critic is F. Scott Fitzgerald's own lament about his most ambitious novel, *Tender Is the Night*: "I would give anything if I hadn't had to write Part III of *Tender* entirely on stimulant [alcohol]. If I had one more crack at it cold sober I believe it might have made a great difference."

No doubt he was right. When he stopped drinking toward the end of his life, he wrote most of the novel that critic Edmund Wilson called his most mature, *The Last Tycoon*. Before he could finish he died of a heart attack at age forty-four—just five years older than Dylan Thomas.

EXPOSING THE BIG LIE

Not until recent studies like Donald Goodwin's *Alcohol and the Writer* and Tom Dardis's *The Thirsty Muse* did the true accounts of the effects of alcohol on writers become publicized. In his study of Faulkner, Hemingway, Fitzgerald, and Eugene O'Neill, Dardis reported that "the writers I consider embarked on writing and drinking careers with deadly effects on their creative powers." This is not just Dardis's outside opinion, but comes from the little-known testimony of the writers themselves.

O'Neill, who is still popularly—and mistakenly—thought of as an alcoholic writer who wrote about alcoholics, explained, "You've got to have all your critical and creative faculties about you when you're working. I never try to write a line when I'm not strictly on the wagon."

The popular distortion of O'Neill's drinking history is surely the most blatant example of how the *mythology* of alcohol as romantic inspiration prevails over the reality of recovery, which is evidently less appealing to the public! O'Neill stopped drinking at age thirty-seven, when his work was getting more verbose and less coherent. It was only after getting sober and writing without drinking that he wrote his great plays—*Mourning Becomes Electra*, *The Iceman Cometh*, and *Long Day's Journey into Night*. After getting off the bottle, O'Neill stayed sober except for several brief lapses, until his death twenty-eight years later. Until I read *The Thirsty Muse* a few years ago, I had thought O'Neill was a lush who wrote while soused, and every time I've told the true story to writer friends they're as amazed as I was to hear that he did his great work while sober.

Until I read Jimmy Breslin's marvelous recent biography of Damon Runyon, I hadn't known that the bard of Broadway nightlife, tough guys, gamblers, and ballplayers had been a binge-drinking young newspaperman in the West, but swore off the sauce *before* he came to New York and made his reputation as a writer. He hung out in bars to get stories, but never touched a drop of booze after coming East in his twenties.

In an introduction to one of John O'Hara's works, I discovered the little-known (by me or anyone I knew) fact that this author I'd always heard about as a hard-drinking, old-style carouser gave up the sauce after getting an ulcer at age forty-eight. He lived another seventeen years and wrote novels I much admired, such as *Ten North Frederick*, *From the Terrace*, *Ourselves to Know*, and *The Lockwood Concern*, as well as continuing to turn out his classic short stories for *The New Yorker*. He also in those years remarried, was a loving husband to his second wife, a good father to his daughter Wylie, and led a full, socially active life, as self-styled squire of Princeton, New Jersey, often photographed in tweedy plus fours and wielding a walking stick. His becoming sober was never much written or talked about—almost as if such information might have detracted from his "glamour," or even his reputation as a serious author. The myth of alcohol and creativity perpetuates its own boozy history.

Mark Twain, still widely regarded as a hard-drinking author who imbibed to create, testified that wine was "a clog to the pen, not an inspiration." He said he couldn't write after a single glass. Twain's experience was echoed in the past decade by the brilliant short-story writer Raymond Carver, who stopped drinking a decade before he died of cancer and reported, "I never wrote so much as a line worth a nickel when I was under the influence of alcohol."

THE POET-KILLER

Not only does alcohol fail as a muse, it actually functions as anti-muse. In his groundbreaking study of the influence of alcohol on the poetry of John Berryman, critic Lewis Hyde goes to the heart of the matter, explaining that alcohol is described medically as "an anaesthetic" and, " 'Anaesthetic' does not just mean a thing that reduces sensation. The word means 'without-aesthetic,' that is, without the ability to sense creatively. . . . An anaesthetic is a poet-killer."

It also kills music and art.

Guitarist and songwriter Richard Thompson, formerly a member of Fair Port Convention, the British folk-rock group whose lyrical work won a faithful audience in America, echoed the experience of writers from O'Neill to Cheever when he said, "I can't remember having written a good song while under the influence of anything. I've written songs about being drunk, but only while I was sober."

Visual artists also suffered from alcohol's debilitating effects. Art historian April Kingsley points out the anti-creative effect of alcoholic anesthesia on painters in *The Turning Point*:

"Paradoxically, instead of releasing the flow of ideas and images, alcohol can stem it for some who suffer from overly stimulated imaginations. Their minds race, their synaptic activity is in high gear, and they need something to push the 'off' button. Willem de Kooning and Jackson Pollock can both be seen anew in this light. Overwhelmed by having to decide moment by moment, stroke by stroke, between this line and that, this color or that, this shape or that, de Kooning was rarely able to finish a picture in his early years. Each small part of the canvas held innumerable alternatives; each image came with an endless ancestry of related images; each picture could be, could have been, countless others. This hysteria of indecision reached its acme in *Woman I*, which he started in 1950 and abandoned as unfinishable before it was resurrected and 'completed' in 1952."

WRITING FOR YOUR LIFE

Under the Volcano is perhaps the most famous novel about an alcoholic written by an alcoholic—factors which have added enormously to its fame. Part of the literary mythology of the book is that it was written by a drunk while he was drunk—an amazing feat, cited as a tribute to the inspirational powers of booze! I was fascinated to learn that Lowry actually wrote the book during the one period in his life when he was at least in partial control of his drinking. He lived during this time in a shack on the beach in Vancouver Bay, rose early to swim and do calisthenics, and limited himself to a few beers during the day. It was during this time that he wrote his famous novel.

The Lowry story made me see through some of the personal mythology of my own drinking and writing history. I was still a big drinker in the early 1970s, when I wrote my first two novels, Going All the Way and Starting Over. I simply catalogued those accomplishments as part of my productivity as a hard-drinking writer. The Lowry story made me think back to that time. I realized, with a jolt, that while I was doing the actual writing of those novels, I was not drinking at all during the day, and having only a beer or a glass of wine when I knocked off work to have dinner at eight or nine at night. Though I drank to excess before and after writing those novels, the actual periods of writing were the most sober times of my adult life up to that point.

I simply couldn't wake up with a hangover and write, and when I was in the act of writing I was so consumed by it, so caught up in the real transport (almost "trance") of the creative act, that I didn't feel the need to drink at my usual heavy, steady pace. The creation itself filled me up, the way the booze did when I wasn't writing. Looking back, I realized that my creative periods had been my times of relief from the steady drinking that seriously threatened my health. It struck me that in a very literal way, writing the novels had saved my life.

JOHN CHEEVER GIVES UP THE BOTTLE

How did so many of us fall prey to the popular myth of alcohol as creative inspiration—and even more puzzling, how does it continue to influence new generations into the '90s?

Not only did the popular press and public mythology perpetuate the old attitudes, scholars of the time took a similarly cavalier approach toward the chemical dependency of writers. Professor Roger Forseth, chairman of the English Department at the University of Wisconsin-Superior and founding editor of the scholarly magazine Dionysos: The Literature and Intoxication Triquarterly, observed that until very recently "if critics and biographers discussed alcoholism at all, they treated it as either a joke or as a horror story. They talked about how many times Hemingway got drunk at Key West or how often Sinclair Lewis threw up in public, but there was no analysis of how these episodes might have influenced their work."

One of the first literary chroniclers to examine the role of alcoholism in a literary life with insight and understanding is Scott Donaldson, whose excellent biography *John Cheever* details the dramatic story of the famous *New Yorker* writer's triumph over booze. At the Smithers Alcoholism Center in New York City at the age of 63, Cheever told his therapist that he could write and drink at the same time, so why should he bother to stop drinking? The therapist asked if what he wrote while he was drinking sounded as good the day after he wrote it, and Cheever said he wanted to think about that. When he came back to his next session he said he had thought about the question, and he was never going to have another drink.

The prognosis for Cheever was "guarded" and the staff at Smithers were not optimistic, but Donaldson tells us, "They did not reckon with his strength of will or his delight in being alive." He went home on May 6, 1975, and recorded in his journal that everything was in bloom: "apples, dogwood, wisteria, lilac, me."

Cheever went to Alcoholics Anonymous, and lived another seven years to finish his most important novel, *Falconer*, as well as his first teleplay, a highly praised drama for PBS called *The Shady Hill Kidnapping*, and also a short, lyrical novel called *Oh What a Paradise It Seems*. That novel has a brightness to it, in the positive theme of the story (the hero saves the beautiful town pond from becoming a dump) and in the emotions of the narrator:

"The sky was clear that morning and there might still have been stars although he saw none. The thought of stars contributed to the power of his feeling. What moved him was a sense of those worlds around us, our knowledge however imperfect of their nature, our sense of their possessing some grain of our past and of our lives to come. It was that most powerful sense of our being alive on the planet. It was the most powerful sense of how singular, in the vastness of creation, is the richness of our opportunity. The sense of that hour as of an exquisite privilege, the great benefice of living here and renewing ourselves with love. What a paradise it seemed!"

As biographer Donaldson observed, "By giving up alcohol [Cheever] opted to live rather than die. But he reminded himself anyway that drink could do nothing to ease his daily passage, that it ruined his writing, that it robbed him of his dignity."

That powerful story of a writer's triumph over his life-long addiction, and the literary productivity that followed, didn't make an impact on most critics and reviewers. When Cheever's *Journals* were posthumously published, most of the reviews spoke of his alcoholism; yet, only one that I saw referred to his conquest of it and the literary productivity that followed. Evidently, such true stories do not fit the romantic image of the alcoholic writer. Cheever seems still branded as the boozing author, rather than the author who sobered up and wrote better than ever.

A LITERATURE OF RECOVERY

The old story of alcoholism with its built-in tragic ending has developed new plot lines in the past few decades with the recognition of recovery as a concept that has entered our social experience and our cultural consciousness. As usually happens in such circumstances, it also now has entered our literature, in fiction as well as reportage.

The realization of recovery as a process, through Twelve Step programs and other treatments, medical and psychological, does not guarantee happy endings but offers the possibility of new kinds of stories in life and literature, dramas that deal with the struggle for freedom from addiction, the striving for wellness and wholeness.

Raymond Carver, recognized as a master of the American short story, drew on his own experience as a recovering alcoholic who lived, loved, and worked in sobriety the last ten years of his life, to dramatize and illuminate in fiction the hard process of recovery.

Carver's story "Where I'm Calling From" tells what it's like for a man who finds himself at "Frank Martin's drying-out facility" struggling to conquer his demons, his addiction, coming shakily out of the physical throes of withdrawal. The fragility and tension, the hope and fear of the process, is conveyed by the narrator who explained at the beginning of the story:

"We've only been in here a couple of days. We're not out of the woods yet. J.P. has these shakes, and every so often a nerve—maybe it isn't a nerve, but it's something—begins to jerk in my shoulders."

We get a gut sense of how delicate, how precarious, how difficult is the battle to withdraw from alcohol.

The lure of drugs and alcohol in contemporary Southern California and the struggle to transcend their enslavement are lyrically told in a series of stories of women in Kate Braverman's collection *Squandering the Blue*.

"Temporary Light" is about the second sober Christmas of Suzanne Cooper, a 37-year-old divorced woman. An interior voice tells her, "One Bloody Mary. It won't kill you. 'Tis the season. . . . You can always go back to AA after the holidays, in January, when the world turns dull and normal. . . ." The next morning Suzanne gets down on her knees and "prays to the God she does not believe in to keep her sober one more day."

Writers like Carver and Braverman have provided other models for writers' lives—ones in which they triumph over the booze and go on to write even better work than before, even enjoying nurturing relationships with loving partners.

MORE SECOND ACTS

Writers are not the only creative workers who are breaking the myth of booze and the muse in their own lives and careers. Though the path to oblivion through booze still retains its lure, and even sometimes its commercial rewards (via notoriety, for Hunter Thompson), the new awareness of the devastation of drugs and alcohol, and the possibility of recovery, are giving the lie to F. Scott Fitzgerald's woeful cry that "there are no second acts in American lives."

Starring together in a revival of the Pinter play *No Man's Land* on Broadway in 1994, Jason Robards and Christopher Plummer reminisced about their younger days when they pub-crawled around New York, sometimes getting so drunk they were thrown out of the bars. Robards recalled that in those days—the 1960s—"The drinking was a mark of manliness in the theater."

Robards stopped drinking in 1972 after a car crash in which his face was shattered and he nearly was killed.

"When you have a real life," Plummer observed, "the pubs don't serve as your surrogate life anymore."

"I have a home life, too, thank God," said Robards, "so I don't go to saloons."

Drinking, they agreed, was no longer a sign of machismo in the theater.

"Not fashionable now," as Plummer put it.

Big boozing has gone out of fashion in the painting world as well. The noted art historian and critic Hilton Kramer, formerly of the *New York Times* and now editor of the *New Criterion* magazine, tells me:

"Most of the painters I know under forty-five aren't heavy drinkers, like the generation before them. They're social drinkers. Only one I know was a serious drinker, an alcoholic, and she's given it up now. There's a tremendous difference today than in the past generation. There's none of the heavy drinking at openings that there used to be. Heavy drinking used to be standard at openings but now everybody's drinking Perrier. People are into health food and all that kind of thing."

The novelist and screenwriter-director Michael Crichton found he had gotten into the habit of drinking bourbon while he was writing, and discovered when he wanted to stop that he could satisfy the impulse for swallowing by switching to Diet Pepsi. He now consumes several quarts of soda, instead of sipping alcohol, during a hard day's work.

The most eloquent testimony to the rewards of sobriety for the working artist comes from Raymond Carver in a poem based on his own experience. It was published in *The New Yorker* after his death from cancer:

GRAVY

No other word will do. For that's what it was. Gravy.
Gravy these past ten years.
Alive, sober, working, loving and
being loved by a good woman. Eleven years
ago he was told he had six months to live
at the rate he was going. And he was going
nowhere but down. So he changed his ways
somehow. He quit drinking! And the rest?
After that it was *all* gravy, every minute
of it, up to and including when he was told about,

well, some things that were breaking down and
building up inside his head. "Don't weep for me,"
he said to his friends. "I'm a lucky man.
I've had ten years longer than I or anyone
expected. Pure gravy. And don't forget it."

Chapter 5

DR. LEARY'S QUICK FIX: THE ILLUSION OF DRUGS

Despite the healthy new understanding of more and more artists who have learned from their own painful experience in the past few decades, there is a powerful surge backward, like a cultural undertow, toward the use and glorification not only of booze, but of the drugs that swept the youth culture of the '60s. The forces of life and death ebb and flow in our society, as they do within our own psyches and personal experience. We move toward wholeness, and then are sucked down again—almost like an undertow—toward fragmentation, *ennui*, and the general direction of self-destruction.

In the early '90s a headline in the entertainment section of the *New York Times* announced, "LSD Is Popular Again." Culture critic Walter Goodman recently reviewed a "48 Hours" TV program called "LSD Return Trip," which reported that lysergic acid diethylamide, known as acid, which was glamorized in the "Psychedelic Sixties," is back as an "in" drug in some segments of the youth culture, particularly in San Francisco clubs where "rave scenes," or "raves," are held.

Goodman wrote of the TV documentary, "The problem with LSD was that while some trippers just dropped out, others freaked out. Tonight's horror stories [on "48 Hours"] indicate that heavy doses can still send users into psychotic states, producing what one doctor calls instant insanity. Nobody seems certain what, if anything, the drug does to the brain, but the unsettling effects have, of course, been given a fancy name, post-hallucinogenic sensory disorder."

That crucial information is omitted from the insidious hip hype in *Mondo 2000: A User's Guide to the New Edge*. An article on "Psychedelic Drugs" claims that "the links between psychedelic drugs and the New Edge culture are deep and subtle. Due to the regrettably silly fact that they are classified as narcotics along with such SEVERELY detrimental substances as heroin, cocaine, and amphetamines, the role of psychedelic drugs in these zero-tolerance times tends to be down-played."

What the article not only "downplays" but fails to mention at all are the real, damaging effects of the drug. It has left people in mental hospitals, in permanently altered states that render them almost nonfunctional—and these are the ones who were lucky enough, if that is the appropriate term, not to have committed suicide while on an acid trip. In one sense, hallucinogens are even more dangerous than "hard" drugs like coke and heroin. At least many people recover from addictions; there is not the same opportunity to recover from drug-induced psychosis.

The article claims that acid enables you to see things from a different perspective, and that "being able to access multiple points of view is an important part of the creative process, thus the popularity of mind-altering drugs with creative artists throughout the ages."

The article does not name those creative artists, nor does it cite any examples of creative works produced by hallucinogenic drugs. The only famous one is Coleridge's "Kubla Khan," a poem which came to him in a drug-induced dream after he smoked opium.

LSD and other hallucinogens are not the only old drugs being rediscovered and glamorized again by the current youth culture. A headline in the February 1993 issue of *The Fine Print*, a biweekly youth paper in Boston, ran a headline "Give Me Morphine or Give Me Death." The "Morphine" referred to is a popular rock group. Their performance at a Boston bar drew "previously converted, adoring fans, who have come to watch the returning heroes back on their (extremely crowded) home turf," the reviewer reported, especially praising one of their new songs, which "revolves around the almost anthemic couplet, 'When they take away the pain . . . (dramatic pause) . . . I'll throw my drugs away!' It's a great song, one of the band's best."

The dark force of numbing is always powerful. The appeal is seductive, strong, and especially magnetic to young people discovering it for the first time—even more so when it is sold with the false propaganda that it's linked to creativity.

Youthful death is still part of the "doomed artist" tradition, tragically acted out in the '90s by the suicide of Seattle rock star Kurt Cobain of the group Nirvana. He sought relief from the pressures of sudden fame, hype, and money with booze and drugs. His own suicide was soon followed by that of another Seattle rocker, the female bassist in his wife Courtney Love's band. They ended their lives in the sick tradition of OD'd stars of former generations like Janis Joplin, Jimi Hendrix, and actor John Belushi. In the same year, young movie star River Phoenix OD'd on cocaine and alcohol.

The student newspaper of Plainsboro–West Windsor High School in New Jersey, *The Pirate's Eye*, discussed that death in a perceptive article by S. Mitra Kalita and Janna Robin, who wrote, "Even though River Phoenix did not necessarily want to be our role model and idol, for many of us he was. And it seemed as though he would live forever.

"And when River Phoenix died, I think a lot of our childhood delusions and illusions died also. We needed to accept that it was drugs, and not some freak accident that took away our hero, and that's painful because it forces confrontation with senseless mortality. People started to realize that no one was above death."

It also forced confrontation with the mythology of the glamour of drugs and alcohol, which still exerts its appeal on new generations.

THE ROOTS OF THE DRUG EPIDEMIC

The alcohol-and-writers myth took a back seat in the '60s to the drugs-and-musicians myth. Death by overdose was hyped as glamorous, and Jim Morrison's early death from drugs became the rock version of Dylan Thomas killing himself with alcohol. As songwriter–guitarist Paul Kantner, one of the founding members of Jefferson Airplane, told Jenny Boyd in *Musicians in Tune*, "in our generation, drugs presented a real problem with moderation, and they got out of control, as alcohol did with our parents' generation and some of our generation as well."

The revised myth was that drugs—especially the newly popular hallucinogens—would open what Aldous Huxley (paraphrasing William

Blake) called the "doors of perception" in his book of the same name (the title inspired the name of the rock group, the Doors). The illusion of salvation by ingestion was hyped by a new breed of fast-talking prophets in hip clothing.

That fantasy evaporated before my very eyes in Allen Ginsberg's apartment on the Lower East Side of Manhattan one Sunday afternoon in 1961. I had gone there to interview Ginsberg for an article I was writing about marijuana, and found a number of poets and writers on hand, including Jack Kerouac. Also present was a young psychologist who had come down from Harvard named Timothy Leary, who told me he was conducting a "scientific experiment" with a new drug called psilocybin. Leary said the drug stimulated creativity, which is why he wanted to give it to the assembled writers to see what amazing results it might produce—perhaps an epic poem on the spot, a sudden story of unimagined eloquence.

Another benevolent side effect of the drug, Leary said, was that it made people "mellow." He suggested I go talk to Kerouac, who was often hostile, but was now mellowed out under the influence of the drug. When I introduced myself to Jack, he recalled I had written an article making fun of a drunken reading he gave at a Village nightclub. He threatened to throw me out the window.

I retreated, deciding the drug hadn't taken effect. Leary urged me to stick around, though, so I could witness what he said was most important—psilocybin's stimulation of creativity. I dutifully stood by as Leary gave Kerouac a pencil and a piece of blank paper and told him to create, to write something in his famous style of "bop prosody." Kerouac groggily turned away, expressing no interest. Leary then reminded Jack that he was taking part in a scientific experiment, and if he didn't do his part by writing, he wouldn't get any more of the drug; if he wrote something, though, he'd be rewarded.

This got Kerouac's interest; he made a grunting sound of agreement, and applied the pencil to the paper as Leary and I looked on with heightened anticipation. Leary hovered over the scene as if expecting a miracle, and for a moment I wondered if perhaps the avatar of the Beats, with the aid of the alleged miracle drug, might spew forth the beginning of his own hallucinogenic *War and Peace* or turned-on *Moby Dick*.

I held my breath as Kerouac drew his pencil across the blank piece of paper; instead of words, he had drawn a straight line; then he drew another. Perhaps the drug had stimulated his artistic rather than literary impulse, and he'd create a breakthrough work of visual art, some kind of mind-blown Mondrian. Jack patiently continued to fill up the paper with these parallel lines; then, thoughtfully, he turned the paper sideways and drew another series of lines through the original ones. Then he handed the paper to Leary and went to lie down. Leary looked at the paper, and laughed nervously. He said there might be another burst of creativity later, but I thought I'd seen enough.

I took it lightly at the time, and only recently did I learn that the afternoon's "scientific experiment" was not just a fiasco for Leary. Kerouac wrote later in an article in the *Chicago Tribune* that he believed the psilocybin had harmed him. Dennis McNally writes in *Desolate Angel* that Jack at age forty-one spoke of his psychedelic experience with Leary as "a frightening descent into lostness that Kerouac now swore had ruined him. 'I haven't been right since,' he confided."

COCAINE KILLS

Though I saw with my own eyes the silliness of the scientific experiment conducted by Dr. Leary that day (even if I didn't yet know the darker, more damaging results), I took LSD three times a decade later, with similarly anti-climactic results. On the last trip, I saw myself going to the edge of a cliff, with only blackness looming below. I vowed that if I could just get back I would never take any more, and after that I was no longer tempted.

During the late '60s and early '70s, I tried most of the other drugs around at the time. I started doing cocaine until a friend went into convulsions and a coma after inhaling it and had to be taken to a hospital emergency room, which dispelled the myth that the worst it could give you was a nosebleed! A doctor friend informed me that an overdose of coke could kill, and what constituted an overdose to any person at any one time depended on that individual's body chemistry. That truth was tragically enacted by college basketball star Len Bias, who "celebrated" his selection by the Boston Celtics with cocaine that killed him.

I JUNK MYSELF

I once inhaled heroin as a substitute for inner peace, and a surrender to despair. I experienced that all-encompassing pseudoserenity, the numbing negation of problems, the waking sleep of stasis—an ultimate state of un-creation. I knew that even one more "recreational" session could put me on the path of no return, the death-in-life of addiction to what the users so aptly label "junk"—and, thus, its victim as "junkie."

When I first stopped drinking I took up marijuana; then I realized I was starting to use it as regularly as I once did alcohol. When I saw it was taking over my life, I packed all I had in a garbage bag and stuffed it in the trash. The myth says pot can't hook you, but I know people who are dependent on it, though they still deny its addictive power. They say they can stop anytime—but they don't.

A SECOND ACT FOR THE LIT BRATS

Cocaine was the '80s version of the fashionable drug of choice, and its use was duly recorded in the literature of the period. Jay McInerney captured the cocaine crowd of hip young New York of that decade in his novel *Bright Lights, Big City*. He was touted as the new F. Scott Fitzgerald, his novel as the new generation's version of *This Side of Paradise*. McInerney's narrator, a disco version of Amory Blaine, explains to himself:

"You are at a nightclub talking to a girl with a shaved head. The club is either Heartbreak or the Lizard Lounge. All might come clear if you could just slip into the bathroom and do a little more Bolivian Marching Powder. Then again it might not. . . ."

Unlike F. Scott Fitzgerald's deluded young hero who thinks at the end of his alcoholic adventures, "I know myself; but that is all!" McInerney's party boy ends up walking the streets of New York at dawn, responds to the smell of fresh bread, and trades his hip Ray-Bans for a few stale rolls. The implication is that our coked-out hero is changing his lifestyle, or, as one reviewer interpreted it, that he realizes "the simple pleasures are the best."

With the heady success of that novel capped by a movie starring Michael J. Fox, McInerney himself became "a star in his own right," as Michael Shnayerson put it in a 1992 *Vanity Fair* profile, "which led to more glittering invitations, more drinking, and more drugs." After two novels panned by critics, McInerney returned to the scene of *Bright Lights*, described by Shnayerson as: "New York—in the giddy, nihilistic months before the stock-market crash of 1987 . . . in that moment after disco and before the spread of AIDS, when cocaine was nose candy and the hardest life choice was Area or Heartbreak."

Looking back on that time from a few years' perspective in *Brightness Falls*, McInerney described his generation of lit brats of those days and their relation to the popular anesthetics of their time and place:

"They'd grown up with drugs, just close enough to the sixties almost to believe in pot and acid as the sacraments of a vague liberation theology but not so close they didn't take them for granted. Not long ago, as putative adults, they were doing coke together at parties and imagining they'd discovered the pleasure principle. Not so long before that they were editing the college literary magazine, going to keg parties, reading Baudelaire."

Unlike Fitzgerald and his friends of the '20s, there are second acts in the lives of Jay McInerney and his fellow survivors of the fast lane of the '80s. Married again and living in Nashville when *Brightness Falls* was published, the thirty-six-year-old McInerney played host to a dinner for ten that in Shnayerson's profile updated the saner lifestyle of the former lit brats now thirty-something:

"It's all clearly emblematic of the new McInerney life—a nice southern evening at home, fine wine but no drugs, not even any margaritas. [The singer Jimmy] Buffet, in fact, is now something of a health nut, despite the musical tributes to drinking in Caribbean climes that continue to earn him millions on tour every year. Slimmed-down and balding, he wakes up at 6:30 every morning, and hurries off to the gym. 'But don't tell 'em that!' he says in mock horror. 'Tell 'em I'm up drinking and doing drugs till four A.M.!'

"For McInerney, it all suggests something truly radical: growing up is . . . in!"

Too bad it wasn't fashionable in Scott and Zelda's time.

A NEW TUNE IN MUSIC

Drugs have been the favored escape, stimulant, and anesthetic of musicians on the jazz, pop, and rock scenes. (Symphonic and classical musicians must adhere to a discipline that simply doesn't allow for the distortions of time and perception induced by drugs.) For jazz musicians, beginning in the '20s, marijuana smoked as "reefers" was the drug of choice, a phenomenon described by clarinetist Mezz Mezzrow in his highly regarded memoir *Really the Blues*. Because jazz was played in nightclubs often run by and frequented by mobsters, illegal drugs were easily available, and fit into a hip culture, with its own argot, dress style, and late-night hours, which proudly differentiated itself from the straight, daylight world.

Also, marijuana and heroin were pushed first and hardest in the black ghettos, where jazz was born, so the African American musicians who pioneered jazz were more familiar with it, and more likely to have had experience with it. Just as young writers drank bourbon in hopes it would help them write like William Faulkner, young jazz musicians tried to emulate Charlie Parker by using heroin. If the star saxophone player took heroin and played great music, maybe by using it they, too, could become as great as Bird. It got them not his genius, but his illness and death. The truth finally spread among black musicians, until, as Miles Davis noted in his autobiography *Miles*, the only musicians who didn't know any better than to use heroin were the white boys.

Just as doomed alcoholic writers were glamorized in the literary world, stories of "clean" jazz musicians were simply not spread. It is little known, for example, that the great innovator of bop, Dizzy Gillespie, never used drugs. It's just not good copy.

Drugs spread like a forest fire in the rock music era, and musicians, like writers, had to learn the hard way that the "creative" effects of mind-altering substances were illusory and finally destructive.

David Crosby, the guitarist of Crosby, Stills and Nash, explained: "What initially happens in the drug experience is that you feel the drugs are helping because they will throw your consciousness up for grabs. And sometimes, early on in the process, that worked for me. The problem with the drugs is, as you become addicted to them, they become so debilitating that the creative process stops entirely. A whole other effect takes place. While I was an addict, for the last three years of my life, I didn't write anything. I didn't have the attention span or the will; it just shut down, as if it had atrophied. And then six months after I quit, I wrote lyric after lyric, and it's been that way ever since. So much for the drugs and hash creativity theory."

A new attitude among musicians, as well as painters and writers, is illustrated by the recent book *Jazz Cooks*, by Bob Young and Al Stankus, whose cover displays a photograph of a saxophone made entirely of vegetables. As Florence Fabricant reported in the *New York Times*, "The jazz world, once rife with controlled substances and uncontrolled cholesterol, now has vegetarian vibes."

At a reception in Soho to celebrate the publication of the book of recipes by jazz musicians, drummer Arthur Taylor, who played with Charlie Parker and John Coltrane, said, "We're all getting older and we've learned that chicken and fish are better for you than meat."

Speaking for a younger generation of musicians, forty-year-old trombonist Ray Anderson said, "I'd rather eat like a health-food person because there's no question it will improve your health." He contributed a recipe for scrambled tofu with vegetables and cheese.

The great sax player Illinois Jacquet is quoted in the book as saying he gave up eating ribs and is on a vegetable diet and feeling "100 percent better." His recipe is for Veggie Roast. Another jazz legend, drummer Max Roach, testifies to the importance of good health as you get older. Vocalist Sheila Jordan, who gave up drink and drugs, told the *Times*, "I've stopped eating meat and dairy products because I have an angina problem. Now I'm grateful for carrot juice. It doesn't mess with your mind or your body." She went on, "You don't want to commit suicide, because you realize how much your music is worth to you."

UPPERS LEAD DOWNWARD

The only time I ever felt that drugs or alcohol were opening up or stimulating my creative powers was when I was under their influence. Sometimes in my twenties, when I lived in Greenwich Village, I stayed up late sipping (or gulping) bourbon and composing short stories—or rather, the beginnings of them, or fragments of them—or leads to magazine articles, which sounded sharp and brilliant at the time, but in the cold, sober light of the next morning were exposed as flat and formless, even incoherent. In those days I also consumed, like many of my friends, the orange or green heart-shaped pills dispensed by my own Freudian psychoanalyst, the uppers called Dexedrine or Dexamyl—legally prescribed amphetamines that wired millions of us in the '50s. There were nights when one of those pills seemed to fire me to marvelous insights and witty, sharp observations, but they, too, failed the test put by Cheever's therapist: Does what you wrote under those circumstances sound as good the next day?

Novelist Herbert Gold captures perfectly the illusion of the upper or speed experience of creativity in his "How to Suffer from Writer's Block":

"You may try drugs, speedy ones. This can move the block at the cost of a desert windstorm of futile words. The brain jangles. The soul dries up. In olden times, people had the chance to sell their souls to the devil, but no one wants to buy a desiccated soul. Chemical gain subtracts."

"It is tempting," wrote novelist Madison Smartt Bell in *Esquire*, "to suppose that a little shot (toke, snort) of something or other might help arouse the friendlier parts of your unconscious, help sneak your right brain out past your left." Looking at some of "the popular options," Bell summarizes:

> *LSD, heavy-duty hallucinogens:* You can't write while you are tripping, you can't even find your pen.
>
> *Marijuana:* Pot-fueled inspirations are hard to remember long enough to write down, and often they don't make sense the next day. Besides, it makes you sleepy.
>
> *Cocaine:* You may actually write on coke if you are nailed in a room with only a typewriter for company. Otherwise you go out and do things that make you ashamed later. People who can afford a steady coke habit probably aren't real writers anyway.
>
> *Heroin:* Why write? Why do anything?

The real "high" of creation comes from—creating.

In *The Turning Point*, April Kingsley notes that abstract expressionist painters Robert Motherwell and William Baziotes were fascinated by the poet Baudelaire's idea that "one must be intoxicated," and then asks with what—"with wine, with poetry, or with virtue?" Kingsley writes of another painter in the group that "Instead of needing artificial stimulants, Clifford Still was intoxicated by Baudelaire's last option—virtue. Witness the following excerpt from Still's diary:

"Quiet. Broken by the stretching of four canvases. A great free joy surges through me when I work . . . as the blues or reds or blacks leap and quiver in their tenuous ambience or rise in austere thrusts to carry their power infinitely beyond the bounds of the limiting field, I move with them and find a resurrection from the moribund oppressions that held me only hours ago. Only they are complete too soon, and I must quickly move on to another to keep the spirit alive and unburdened by the labor my Puritan reflexes tell me must be the cost of any joy."

This high came from nothing but the act of painting itself—no drug, no magic potion—only the true, clear magic of creation.

Writer Reynolds Price, in excruciating pain from cancer of the spinal cord, left the comfort of his home, taking his first plane trip since surgery, to be involved in the production of his first play. He reported, in *A Whole New Life: An Illness and a Healing*, that as he worked with the cast, director, and stagehands, who "politely but firmly demanded my submergence in the task at hand," making revisions as they worked past midnight, he found the "home truth" that "a thorough immersion in absorbing and, if possible, non-stop activity is far more narcotic than any drug."

CREATIVE HIGHS AND HEALTH

The high of creativity is not an illusory sensation, or one that leaves you feeling worse the next morning. In fact it has a positive long-range effect on your body as well as your mind. Recent studies show that some kinds of creation—writing about deep thoughts and feelings—not only make you feel better at the time, but have a positive effect on your overall health and in particular on the immune system!

In *Opening Up: The Healing Power of Confiding in Others*, James W. Pennebaker reported on a study conducted by the psychology department of Southern Methodist University. When students from a psychology class wrote for four days in a row, only fifteen minutes a day, there was a measurable improvement in their health.

Four months later a followup study showed that those same people had improved moods, a more positive outlook, and greater physical health.

In another such study, an immunologist drew blood from fifty students just before they wrote in a similar manner for twenty minutes a day on four consecutive days, again after the last writing session, and a third time six weeks later. The study found evidence of "heightened immune function" among those who wrote about their deepest thoughts and feelings.

We express and deal with our deepest thoughts and feelings not only in writing, but in painting, sculpture, dance, music, and theater—in all the creative arts. I suspect that any kind of sincere creative activity makes us feel better, not only in the act of creation, when we find ourselves in the flow of the experience, but after, in the affirmation that comes from using our natural gifts.

Certainly, creativity makes us feel more human. It is part of our humanity, and neglecting it allows a vital part of us to grow stale and to atrophy. The use of our creative powers in artistic expression can also carry over into other areas of our life, giving us the opportunity to deal with our work, family, and relationships in more creative ways.

So how do we find our true creativity? How do we go about creating, without the alcohol, drugs (prescription as well as illegal), or other stimulants we once may have imagined were the secret ingredients of true artists?

What if the key is clarity?

What if the secret ingredient is *no ingredient at all?*

Part Three

The Keys to Creation

Chapter 6

EVOKING THE
SPIRIT: THE POWER
OF CLARITY

A barrage of distracting and deadening forces from both outside and inside constantly assaults us, in a way that disturbs and even destroys our clarity of mind, body, and soul: the abuse of alcohol or drugs; food, when overconsumed to the point of discomfort or vomited out in bulimia, or underconsumed in the way that leads to anorexia; sex, when used as a kind of anesthesia, or performed in compulsive, loveless repetition in anxious pursuit of new partners; even relationships, when they become a kind of addictive distraction. Television, too, is a narcotic when automatically turned on for the comfort of noise, words, pictures, regardless of what is being shown. We use these things to numb our senses—and our sense itself.

Don't worry: I'm not advocating that you give up all these things and become a saint. I wouldn't know how to tell you to do it, or want to do it myself, even if I could! What I want is to provide some clues for tapping into your creativity by first "clearing" yourself of the accumulated debris of substances and practices that clutter and deaden the mind and the senses. To me, the most powerful key to accessing creativity is clarity. Clarity is the compass that orients you, the lens that focuses, the "sword in the stone."

Retreats at Buddhist or Christian monasteries, yoga centers or ashrams, meditative weekends sponsored by synagogues or churches or adult education programs, classes in meditative disciplines such as tai chi or yoga, all can provide a space in our experience out of the rush and jangle of everyday life. Such "time-outs" interrupt our rote behaviors, and provide the chance to get in touch with our deeper levels of consciousness. They open a clearing in which to create.

All these experiences have opened up my life in the past decade and a half—experiences that once would have put me off, even frightened me. I wouldn't have admitted the fear to anyone. I joked about such activities and made fun of people who engaged in them. Silence can scare the wits out of people who've kept their minds stuffed for a long time.

Many people think practices like tai chi or silent retreats are only for monks and yogis. But let me tell you my honest belief that if I can do them, anyone can do them! I have an easily distracted mind in a nonathletic body, and I'm trying (like most people I know) to live in a fulfilling way and make the most of my brief time on earth. I've been blessed with some happy accidents and a lot of what I can only call grace to be here, feeling better than I ever have in my life at age sixty-three, after abusing my body and mind for many years with booze until my own "turning," when I was forty-eight years old.

THE ROAD BACK

My crash came in Hollywood, where I'd gone to work on the NBC-TV series I had created, "James at 15," and stayed two and a half years. I was pouring down increasing amounts of wine every day to numb the growing anxiety of trying to "pitch" myself and my work to the buyers of filmland, watching projects collapse around me, and finding my own work harder to do as my "resting pulse" raced to 120, roughly twice what it ought to be. Finally I split for Boston, also splitting the longest relationship of my life with a woman I thought I would be with forever; then I went to my father's funeral, and then my mother's six months later.

I found solace by the pond in the Boston Public Garden, where the words of the Twenty-third Psalm seemed to have led me: "He maketh me to lie down in green pastures; he leadeth me beside the still waters. He restoreth my soul." I was also restoring my body in a program of diet and exercise guided by Dr. Howard Hartley. I lost twenty pounds and reduced my pulse to eighty, dried out for a month without booze and reduced my pulse to sixty, then turned toward a spiritual path that led me back to church.

MEDITATION OR PRAYER IS THE KEY

Since spirit and spirituality are part of the title and subject of this book, I want to make clear that it is not my intention, ever, to impose my own faith on you.

As a baby I was baptized with a sprinkling of water in a Presbyterian church. I attended a Presbyterian Sunday School near my father's drugstore in Indianapolis until about the age of nine or ten, when I went with a friend to a Baptist Bible study class. I was so drawn to the vigorous hymns ("Throw out the lifeline, throw out the lifeline, someone is drifting away!") and the powerful stories of Moses and Jesus, that I asked at age eleven to be baptized by full immersion. In college I turned away from the church and became an aggressive intellectual atheist, a position I more or less adhered to until 1980 when my life started coming apart and I returned to church. I joined King's Chapel in Boston, where I've been a member ever since. King's Chapel is an anomaly, a Christian church in the Unitarian Universalist Association, whose membership is largely humanist. I like the combination, for my roots are Christian, and the Unitarian outlook is open to a great variety of beliefs, requiring no rigid dogma, and emphasizing "the interconnected web of the universe."

During my years outside the church, my anti-religious feelings were most inflamed by proselytizers who tried to impose their own beliefs on me and others. The people who kept my respect for religion and spirituality, even during the times I was most hostile to it, were those who never tried to recruit me to their faith but simply lived it— people like Reverand Norman Eddy of the East Harlem Protestant Parish, and Dorothy Day, whose Catholic Worker movement in the Bowery fed the hungry and gave shelter to the homeless in the midst of an affluent, indifferent society.

When I recently talked about creativity and the spirit with Reverand Eddy he said, "Meditation or prayer is the key. It doesn't have to be through Christ or Buddha or the Sufis. It's finding the way to the core of our being, to become a cocreator with God. As the years go by, I feel one needs a guide. Jesus is the guide for me, while others find it in Buddha, or Mohammed. All religions embody the spirit in different forms."

I would go even further to say the spirit is also embodied outside formal religions, sometimes in mentors of the far or even recent past, men and women of the spirit whose lives and work enlighten and inspire our own. They could be creators of art, literature, or music, who touch the deepest part of our soul, our longing and aspiration.

I think of spirit as in "spirited," always as a life force and a blessing, never as a damper. Some people put a restrictive connotation on "spiritual," as if it means "taking the veil," retreating from life, putting a protective screen between you and the world. I think of it in the opposite sense, as bringing you into the world in a full, joyous way, opening your eyes and ears and mind and heart to the wonders of creation, in all their glorious presence; the power of being present to our senses, our natural perceptions and powers.

LIFE WITH NOTHING ADDED

I had cut down on my drinking on my doctor's advice, and was measuring the number of glasses I could consume in a night (one, or two at most) without my pulse rising, but it was a constant struggle, a battle of will against a habit based on a lust for the old numbing. I felt I had it under control though I noticed the glasses I drank from tended to get larger, growing into fishbowl size, which I still counted as one glass. I slipped periodically, then renewed my efforts at abstinence, all of which consumed a lot of energy, but I consoled myself that at least I didn't get drunk anymore.

In the spring of 1984 I did "est," that controversial program for personal growth often panned in the media. (The one fact about est that stuck in the public mind was that participants weren't allowed to go to the bathroom. The discipline of not being able to leave the room during sessions was an effort to hold people's attention. It later was dropped, though not until it was immortalized as a joke in the movie *Semi-Tough*.) Despite the bad press, I listened to some friends I respected who told me how valuable the est training had been for them, and I plunged in as part of my own search for growth. Before signing up, I wondered if this work would in any way be counter to spiritual growth, and I was assured by a Trappist monk who had done the program that "whatever genuine spirituality you bring to this will be deepened by it."

That was my experience. The program opened me and freed me up in many ways, resolving troubled feelings and fears left over from an old, destructive experience in Freudian psychoanalysis. I came away with a new sense of energy, excitement, and possibility. I took a follow-up seminar called Be Here Now, whose purpose was to teach people to "live life with nothing added." I realized for me that would mean not "adding" alcohol. What followed this realization was a lifting of the desire to drink. The lust for it was gone.

I didn't make a pledge not to ever have a drink again. I just didn't want to drink. A few times in the next few years I had a glass of wine or champagne at a wedding or birthday party, but it made me nauseous. I felt I'd become allergic to alcohol, and a doctor told me that was possible, that sometimes pregnant women develop such an allergy, as their bodies "know" it is bad for them.

I don't know of anyone else who has had this particular result from est, nor do I necessarily recommend it for that or any other problem. All I know is, *that's what happened to me*. Frankly, I wish it had happened somewhere else, somewhere less controversial, like a church basement or the YMCA. But it happened where it happened and I can't deny it—though I've sometimes had mention of it excised (censored) from magazine articles I've written. The stigma associated with programs like est is that they are cultlike, that they brainwash people. That was simply not my experience with the est training. I did not come out of it believing anything different than I had before. In fact, I found my basic beliefs reactivated and strengthened, and I returned to my church and community with renewed commitment and enthusiasm.

One of the goals people have in taking such seminars, and perhaps the greatest benefit from taking them, is to "get clear"—to experience a process powerful enough to thrust us out of the confusion that grows up around our lives so we can see through the underbrush of excuses, dilemmas, stories, stuck-ness, repetitions, and addictions that blind our vision and clog our action. One reason people return to such programs or do new similar work is because inevitably the confusion grows up again, like jungle vegetation.

For me, living life with nothing added enabled me to eliminate alcohol. A friend was able to stop "adding" new wives! He had been divorced once, remarried a younger woman, and was about to begin a new affair with a still younger woman. When he took the seminar about living life with nothing added, he saw that if he started the new affair he would simply keep repeating this behavior in cyclical fashion for the rest of his life, "adding" new wives and children every seven years. When he saw this (or in a deeper way, he "got it," in the jargon of the program), he did not proceed with the new affair. He persuaded his wife to do the same program, both recommitted to their marriage, and are still together twenty years later.

DOES IT CALL TO YOU?

Transformational programs are not for everyone. Some people are traumatized or offended by such processes, though others are inspired by them. Every method of change involves risk—not only programs like est, but even Freudian psychoanalysis, which in my own case was harmful, while for others it can be healing.

A good subjective test was suggested by Werner Erhard himself, founder of est, when he still was active in the program. (After a controversial "Sixty Minutes" exposé-attack on him in 1991, Erhard left the country and sold his firm to the program leaders, who formed Landmark Education to present The Forum and other seminars.) Before a packed house at the Armory in Boston in 1988, Erhard said after making his pitch, "The work I've just described may 'call' to some of you—it may sound like something you want to engage in. If that's the case you should do it. There are others who simply don't feel any response, or you just didn't like what you heard—it didn't 'call to you.' In that case you should *not* do it."

This is a good rule for any course of action, from personal relationships to deciding on a job, a school, or a place to live. Remember as well that when your senses are numbed, it's hard to hear *any* kind of "call." Being clear is the optimal way to be attuned to what really does call to you, in a positive, life-giving way.

I wish I'd abided by the rule of responding to what called to me—and rejecting what did not—back in the 1950s when I was about to go into years of psychoanalysis. I asked the psychoanalyst if it mattered that I didn't like him. No, it didn't matter at all, he said—that's something "we can work with." My entire instinct told me this was wrong, that this man would not be able to help me, but I looked at his professional degrees and certificates on the wall and feared that I was only "resisting" this crucial treatment. Surely the doctor, like father, knew best. I have come to believe since then that there is no way to get help from someone you don't like and trust. I have also learned time and again to trust my own deepest gut instincts; when I've forced my will against them—and I sometimes have, even after I was clear of drugs and alcohol—I've met with disaster.

From time to time I have gone back and done personal growth seminars. While none have had the impact of my initial experience with est, most of them have been valuable in providing new ways of seeing problems, renewing commitments, clarifying vision, and getting new methodologies to use in my search for growth. I have also enjoyed the people I've met in this work—doctors and waiters, lawyers and truck drivers, ministers and secretaries, black and white, gay and straight, all committed to looking for further personal growth, to finding ways of being more effective in their lives and work, to breaking up old patterns and seeing new possibilities.

I've also had crucial, creative recharging from church retreats, Bible study, prayer and meditation groups, a weekend of "sitting" at a Zen monastery, tai chi lessons, yoga classes, a week at a health spa, and other such programs.

Again, what path you follow, what voice you listen to, ought to be those that call to you. You may hear a message a hundred times and have it seem irrelevant, then hear it again in different words by someone else in another setting, and it may come alive for you. Books act on us in a similar way; as novelist Elizabeth Bowen observed, "Certain books come to meet one, as people do."

Reverend Joan Gattuso, minister of the Unity Church of Greater Cleveland, had that experience when the spiritual text A Course in Miracles "came to meet" her. Though she had heard its messages in many forms before, somehow this reached her in a way that nothing else had. She wrote in her own powerful book A Course in Love, that after encountering A Course in Miracles, "I stepped upon a new path that led me into a number of trainings, teachings, and spiritual adventures. My life began to radically transform, and I began to view all life from a different point of view, seeing relationships radically different from the way society and psychologists do." This path led her to her own "soulmate" and husband, and a rich new way of counseling others on relationships.

NO BURLAP NECESSARY

Though my own path has led me to a release from the alcohol that I consumed as daily fuel for more than a quarter century ("You use it like a car uses gasoline," one therapist told me in my hard-drinking days), I'm not a modern male incarnation of Carry Nation, taking an axe to the bars and preaching damnation of all who drink. Many of my friends have found relief and an increase in energy and appreciation of life in giving up alcohol altogether. I also have many friends who enjoy wine and spirits in moderation, including my own minister, as well as colleagues in the arts who do their work without the sort of overindulgence that would cloud their creative clarity. I have no desire to reform them or urge them to give up a part of life that is pleasant and nondestructive for them.

When I gave one of my first workshops in Creating with the Spirit a participant spoke up with some anxiety when I asked for a discussion of views on alcohol and creativity. This man said he'd read an article that quoted Joan Didion as saying one of her favorite times of the working day was in the late afternoon when she read over what she had written while drinking a glass of white wine.

"So what do you think about *that?*" the man asked me in a challenging voice as he leaned forward like a prosecuting attorney.

"I think it's just fine," I said.

I meant it. I know and respect Joan Didion and her work, and I know her artistic integrity would never allow her to lose her own sense of clarity, which is one of the hallmarks of her powerfully lucid style. If she enjoys a glass of wine while she reads over her day's writing, I'm glad. What bothered me about the man's question was the tone of worry and challenge, fear that I was going to deprive him of something that he couldn't do without. That's the danger signal of addiction.

I'm making an assumption about that man because of his attitude, and my own experience as a former drinker who also would have jumped to the challenge if anyone suggested taking away any of my booze habits. I may be wrong, though, and the only one who knows that is the man himself. If he is "in denial," the people who love and live and work with him will know, though even those closest to the one with the problem may be reluctant to tell him.

To find your own clarity and creativity you don't have to put on a burlap shroud and exist on a diet of boiled locusts and beet greens. Part of being creative in one's daily life is to savor the natural pleasures of it, the awakening of the senses—rather than crushing them with so much overload they go numb. There is or ought to be real pleasure in tasting one's food—even preparing it—whether your diet is nouvelle cuisine or middle-American meat and potatoes or New Age vegetarian. You can ruin any taste by overindulgence, or heighten it by savoring.

One of my favorite magazines is Gourmet, because of the loving, appreciative way its writers and photographers approach that wonderful subject—food! Gourmet is not just about fancy, expensive meals, but the deep pleasures of simple, basic tastes and their comfort and fulfillment in different seasons. The late Laurie Colwin, a talented novelist who wrote marvelous essays for the magazine, once did a piece on her passion for tomatoes, along with a few of her own favorite recipes thrown in as a bonus! Here was a person who was making the fullest use of her sense of taste, and her genuine appreciation of one of the "ordinary" gifts of our abundant life, one we take for granted, like background music—the common tomato that can grow in your own backyard:

"One of the joys of summer is to go roaming through the garden, pulling ripe tomatoes off the vine and biting in. Juice and seeds drip all over your nice white shirt, but who cares? . . . On one of the great days of my life, a friend with an enormous garden invited me and a pal to wander through his tomato patch and take as many plump specimens as we wanted; it was the end of the summer, and he had over-planted. I felt like the person in the Andrew Marvell poem 'The Garden,' about whose head ripe apples fall, except that these were tomatoes— in this case sharp, ripe, juicy cherry tomatoes.

"In this world of uncertainty and woe, one thing remains unchanged: Fresh, canned, puréed, dried, salted, sliced and served with sugar and cream, or pressed into juice, the tomato is reliable, friendly, and delicious. We would be nothing without it."

As I read Colwin's paean to tomatoes, an old memory rushed to my mind: My cousin Junior, just before he went off to serve in the Air Force in World War II, walked with me through our backyard Victory Garden, plucking the biggest, fattest tomatoes, shaking salt on them, and eating them right there on the spot, urging me to do the same. I did, enjoying this wild way of eating tomatoes—not in the tame confines of the family kitchen, all sliced and served with a meal (much less packaged in contemporary supermarket cellophane!), but plucked from the vine, from nature itself, straight to my mouth, almost like a forbidden fruit, and tasting all the more glorious for it.

FINDING OUR OWN BALANCE

Don't deny yourself the natural pleasures given us as part of the human condition—don't take the simple, sensuous pleasures for granted, but rather, savor the hot bath, the cold shower, the scent of woodsmoke, the comfort of blankets, the sweet taste of honey, the soothing sound of string quartets or early morning birdsong, the sudden flesh-to-flesh thrill of a kiss. This galaxy of wonders we take for granted is given to each of us, yet we often ignore it.

Become aware of your senses, "try them out" consciously, experiencing the clarity that comes from attention. In this state of awareness, eat a peach, listen to a piece of music you like, feel the bark of a tree, smell a rose, look at your own hand. You'll taste, hear, touch, smell, and see things in a way you haven't before, or maybe in a way you've lost since childhood. "Be with" your senses as an exercise. It's one of the accessible keys to clarity, available to all of us.

Don't let the enjoyment of your senses fade into a neutral background of nonexperience. Nor should you overindulge in their pleasure until it turns to need, and the need grows into an out-of-control addiction. Every so often, to continue enjoying our pleasures, we need to make a reality check to see that they haven't got out of balance, haven't tilted our behavior off course into a mindless and sense-numbing consumption of booze, or sugar, or television, or indiscriminate sex. I am not suggesting abstinence, but balance—the kind of balance that allows you to enjoy and appreciate the use of your mind and body for creating a meaningful life.

Unless your habits get so out of hand that your loved ones or colleagues are brave enough and caring enough (as well as fed up and frightened enough) to challenge you, then you are the only judge of your own balance. And it's easy to fool yourself. The smarter you are the easier it is to think up ingenious ways to excuse your addiction.

My denial was much like the experience journalist Pete Hamill describes in his memoir: "I never thought of myself as a drunk. I was, I thought, like many others, a drinker. I certainly didn't think of myself as an alcoholic. But I was already having trouble in the morning after remembering the details of the night before. It didn't seem to matter; everybody else was doing the same thing. We made little jokes about having a great time last night—*I think.* And we'd begun to reach for the hair of the dog."

It is rare that even friends and loved ones dare speak the truth to someone about overindulgence or addiction. It takes tremendous courage and "tough love" to confront a person who is falling into dependence, for defenses are sometimes impregnable, and responses of people who feel themselves challenged or accused can be angry, and even violent. It is safer to flow with the status quo, even when someone is harming himself and others.

We depend on friends, and they on us, for the accuracy of our sense perceptions. There is clarity in the truth, hard as it may be to hear the warnings or challenges of friends who care about us. It's important to have some friends whose senses are alert and clear, whom you can depend on for an accurate reading of your own condition. If our friends' perceptions are dimmed by drugs and alcohol, however, we can't depend on them in such matters—or perhaps we depend on them to confirm us in our addictions, knowing they would be the last to know, and the last to want us to turn from the habits they join us in.

At one point in my heavy drinking days I became aware enough of my own drink-inspired troubles, from sick hangovers to booze-fueled arguments, to ask several friends if they thought I was an alcoholic, or needed to do something about my drinking. I was (falsely) assured that there was nothing wrong, that "everyone" drinks, especially writers, and there was nothing to worry about.

Only one person spoke the truth to me.

The late John Ciardi, a marvelous poet, powerful lecturer, and dedicated director of the Bread Loaf Writers Conference for many

years, wrote me in 1972 to explain that the reason he hadn't invited
me back to serve on the staff of Bread Loaf, as I had every alternate
year since 1962, was that in 1970 my drinking had become so out of
control that it was affecting my lectures, which had become "fuzzy" on
the mornings after my furious consumption of vodka. (I had taken to
carrying a half-gallon jug around with me from one party to another,
so as never to be out of booze.) As director, John felt he had to
be "faithful to the ghosts" of the writers like Robert Frost who had
founded the conference and its traditions, to see that only the highest
quality of performance was offered by those on the staff. My drinking
had disqualified me. I was shocked at the time and offended; yet, I later
came to appreciate Ciardi's honesty and courage. It stuck like a burr in
my consciousness, one of the first promptings in my own head that the
time was coming when I had to stop if I wanted to continue to work—
indeed, to live.

I count myself lucky to have had such a friend as Ciardi who was
willing to speak the truth to me. (I'm happy to say I returned to teach
at Bread Loaf again when I'd given up alcohol, and experienced the
conference sober for the first time!)

EDITING OUT THE WORLD

If you're getting out of control and you have a friend as wise and tough
as John Ciardi to tell you so, you're lucky, but you can't count on such
outside influences. The most you can hope is that a clearheaded friend,
if asked, will tell you the truth. But you can't depend on anyone else to
take responsibility for your own behavior and performance, personally
or professionally. After getting opinions from people you trust, in the
end you are the one who must finally determine whether you are working and living at your peak condition, in the optimal state to achieve
the greatest clarity when you want to create.

The Reverend Norman Eddy said recently, "I see marvelous
people, moved by the spirit, unconscious of it, trying to see what it
means, and if they would just look within, the best in them is telling
them what to do!"

You always know, though, of course, you can always deny the truth.

It's easy to fool yourself. Like other writers and artists, Pete Hamill justified his drinking with a favorite refrain that my fellow boozers and I used to croon with great self-righteousness: "If I was able to function, to get the work done, there was no reason to worry about drinking. It was part of living, one of the rewards."

Growing up Irish in Brooklyn in the '40s, Hamill learned that "part of being a man was to drink," and started guzzling beer in grammar school. He recalls that even then, "It was as if the beer were editing out the world, eliminating other elements, such as weather, light, form and beauty."

He drank through his early years as a star reporter for the *New York Post* in the '50s and '60s, but in 1972, he began to notice little signs of deterioration in his work: "Typing a column or a script I would misspell simple words, not just once, but eight or nine times. Sometimes my fingers felt like gloves filled with water and typing was a plodding effort of physical labor.

"My hands trembled too, and there were little odd twitches in my legs, little spasms of protest, or I'd wake up with no feeling in my legs. I shook off most of these signals. I was just getting older, I told myself."

He was thirty-seven.

That New Year's Eve he watched his hands trembling in the mirror of a bar as he tried to light a cigarette. Later in the evening he looked down at the vodka-soaked lime at the bottom of his glass and he said to himself: *"I'm never going to do this again."*

He began a new era of sober and successful productivity of novels, movie scripts, and nonfiction books. In *A Drinking Life*, Hamill reports that after a while the temptation grew weaker, and one day he gratefully realized that "somehow, I'd replaced the habit of drinking with the habit of nondrinking."

Just as numbing ourselves can be a habit, so keeping ourselves awake and clear can be a habit as well. The choice is always there to set on one path or another. We can pick up a bottle or tune in some mindless television and get in the habit of blanking ourselves out, or we can wake up one morning, take a deep breath, and set on a new, fresh course that will bring our senses and spirit back to life. The choice is ours.

FINDING THE "MISSISSIPPI OF FRESH SPIRIT"

Everything in our society seems arrayed against us in the search for clarity and creativity. Everything is done for us, prepackaged before we can create it, from entertainment to food, so we are separated from our natural creativity, the way it showed up for people in daily life routines up until the second half of the century. Back in the '50s my old mentor and professor at Columbia, the sociologist C. Wright Mills, struck a nerve of public pain and response in his book *White Collar*, when he illuminated the plight of the new middle class of office workers, men and women who no longer created or consumed the fruits of their own labors, but became anonymous functionaries cut off from the meaning of their work.

Rebelling against that restricted, increasingly robotized kind of life himself, not only intellectually but experientially, Mills used to roar in to Columbia on the BMW motorcycle whose motor he learned to repair himself. He built his own house in Rockland County with his own design and his own hands, and enthusiastically learned to cook, taking special pride and pleasure in baking his own bread. Pacing the classroom like a restless prophet, he foresaw the communal spirit of the '60s when he urged a return to the land, to small communities where people would learn to use their own tools and talents to grow their own food, create their own arts and crafts, and make their own forms of community.

In Mills's class I wrote a paper on the new mass society that was forming the kind of future predicted in W. H. Auden's great poem "September 1, 1939": "faces along the bar / cling to their average day / the lights must never go out / the music must always play." That was in the pretelevision era. Now with the installment of the tube as a kind of psychic life-support system for the public, an all-pervasive tranquilizer, numbing night and day, providing its own glimmering light, its never-ending babble of noise, its faster flashing images and ten-second "sound bites," its increasing violence, Auden's vision has been not only realized but surpassed.

We must consciously fight for our clarity and reclaim our creativity. What for? To be human, to enjoy and experience the sights, sounds, tastes, touches, smells, and emotions given us as part of our humanity. Giving up the habits that blot out those senses is not a loss but a recovery. We recover feeling, and we see with more than the eyes. In this kind of clarity I see much more powerfully the role that friends play in my life, and enjoy a much greater appreciation of the gifts that other people are in my own journey. What a desert it would be without them!

Clarity enables you to blink and see how much you have, how rich are your resources, no matter what your station in life or position in the economy. The substances that temporarily numb our pain also numb our pleasure, and for a much longer time. The novelist Donald Newlove, in his powerful and myth-breaking book *Those Drinking Days*, conveys a sense of joy in the kind of clarity I am talking about: "Yesterday I had a day I couldn't buy for a million. I didn't drink. Today I have today, a Mississippi of fresh spirit flowing through me moment by moment from my first waking second."

So do I. As I write this book I'm looking out a window onto San Francisco Bay. I've been working here all summer at the home of a friend, writing in the mornings and biking every afternoon to the Golden Gate Bridge. The wind blows clean and cool off the water as my wheels crunch over the gravel path, and I take my hands off the handle bars, feeling I'm floating, like I did as a kid. Last night we had dinner at a small Vietnamese restaurant in the neighborhood and the food was great—light and delicate. I tasted every bite. Tonight we're going to a yoga class, and I'll awaken muscles I didn't even know I had a few years ago. I wake in the morning to have a bowl of fruit and cereal, whose flavor I savor as I look at the papers, then set to work.

Or is it play? When I sit down at this keyboard of my laptop computer I feel true pleasure in calling up the file, tapping out the words, "hearing" them in my mind, reworking sentences to get the rhythm right, expressing thoughts through a medium I've loved and created in since I was six years old. I am blessed. And I am grateful. I still make mistakes, wrong choices, have aches and pains, doubts and worries, lapse into sloth, and drag myself back to awareness again. One thing I know: working and living clear sure beats the old way.

I also see how creativity is not restricted to words I put on the page. After giving my workshop on Spiritual Autobiography for several years, I was asked by the Paulist Center in Boston to present a daylong program that might be useful for people recovering from alcohol dependence. I devised (created) some exercises that became the beginning of a whole new workshop, one that broadened beyond alcohol to all forms of creativity. In working "clear," ideas seem to sprout naturally, and there's a flow that leads from one idea to the next. When you're "in the flow" you seem to meet the people you need to help you carry on the next project, and the currents of your work take you to the next right place to develop it.

I think this flow is part of the feeling Donald Newlove was describing when he spoke of the "Mississippi of Fresh Spirit." It's available to all of us, all the time, if we take the trouble to seek it—or as Huck Finn would say, to "light out for it." You can't find your way if your head isn't clear, if your senses are not alert. Having emptied ourselves of alcohol and drugs, and the myths that promote them as the key to creativity, we've cleared ourselves to find what Mark Twain called, in another context, "the territory ahead."

Having cleared ourselves, we find in some sense that we are empty. It's a shock, and it can be frightening. What will we do without our old crutches and supports? How will we get through the day—much less the night? But emptiness is only temporary; Spinoza reminds us that "nature abhors a vacuum." Jesus tells a parable of a man who cleans his house of demons, and seven worse ones come to take up residence. Emptiness can be dangerous—but it can also be powerful.

The Buddhists talk of the need to "empty" ourselves to gain enlightenment. This kind of emptiness can lead to filling up. I'm not speaking of gas tanks or energy, but movements of the spirit, the force of creation.

Chapter 7

EMPTYING

An often repeated Zen story tells of a learned professor who goes to visit an old monk, famous for his wisdom. The monk welcomes the professor, invites him inside his temple, and offers him a comfortable seat on a cushion. The professor says he wants to learn from the monk, to gain some of his wisdom; before the monk can say anything, the professor launches into a long and proud account of his own accomplishments, his own theories, his own knowledge. The monk listens quietly, then asks politely, "Would you like some tea?"

The professor nods and smiles, continuing to spout his ideas, and the monk hands him a teacup. The monk takes a large pot and pours tea into the cup held by the professor. The tea rises almost to the very lip of the cup, and the monk placidly continues pouring—as the professor continues chattering. Only when the tea overflows and the monk continues to pour does the professor finally notice and stop his monologue. He leaps to his feet and demands, "What are you doing? What's going on?" The monk replies, "This cup is like your mind. It can't take in anything new because it's already full."

The story is a dramatization of the idea that "being full" (in this case full of yourself) is not always desirable, and that "emptiness" can be a valuable, even essential condition, a state in which we can *receive* much that is of value. If our cup is already full, nothing can be added— it simply spills over and is wasted, like the tea poured in the story.

"Emptying" is a crucial process in the spiritual path, the path to creativity and wholeness that the Navajos refer to as being "on the gleaming way." This kind of emptying is part of the process described at the beginning of the book: the model of successive stages that lead to a new discovery of our creativity: "Breaking the Myth," "Emptying," "Filling," and "Creating."

There are different kinds of emptying. Some are very destructive to the mind and body, and one must be careful to *discern* what acts are really in the service of the spirit, the creative force. Bulemics, who force themselves to vomit their food are, strictly speaking, emptying, but obviously not in any life-enhancing way, nor are anorexics, who keep themselves empty of needed nourishment. Couch potatoes remain empty of knowledge and experience by vegetating in front of the TV.

One of the keys to emptying is awakening our senses, as described in the chapter on clarity. If we are overstuffed with food, booze, drugs, television, ear-blasting music, telephone chatter-gossip, continuous computer games, or any other sense deadener, we need to empty in order to receive—ideas, inspiration, information, experience, knowledge, love.

At first the very idea of becoming empty sounds unappealing, even frightening, or perhaps painful. Isn't that the opposite of what everybody wants? Don't we all really want to have everything, be full, and therefore satisfied? Yet, we all know times when emptying our minds through meditation, or our bodies through a healthy, regulated diet or fasting, can be refreshing, awakening us to heightened perception and aliveness. When we are in good shape, sharp, and clear is when we feel most alive, when we're open to experiencing the natural highs of life.

THE JOY OF SPINACH

Emptying doesn't necessarily mean, as we usually are quick to assume, loss or deprivation. Emptying can bring a fuller appreciation, even fuller sensation, an expanding of the senses. I unexpectedly experienced this in a small way when I started to cut down on fat in my diet. I steamed vegetables for the first time, eating them without any butter or sauce. I assumed this would make them tasteless or bland, but to my amazement, when I ate my first steamed vegetables I felt I was actually

tasting them for the first time. No wonder I had never liked spinach—
I had never really tasted it! The butter and sauces I was accustomed to
having vegetables drowned in by restaurants and popular recipes had
blotted out their true taste. The steaming brought out their natural
flavor, enabled me to really know it for the first time. This simple experience opened up a whole new area of enjoyment for me. Less was
more, what seemed like deprivation was enhancement, discovery of
new pleasure.

Depriving ourselves—emptying—can sometimes be a method of
bringing a spiritual sense to our experience. This intriguing subject has
been illuminated by Rabbi Harold Kushner. In his latest book, *To Life:
A Celebration of Jewish Being and Thinking*, Rabbi Kushner explains
that the real significance of the Law in Judaism, is that it teaches "how
to take the ordinary and make it holy."

Writing of the often misunderstood dietary laws of Judaism, Rabbi
Kushner says that "We sanctify the act of eating" by keeping Kosher.
Rabbi Kushner views the rules for cooking and eating Kosher as a
means of celebrating, not being deprived or punished. When he has
lunch with a non-Jewish friend in a restaurant, he doesn't feel sorry for
himself and think about a horrible God who wants to deny him the
pleasure of eating pork products. Instead, he is thankful that there is a
God who, despite all the other concerns he has about his creation,
cares about what the Rabbi is having for lunch.

Illuminating the idea of freedom being achieved by restriction,
Kushner points out that the Torah—even with all its rules and regulations—"is a source of freedom." For instance, if he dines at a restaurant
with a non-Jewish friend, his companion has far more choices than
Rabbi Kushner, whose choices are limited by observing the Jewish dietary laws. How can it be, then, that the observant Jew is more free than
his friend? Rabbi Kushner compares the freedom the Law offers to the
freedom athletes feel in disciplining their bodies, enabling them to perform physically in a way that many people can never experience. It is the
freedom of being "the master of the appetite rather than the slave."

By eliminating from his diet the foods proscribed by his religion,
Rabbi Kushner is adding a sense of the sacred to his every meal, and increasing his own self-discipline, his own power to control his appetite.

The idea of emptiness is a paradox, and sometimes we have to em-
brace it, to understand different aspects of it, before we're able to enjoy

a sense of fullness of spirit. Before we can even look for the spiritual path we need to first empty ourselves of the substances and habits that numb us to our own deepest feelings.

A SPIRITUAL IMPULSE

Like many other people, my own interest in anything spiritual didn't begin until I stopped drinking for a long enough period of time to really be sober, not just recovering from a hangover. I had gone for about three weeks without a drink—the longest time without alcohol in my adult life—when I overheard a man say he wanted to go to church on Christmas Eve. I suddenly had an impulse to do that, too. This urge came as a shock to me, since I hadn't been inside a church for more than a quarter of a century—roughly the same period of time during which I'd made alcohol part of my daily diet.

A woman I met on a book tour told me how she and her husband quit drinking after going to the edge of physical abuse and realizing the danger they were courting, the road they were heading down. It was her custom to make a big breakfast on Saturday when they both had hangovers, and one Saturday, after they'd both been clear and sober for several weeks, her husband came to help—something he'd never done before. When they sat down to eat he said what a beautiful morning it was, and she agreed, and then they both looked out the window and started laughing. It was rainy, stormy and dark—outside. Inside, in their new lives, it was a beautiful day. Others have told me similar stories. It makes sense. When you're drinking, as I was, to numb yourself on a regular basis, to blot out the psychic pain of life, you are also blotting out the natural instinct for any sort of spiritual experience. By "spiritual," I emphasize again, I don't just mean going to church or synagogue or adopting any particular faith.

Whatever our creed or spiritual practice may be, one of the most common ways we numb ourselves to the spirit is through noise, outer and inner. The outer noise is the daily rush and bustle of getting up, radio, talk, traffic, work, meetings, discussion, phone, lunch, business, Muzak, shopping, dinner, TV. Hopefully, there are many more loving and satisfying pauses and interruptions in the day, but it is rare that the noise ever stops, the everlasting distraction.

GIVING UP NOISE

In one of his midweek sermons at King's Chapel just before Lent one year, Rev. Carl Scovel suggested that instead of sacrificing sweets, or undergoing any such customary deprivation of food or drink during the coming season, we give up—noise. Turn off the TV. We smiled. A shocking idea. Original, though. And maybe not too hard. Just think, we could stuff ourselves during Lent, but in silence; yes, that's what Carl was recommending we expose ourselves to—silence. Of course, we'd be able to hear ourselves chewing as we smugly ate all that fudge and those cookies and even the Valentine candy, or double-rich ice cream. Was that the idea—we'd hear ourselves eating, and be embarrassed? We'd be aware, we'd realize what and how much we were eating because there wouldn't be any TV to take our mind off what we were doing. Another one of his tricks, no doubt. No TV? Insidious. Radical.

Still, I decided to give it a try. There weren't any programs I was dying to watch, anyway. So what was the big deal? It ought to be a snap, and evidently would look good on my record (with God, in that enormous account book he keeps). The first night I came in and started to flip on the tube like I always do, no reason, just to see what's on—or maybe not even to see what's on. Maybe just to have something on—anything. Why did I do it? I always did, I'd gotten in the habit of it during the past—how many years? I wasn't sure.

I began to ask myself questions. Why was I turning on the tube when I wasn't even watching it? Voices? Maybe. I was living by myself, maybe the voices were a kind of company. Welcome, too. Keeping me from my own company, my own thoughts. Resisting the urge to turn it on wasn't easy. I was used to turning it on automatically—another addiction. But harmless, surely? Or was it? Anyway, I kept my pledge, left the screen blank. I lay down on my bed and read for a while. I noticed how quiet it was. Wow. Kind of peaceful. Restful. Not bad. In fact, a relief.

After that, when I came home I would get out a book and lie down on the bed to read, instead of clicking on the TV. I began to look forward to the silence. Even after Lent, I was comforted by knowing that silence was there, a kind of haven, or mental meadow, or pasture of the soul. I entered it, gratefully, thinking sometimes of the psalm: "He maketh me to lie down in green pastures. He restoreth my soul."

BILLIE HOLIDAY KICKS TV

A few months after I gave up TV, I found myself turning the tube back on in that automatic way, sinking back into the habit, the numbing. Like all other addictions, this one isn't beat just because you conquer it once. It creeps right back into your life and takes over. It's a serious drug, a narcotic of mind and soul. No one articulated this better than Billie Holiday, in her autobiography, *Lady Sings the Blues*. She is speaking at a period when she has again kicked her heroin habit, and reflects:

"This time, the doctors have told me, with any kind of luck, I should be able to stay straight for two whole years. . . . But no doctor can tell you anything your own bones don't know. And I can let the doctors in on something. I knew I'd really licked it one morning when I couldn't stand television any more. When I was high and wanted to stay that way, I could watch TV by the hour and loved it. Who can tell what detours are ahead? Another trial? Sure. Another jail? Maybe. But if you've beat the habit again and kicked TV, no jail on earth can worry you too much."

Does this mean we must hock our TVs if we want to be spiritual people? I don't think so. TV can be beneficial when used thoughtfully, to watch a program we know we'll be interested in, even a regular weekly show. The challenge is to not be pulled under the steady influence of the tube as a companion, as a mental and spiritual narcotic that we can't do without. The gift of silence, with all its refreshment, can be forgotten, lost, if we return to the easier numbing of available noise.

SUPPORT FOR SILENCE

It's hard to stay alert to our habits, to battle the addictive, noncreative ones on our own. That's why community is so crucial to the spiritual path. One of the benefits of being part of a spiritual community is that it supplies you with other ways of getting back on the track, of coming awake again, of practicing your discipline.

Sometimes at King's Chapel we had a Silent Day at the Parish House, on a Saturday, beginning at around nine in the morning and lasting till three or four in the afternoon. There would be books of spiritual readings around, or you could bring a book yourself, or a notebook to write your thoughts in, or just sit and look out the window, or simply close your eyes and rest. We had lunch in silence, too, eating together around the table, smiling perhaps, or exchanging glances or silent greetings, but not talking. There was something extra in this, in being silent with other people, as if the others' silence gave a greater weight and meaning to your own, as if your own could be shared, and mixed in with these others, as they, too, chose to be with fellow seekers, in community, in a common experience of respect, contemplation, prayer. I would leave those occasions feeling closer to the others who were there, as if I knew them better, in some deeper way than discussion would have given us. I always left feeling refreshed, too, as if I'd taken a dip in a fresh spring.

If you are part of a church, synagogue, or any kind of faith community, suggest your own kind of Silent Day if there is no equivalent in your program. If you aren't part of a faith community, try it with whatever kind of community you are part of, or want to organize—a Twelve Step program, a writer's group, or even people you get to know at work. Perhaps they, too, feel a need for respite from the sound assault of the workplace. You might even suggest it to your boss—a day, or even a morning or afternoon set aside for people who wish to sit in silence, with reading available of a meditative nature, or whatever each person wishes to bring to share, set out on a table anyone can choose from. I know, it sounds impractical, yet, perceptive administrators know that any exercise that lowers stress and brings a sense of calm to people will eventually enhance their work.

Silence can even enhance performance in team sports, according to Phil Jackson, coach of the Chicago Bulls, in the powerful book he wrote with Hugh Delahanty, *Sacred Hoops: Spiritual Lessons of a Hardwood Warrior*. Coach Jackson is a Zen practitioner who teaches meditation and Buddhist techniques to his team, and he has found that "the experience of sitting silently together as a group tends to bring about a subtle shift in consciousness that strengthens the team bond. Sometimes we extend mindfulness to the court and conduct whole practices in silence. The deep level of concentration and nonverbal communication that arises when we do this never fails to astonish me."

Another way to experience silence with a group is to invite a few friends to your own house or apartment for a day or a morning on the weekend. Unplug the phone, radio, and TV, provide some of your own favorite books or articles that inspire contemplation, set those out, along with tea or coffee and perhaps some fruit, and share some hours of silence together.

Giving ourselves the gift of silence sometimes solves problems, leads to new insights or understandings. Business leader Arnold Hiatt told me that when he was a student at Harvard he was torn about whether to study medicine like his brother, though it wasn't what he wanted to do. One afternoon he was walking along the Charles River and noticed the monastery of the Cowley Fathers on Memorial Drive. "I went in," he recalled, "and I sat down, and it was very peaceful and calm. It was like 'hearing silence.' I decided I wasn't going to pursue this course I was on, that I really didn't want to do it. I went out very relieved."

Our great nineteenth-century novelist Herman Melville wrote, "All profound things and emotions of things are preceded and attended by silence," a thought that affirms Hiatt's experience. Melville went on to say, "Silence is the consecration of the universe. Silence is the invisible laying on of the Divine Pontiff's hands upon the world. Silence is the only voice of our God."

The silence of the Quakers is their way of worship. In an essay on "The Eloquent Sounds of Silence" in *Time* magazine, the Indian-born author Pico Ayer wrote, "Silence is an ecumenical state, beyond the doctrines and divisions created by the mind. If everyone has a spiritual story to tell of his life, everyone has a spiritual silence preserve."

NIGHTS AT A MONASTERY

Besides one's own spiritual community—which may be a church, a synagogue, a Quaker meeting, a Twelve Step group, a support group born out of any number of empowerment or adult education programs—spiritual resources exist in the larger community around you which can be of tremendous value on your own journey, in staying on the path and strengthening your commitment to creativity and wholeness. The religious education committee of my church once under-took the project of compiling a pamphlet of resources in our own com-munity. We asked everyone to contribute ideas to the list—places, people, and events that they had found to be enriching—it's a useful kind of guide to have for any group. One of the first places we put down was Glastonbury Abbey, a Benedictine monastery in Hingham, Massachusetts, about forty-five minutes from us in Boston.

Experiencing the silence and peace of a night in a monastery can provide a marvelous deepening of spiritual enrichment. Inhabiting the sacred space of any religion or spiritual discipline helps us empty our minds of the worldly concerns of accumulating, achieving, competing, conquering, climbing (socially and/or professionally). It offers rest for a while in the peace that lies beyond all that, in the realm of the spirit where none of that earthly struggle counts, but is seen as fleeting, ephemeral.

You needn't be a Catholic or even a Christian to spend an evening or a weekend at a Benedictine monastery, nor do you need to be a Buddhist to spend such quiet time at Zen Mountain Monastery in Mt. Tremper, New York, or other places like it. You needn't be rich or privileged, either. Monasteries usually ask for a *contribution* in the range of $20–$25 for a day and night, including three meals and all services and facilities, but if you can't afford that, and feel a sincere need for this kind of experience, they will accept whatever you are able to contribute.

In the early 1980s the religious education committee was looking for new places to hold our semiannual retreats in spring and fall. Two of the "scouts" reported back favorably about Glastonbury, with one concern. "There are crosses all over the place, a cross is in every room, and this might be disturbing to some of our Humanist members who are good Unitarians but aren't Christians."

The attributes of the place were so great that we decided to take the risk. We explained to people clearly that it was a Roman Catholic monastery and the cross and Christian symbols were naturally promi-nent throughout the place. As it turned out, no one who stayed at Glastonbury was bothered at all by the Christian symbolism. There was no pressure to take part in any ritual or state any belief; the place was simply at the disposal of guests to take what parts of it they wished to enjoy according to their own beliefs and inclinations. All were impressed by the gracious hospitality of the community, and we weren't surprised to learn that hospitality is the "specialty," or mission, of the Benedictines, as teaching is of the Jesuits.

Glastonbury became a favorite place for our retreats. We came to know some of the resident community, who always welcomed us and made us feel at home. Some of us have even gone there for individual retreats, to spend a night or two in the quiet, peaceful atmosphere of a monastery, a place of prayer. We were welcome to join the monks in the chapel at their offices of prayer, held at regular intervals through-out the day and evening, as they chanted and sang the psalms and prayers of their devotions. Glastonbury is not a "silent" monastery, as some are, and there is conversation at meals, but the place itself is of course one of quiet, and contemplation.

Thomas Merton wrote in *The Seven Storey Mountain* that when he saw some of the monasteries of Europe as a young man, he thought them a kind of oddity, relics from the past. Later, when he turned to his own spiritual path, eventually joining the Trappist monastery of Gethsemane in Kentucky, he began to appreciate monasteries as focal points of powerful prayer. He came to believe that monasteries, rather than being superfluous, are essential to the world; that perhaps the concentrated prayer from these places, like a kind of spiritual atomic power, is what keeps the earth going around, what keeps the whole hu-man enterprise continuing.

I find that after spending quiet time at a monastery, it is easier to practice silence at home. The ability to be silent is—like every other ability—strengthened by practice and discipline. The ability to be silent is like a muscle that needs to be exercised.

THE CHALLENGE OF SILENCE

Silence is a challenge, and it can be disturbing for some people. On one of our church's retreats at Glastonbury, part of the program was to have the midday meal without speaking, with music playing in the background. One man, a professor, looked nervously around the room, then picked up a carton of orange juice that was on the table, and be-gan to read the wording on the sides of it. He read those words over and over, studied them, dwelt on them, in a desperate effort to fill up his mind, to avoid the emptiness of silence, or the simple, wordless message of the music. A woman, who looked increasingly disgruntled, expressed her anger to one of the retreat leaders after the meal, for being subjected to this experience. She said she "hadn't come here for that," and was so disturbed that she left, escaping even the memory of less than an hour of silence.

In my own pursuit of spiritual growth, I went on a personal silent retreat for five days, under the guidance of a spiritual director. A spiritual director is usually a priest, nun, or minister who is trained to lead lay people into a deeper experience of prayer, meditation, and awareness of God, meeting with them once or twice a month, engaging in discussion about these matters, and offering suggestions for developing that dimension of life. The process might be thought of as a therapy of the soul.

My own spiritual director at that time was a member of the Society of St. John the Evangelist, an Episcopal order of monks. My director had explained at the outset that he asked those he met with to do a personal silent retreat once a year at the order's retreat house in Newbury, Massachusetts.

I went on this retreat eagerly, yet with apprehension. I wondered if I'd get bored, or anxious, or depressed; though I hoped I'd be relaxed, comforted, calmed, perhaps even inspired. I took lots of books, a notebook to write in, and plenty of pens. I stayed in a new retreat house by myself, took my evening meal with the Brothers in their large farmhouse, and talked to no one except the spiritual director, whom I met with for an hour each day.

It was one of the loudest times in my life. With other noise shut out, it was as if my own head grew more raucous, with contending interior voices yelling for attention. It was fascinating, never dull, and in fact, pretty tiring! I felt I had gotten in touch with a whole aspect of myself that had been drowned out, or shut up, and it felt healthy to experience all the complexity of my own mind when given free rein. The once-a-day meetings with the spiritual director were a kind of anchor, or focal point, and he always recommended psalms or texts to read and meditate on, which I did, engaging them much more vigorously in this state of silence, with only my own voices going at it, than when I was speaking with others in a group.

Though it was sometimes exhausting, it was invigorating, too. I felt like Jacob wrestling with the angel. That's, in fact, what the five days seemed most like in retrospect—a kind of extended wrestling match, with different parts of my self, and God. It also seemed a relieving process—an emptying—of all those voices that rose up in my mind when I exposed myself to a state of extended silence.

THE ART OF EMPTYING

Monasteries, of course, aren't the only places for finding silence, meditation, and contemplation. There are a number of ashrams in this country now, open to people of all faiths who want to experience with other seekers a break from daily life. Removing ourselves from that routine temporarily can be a relief, a kind of healing, a process of emptying ourselves of habitual patterns of thought and behavior.

Living in Boston, I had heard about the Kripalu Center in Lenox, Massachusetts, in the Berkshires, and I had seen their catalogues in coffeehouses and stores on Charles Street on Beacon Hill. The catalogues always showed healthy men and women doing yoga or climbing mountains or splashing in a lake, smiling and obviously enjoying themselves in a lovely natural setting. I decided to go for a weekend and drove over with a friend who was also curious about the place.

The building and grounds of Kripalu were originally a Roman Catholic retirement home for Jesuit priests, known as Shadowbrook, and was bought in the late '60s by Amrit Desai, known to his followers as Gurudev ("beloved teacher"). Desai came from India to teach yoga, developed a following at his first ashram in Pennsylvania, and established this larger center in the Berkshires.

In 1995, Desai was ousted from the institution when he admitted sexual relationships with followers that he had previously denied. Kripalu survived the ensuing crisis, and the resident staff, who live and work there year-round and run all aspects of the operation, have continued the programs and work of the center.

During my four visits to Kripalu, the resident staff was hospitable and friendly, but never tried to impose their beliefs on the guests. I felt perfectly comfortable there and was never pressured, even to attend the program or classes I had signed up to take. I enjoyed the abundant and tasty vegetarian food, the sessions in yoga and meditation, and special programs for empowerment in particular areas. Friends who have been there in the post-Gurudev era tell me it's operating well.

Kripalu is one of those places that provide a context for "emptying," for breaking free of destructive habits you haven't been able to shake. A woman I know was sent there by a friend who was worried about her drinking and smoking and increasing depression. There is no alcohol, tobacco, or caffeine at Kripalu, so going there automatically means emptying those substances from your body. Like most people, I got a headache from caffeine withdrawal the first time I went.

My friend at first rebelled, laughing at the staff and calling them escapists, but they just smiled, and by the end of the week she felt better than she had in a long time. She decided to go again for the three-week yoga teacher training, gave up alcohol and cigarettes, and became a popular yoga teacher herself! That's how powerful an exposure to a new way can be.

YOGA IN PARADISE

For months I had studied with fascination a full-page ad with photographs on the back cover of *The Yoga Journal*, for an ashram in the Bahamas. The pictures looked too good to be true, and the price also seemed too good to be true for what looked like a beautiful beachside resort. I didn't go until I discovered a friend who had actually been to the place.

"It's like spiritual boot camp," Cheryl told me. She said if I didn't mind getting up at five-thirty in the morning for the early meditation, and going to two meditations and two yoga sessions every day (attendance is required, to ward off people who just want to take advantage of the great beach location at a low price), I'd probably enjoy the experience.

The Sivananda Ashram Yoga Retreat on Paradise Island turned out to be as good as it looked in the pictures. Doing yoga postures on a platform on the beach, with the spray of ocean waves wafting over you and the warm sun beaming down, is hard to beat. When the surf gets too loud, class is transferred to a platform on the bay side of the island, an idyllic spot itself, with gentle waves lapping and cruise ships passing by.

Attending the two-hour meditation sessions in the morning, sitting on pillows on the concrete floor of the temple, with chanting and singing in Sanskrit, facing candles and framed photographs of gurus, would not be everyone's idea of a vacation. If you let yourself sink into it, though, using the time to relax, clear the mind, and empty yourself of the usual worries, fears, and concerns, it can be a beautiful way to begin the day.

After that mental emptying, followed by emptying the body of soreness and fatigue in morning yoga, you can fill your body with fresh breads and muffins, hot and cold cereals, fresh fruit and salads, tea, and milk, at an abundant brunch at ten o'clock. The ashram asks for people to volunteer for taking turns at cleanup, dishwashing, and food preparation, but aside from those alternating minor duties you are free then to enjoy the beach or go into town until the afternoon yoga session at four o'clock. Dinner is at six, followed by evening meditation, which is usually lighter than the morning chanting, like a meditation walk, a bonfire on the beach, or reading stories aloud from the Hindu tradition.

To emphasize their welcoming and respect of other faiths, the residents and teachers at the ashram encourage visitors to sing or lead hymns from their own religious tradition during walks or evening get-togethers. Never when I was there was there a hint of any attempt at conversion, or that most dreaded of all things we fear when we have to go to a place whose traditions are foreign and mysterious to us— brainwashing.

My fellow retreatants were an interesting and congenial group of people ranging in age from twenty-something to seventy-something, from the U.S., Canada, Germany, England, Australia, with varied backgrounds, from a retired entertainment lawyer to a United Nations guide, a Soho painter to a Washington, D.C., housewife. I stayed a week and left invigorated.

While it's great to go to the Caribbean, it isn't necessary to go to an exotic place to do yoga. I took my first classes at the Boston Center for Adult Education, and the benefits to mind, body, and spirit were just as great. Most adult ed centers, as well as Young Men and Young Women's Christian Associations, and Young Men and Young Women's Hebrew Associations in most cities offer classes at modest prices. If you can't find any classes in your area, a copy of *The Yoga Journal* lists teachers from every state in the back of the magazine, and even if one isn't in your own city or town, calling or writing them is likely to lead you to the nearest yoga class.

Nor do you need to go to ashrams or monasteries to find silence. Rev. Carl Scovel loves to hike in the White Mountains of New Hampshire, especially enjoying the silence of it, the natural meditation that goes with the experience. He most enjoys going by himself, and doesn't encourage conversation when he leads hikes for parishioners and friends.

Sometimes wordless times come as a surprise and relief. The writer and stand-up comedian Mary Beth Coudal told me she was taken to a dance recital recently, and what she most enjoyed was the spectacle of this kind of dramatic art *without words*. Words are her stock-in-trade, yet sometimes they seemed to overwhelm, clutter, and distract; this experience of watching a different kind of artistic performance, with no words at all, was especially restful to her.

"There wasn't any 'blah, blah, blah,' and it was great!" she explained.

CENTERING WITH MEDITATION

When we shut down the outer noise of the world—the traffic, boom boxes, televisions, radios, stereos, speeches, discussions, songs, conversations—then we are left with another kind of noise, the nonstop chatter of the mind. This constant, clamorous inner voice or voices reminds us of what to regret, what we ought to do, didn't do, what might be done, what has to be done, what was done to us twenty years ago, what we should have said to the person who did it and what we could say to anyone who tries it again—I have even caught myself talking out loud walking down the street as I play out some of these dialogues of the mind. I have heard this constant noise described as sounding like a foreign radio station whose rat-a-tat messages are meaningless if we don't know the language, or like the chatter of a horde of monkeys at the top of a banana tree, or a personal Tower of Babel.

Everyone agrees this interior babble is annoying, exasperating, crazy (and human)—all right, but how do we turn it off? How do we get some relief from it? Maybe that's why we turn on all that outer noise—to drown out the noise inside our own head. Maybe that's also a reason we drink, do drugs, overeat, over-sleep, over-work, over-sex—engage in anything that distracts us, anything that takes our mind off—our mind!

The other way to try to silence it is meditation—the conscious effort to empty our mind of all that detritus.

Humans have attempted for centuries to devise methods to still the mind, to try to remove ourselves from the chaos of the long-running record inside it. Today we are not discovering new and better ones but rather continuing or rediscovering the oldest ones. In this area there is no scientific advance, there is only the discipline of the ancient techniques.

Concentrating on a still point, a light, a candle flame, is one of the ways of focusing the mind for meditation. Mantras—words with sacred connotations or with no connotations at all—are repeated to focus the attention, and to "bring the mind back" to a point of concentration, nondistraction. Transcendental meditation, brought to this country by Maharishi Mahesh Yoga and his followers in the '60s, uses a mantra to keep coming back to, usually a Sanskrit word of one or two syllables. Some yoga meditations suggest simply concentrating on the breath, as it passes in and out of the nose. A Japanese technique counts to ten backwards, and then repeats it over and over.

Centering prayer, a kind of Christian version of TM, begins by asking God or Jesus to be present, and then uses a mantra such as God, Peace, Love, or Jesus. Instead of repeating the mantra, the meditator lets it go, and uses it again only when thoughts wander off, to bring the mind back to the focus, the still point. Father Basil Pennington, a Trappist monk, has been instrumental in spreading the practice, and illuminates the process in his key book, *Centering Prayer*.

All the meditation practices, from centering prayer to yoga, emphasize the importance of breathing. In fact one of the systems of yoga, called Pranayama, studies the link between breathing and consciousness and gives exercises to balance mind, body, and spirit through breathing. Michelle Hebert, an outstanding yoga teacher in Southern California, wrote on "The Breath of Life" in *Idea Today*, that we have the ability to control our breathing patterns, "to quicken our breathing or slow it down," and that "breath can change energy levels from low to high, from sluggish to revitalized. . . .[W]hen a person is in a state of anxiety, fear, or stress, his or her breathing is often shallow or uneven." Breathing exercises can shift those conditions to "a calmer, more balanced state."

Health pioneer Dr. Herbert Benson of Massachusetts General

Hospital explains in *The Relaxation Response* that the body cannot be in a state of stress and relaxation at the same time. By controlling the breath and focusing the mind on a single point, anyone can create physical relaxation. Dr. Dean Ornish, author of *Reversing Heart Disease*, found that such relaxation techniques can reduce both blood pressure and cholesterol levels.

What's the big deal? Don't we all breathe automatically? Isn't that one thing I don't have to *learn*? Well, you do, if you want to have some influence over it, and over your body and mind. Left to its own devices, the breath, like the mind, simply whirls out of control. Breathing techniques can be learned at any yoga class, or through a number of instructional tape cassettes.

THE WANDERING MIND

The mind always goes wandering off. One meditation technique is to watch it wander off, to be the observer of your own mind, separated from the gabble of it. But the gabble always rises up, just as powerfully for people today as it did for Abba Isaac of the Desert Fathers, who wrote in his instructions on this way of prayerful meditation:

"Perhaps wandering thoughts surge about my soul like boiling water, and I cannot control them, nor can I offer prayer without its being interrupted by silly images. I feel so dry that I am incapable of spiritual feelings, and many sighs and groans cannot save me from dreariness. I must needs say: 'O God, come to my assistance; O Lord, make haste to help me.' "

As it was in the first century so it is today!

Geoffrey Wolff, in his article on "Writers and Booze," speaks of the clamoring voices in the head as something peculiar to writers, when he explains their temptation to drink: "Writing is hard. I don't mean it's harder than everything, because it's not; I mean only that it's uphill work to write. And what's toughest is the din that echoes in a writer's ears after the day's work is done. A writer can't shut down the damned noise, his characters' voices, their competing complications. . . . Booze will send me to never-never land, dress me in thick wool, earmuff me against the voices, blink off the light, give rest and sleep and peace. Just what I must have wanted. Just what I don't want."

I would argue that it isn't only writers who "can't shut down the

damned noise" in their heads, it is all human beings. I would bet that
when Mr. Wolff is in between projects, he still can't shut down the
damned noise without conscious effort. The lure of drink to "earmuff"
a person against the interior voices is also why others turn to alcohol—
businessmen and housewives and pole vaulters and auto mechanics,
who also want to "blink off the light" and go to "never-never land."

It is much easier to pour a drink than to find a quiet spot, take a
breath, and devote twenty minutes to trying to clear the mind through
meditation! Meditation, meditative prayer, whatever the name we
give to that effort to still and empty the mind, is extremely difficult
and challenging. Doing it for twenty minutes twice a day, once in the
morning and once in the evening (as TM and centering prayer recommend) is a major commitment, one I have had a hard time keeping. I
followed a single twenty-minute prayer schedule every day for about
five years, then stopped for a few years, and have started again with
only ten minutes, hoping to flex this "muscle" of meditation and work
my way back to twenty minutes.

HEALING WITH MEDITATION

For most people, this kind of prayer or meditation is a struggle. The ef-
fort to empty is a challenge, yet it brings great benefits: a lessening of
tension, a relaxation, greater ease in personal and business dealings.
Few have had as dramatic results, though, in as short a time as Joan
Borysenko, the author, lecturer, and cofounder of the Mind/Body
Clinic at Massachusetts General Hospital.

In her bestselling book, *Minding the Body, Mending the Mind*, Joan
tells us that when she was twenty-four years old, working on her doctorate at Harvard Medical School, she was living on coffee and cigarettes, trying to cope with a troubled marriage and an infant son for
whom she had "too little time." She goes on:

> I was also a physical wreck. Troubled by migraines all my life, I
> found in college that the intense competition had added crip-
> pling stomach pains and vomiting to my list of psychosomatic
> illnesses. As a graduate student, I also came down with severe
> bronchitis four times in two years and had to study for my doc-
> toral exams while my head spun in a fever. If this weren't

enough, I also developed the high blood pressure that ran in my family.

My marriage fell apart during this year. I was now a single parent plagued with fainting and crippled by abdominal pains that were diagnosed as spastic colon. I was given antispasmodics, painkillers, and tranquilizers—all to no avail. Then a viral infection in the lining of my lungs created suffocating pain that took me to the emergency room of the nearest hospital.

There was no Mind/Body Clinic for me to go back to then, but there was a friend in the lab where I conducted my graduate research who was excited about his new hobby—meditation. He compared it to a mini-vacation in which he could switch off all his cares and concerns and come out refreshed and ready to tackle whatever came up. My first thought was that meditation was for ascetics who lived in caves. I was a hard-headed scientist, literally killing myself to master the ways of the medical establishment.

Nevertheless, I gave it a try—largely out of desperation—practicing each day. The test came a few weeks later while I was sitting at an electron microscope, trying to unlock the secrets of cancer cells. I felt the familiar stabbing behind my right eye, the light sensitivity and nausea that heralded a migraine. It was time for an experiment.

Retreating to my office, I pulled the shade and shut the door. I settled into a chair, relaxed my muscles from head to foot, shifted my breathing from tense chest breathing to relaxed diaphragmatic breathing, and began to meditate. In time the pain subsided. After the meditation was over, I was left with a feeling of having been washed clean, like the earth after a heavy rain. I ran around the laboratory announcing that I had performed the most important experiment of my life. It was the beginning of a great change in my life.

Another kind of meditation technique, one which Joan uses in working with people who are trying to attain a more calm lifestyle, is called "mindfulness," sometimes described as the "be here now" approach. It focuses on whatever you are doing at the moment, whether it is washing the dishes, eating a piece of bread, or crossing the street—

being present to the experience, emptying yourself of all the distractions of the past and future.

Joan writes, "During a full day session that occurs at the midpoint of the Mind/Body program, we take a long walk in a park by a river near the hospital. There is no 'purpose' to the walk—nowhere to go and nothing to accomplish. The accomplishment is being present in the process of walking. Our patients are usually amazed at how incredible the commonplace is. They hear sounds and see sights with new ears and eyes, with the kind of enjoyment a child experiences."

WESTERN ZEN: EMPTYING
AND EMBRACING THE HOLLOW

There are other simple techniques to experience the calming effect of silence. Singer Judy Collins told me, "I use exercise and breathing to center and clear my head. I like to run and swim—those are the Western forms of Zen."

Running is one of the most popular contemporary ways of clearing the mind, and you don't have to be a marathon champion to have the experience. Oregon professor Robert Grudin tells in *The Grace of Great Things: Creativity and Innovation* how "a long jog, with its strong rhythm and sense of physiological expressiveness" is one of the everyday methods he uses for clearing his mind when he's blocked or confused, and adds, "Contrapuntal music works on me similarly, and sometimes a glance out of my office window, of the graceful Douglas firs that stand to the south, is enough to clear my head."

Swimming is the key practice for Constance H. Gemson, who took part in one of my Spiritual Autobiography workshops at the 92nd St. Y in New York. She published her first article in *New York Newsday* on her experience of swimming "to find serenity."

"Others may attend church or meditate," Gemson wrote, "but for me, swimming provides the peace and serenity I need.

"By swimming, I am creating and keeping the silence as I glide through the familiar water in a pool on West 86th Street in New York City. Each experience is the same, yet different. I go back and forth, back and forth, to finish this cycle sixty-six times, or a half a mile. . . . I swim three times a week in my search for a clearer, calmer life. . . .

"By swimming, I find my own rhythm and silence. In my crowded life, this is vital. In my secular city, I swim and I'm refreshed."

Kurt Vonnegut has suggested (in an introduction to a collection of stories by Budd Schulberg) that another Western form of meditation is simply reading short stories—in this process the pulse beat slows, the mind concentrates on the immediate word being read, the static of interior chitchat is turned off, and we experience the same benefits as those of the more rigorous exercises of "pure" meditation emphasized by the Eastern traditions.

When I started expounding the virtues I had found as a beginning yoga student to my old friend Ted "The Horse" Steeg, a great athlete who was a "little-All-American" (an athlete from a small-enrollment school) at Wabash College, and a champion in all town sports from softball to basketball in Woodstock, New York, he began to laugh. At first I thought he was trying to joke away my enthusiasm for living in the moment and shutting off the noise that the yoga postures provided. But that wasn't it.

"You yo-yo! Why do you think I've been playing sports all these years?" he challenged. "That's what it does—puts you in the moment and shuts down the mental noise!"

"Oh, yeah—I guess it does," I sheepishly admitted, healthily shedding some of my false guru-ship.

Coach Phil Jackson affirms that "What makes basketball so exhilarating is the joy of losing yourself completely in the dance."

Whatever the process—from swimming to playing basketball, reading short stories to centering prayer, Quaker meetings, Zen sitting, and Transcendental Meditation—the stilling and focusing of the mind empties you of distractions, puts you in the present, a phenomenon described by Annie Dillard in *Pilgrim at Tinker Creek*: "Experiencing the present purely is being emptied and hollow; you catch grace as a man fills his cup under a waterfall."

By emptying, we are preparing ourselves to be filled.

THE WISDOM OF BODYSPIRIT

Some people in search of a spiritual dimension to their lives may start taking a course in yoga or tai chi, the most meditative of the martial arts. Both of these physical practices help empty the mind of distraction, and at the same time tone and strengthen the body. Sometimes students come to these practices strictly in search of physical empowerment, and in the process are awakened to the spirit.

All will discover that discipline of the body is also a way to discipline the mind, and that these practices themselves are a form of meditation. When you hold a yoga pose you are focused on your body holding the pose, rather than your ongoing mind-gabble. When you concentrate on performing the movements in tai chi, you are similarly freed from the interior babble stream.

The turn toward a spiritual path often—though not always, and not by some kind of hard-and-fast rule—involves an awareness of the body, an attention to one's physical condition that may not have been present before.

This, too, makes sense, and is illuminated by Nancy Roth, an Episcopal priest who writes, "In the Hebrew scriptures, human life is understood as one indivisible unity of body and spirit, which in Hebrew is expressed in the word *nefesh*. The closest equivalent we can manage in English is 'bodyspirit,' without the space between the words."

Bodyspirit. The two concepts were indeed joined in my own experience.

Though I'd gone to my first tai chi class purely, I thought, as a way of learning to use my body in a better way, when I slowly lifted my arms with palms upraised in the opening movement of "the form," as it's called, I sensed at once this was also prayer. ("The form" of tai chi is a series of flowing movements like a slow dance, that look like David Carradine's slow-motion movements in his "Kung Fu" television episodes.)

The Episcopal priest Nancy Roth explains in *A New Christian Yoga* that she began taking yoga classes because she wanted to make her body stronger and more supple in order to be a better dancer. She had found that "the absolute attentiveness" required in a strenuous ballet class "had a centering and calming effect that I could only describe as 'spiritual.' " When she enrolled in yoga class she had a similar experience, finding that "the exercise affected both my body and my spirit," and that the relaxation posture at the end of the class became for her "a doorway into prayer."

MY BODY, MY BURDEN

This whole idea of "bodyspirit" seemed, suddenly and marvelously, a revelation to me, which was not surprising since I had gone for most of my life without seeing (and vehemently denying) any connection between the body and the mind, much less the spirit.

That the mind and body are connected seems, of course, the most obvious truism imaginable—after all, the mind isn't floating outside you somewhere, in a separate compartment! But still, that concept is difficult to grasp when you've been brought up in a culture that until the last few decades separated those spheres of being. Dr. Herbert Benson had to battle to get his theories of direct mind-body relationships—like meditation lowering the pulse and blood pressure—accepted by the medical profession, even after they were tested and proved.

It used to suit me just fine to believe that the mind and body had no connection, since my mind—or at least the imaginative part of it, the part that enabled me to write—had served me pretty well. My body, on the other hand, while it had all its parts in working order, in high school was not strong or big or agile enough to make me a good athlete (a circumstance that, happily, turned me from trying to play football, to what for me was the more natural occupation of writing about *other* people playing football).

From my teenage years onward, I simply regarded my body as a necessary if annoying adjunct to whatever I thought of as "me"—a sort of burden to be fed, clothed, and washed as cursorily as possible, with the least bother. From my early twenties until age forty-eight I abused my body with tobacco and alcohol to such an extent that when I finally paid attention to it by starting that exercise program and getting off booze, I was told that if I had waited another six months I would have done permanent damage to my heart.

Even so, at first I looked on my new attention to my body simply as a practical measure, to enable me to live longer to use my precious mind and imagination. It didn't dawn on me that a person's physical and mental capacities were connected, and influenced one another—and even had to do with the spirit, an element I had denied altogether all those years. I began to see the interconnection when I started taking the tai chi and yoga classes.

PUTTING THE PARTS TOGETHER

"The word 'yoga,'" Nancy Roth explains in *A New Christian Yoga*, "comes from the Sanskrit word *yug*, which means to 'yoke' or 'join together.' For Hindus, the various disciplines of yoga help to join together body and mind, the human being and the divine, and the self and the world."

After coming back from the ashram in the Bahamas, I wrote that "waking to a tinkling bell in the dark at 5:30 in the morning, with the sound of the surf outside, going to meditation in the chapel, and on to yoga on the platform by the beach, with the sun and sea spray blessing our bodies, I soon found I wasn't making any distinctions between the purely physical and the rest of my being. All of it felt comfortable, calmed, alive."

The resident swami at the ashram, Swami Shanmugananda, had told me, "There is only one yoga. It is all for mystical union. Don't overemphasize the *asanas* [postures], that is a misunderstanding. People are attracted to Hatha yoga, taken by the physical postures, but what's behind it is mystical practice. The purpose of the postures is to facilitate the body to be steady during meditation. If the mind is not pure, then even if you're doing the most excellent postures, it's meaningless—it's like having a car in good condition, and the driver is drunk."

At the last yoga session I attended on the island, the instructor ended the session by quietly offering a prayer for "the *asanas* and what they teach us." They taught me in my bones as well as my mind what I should have known all along—that the body, spirit, and intellect can't be split into isolated compartments. What nurtures any part nurtures the whole.

In yoga, in joining together, I began to see—or rather, experience—the interconnections of all those elements of my life I had looked on and experienced as separate. This included, finally, the creative, which I held out longest of all as a separate realm, a sort of magic kingdom which the elect were privileged to enter and work in—the elect being people like myself who were "professional" creative people, those who made a living as writers, painters, sculptors, musicians. In yoga class, finally, I experienced in a small but obvious way that brought home to me the connection of creativity as part of the whole, a function of bodyspirit.

IDEAS FROM <u>ASANAS</u>

A few years ago I was commissioned to write a movie script based on my novel *Selling Out*, about a writer in Hollywood who was going to pieces as he used more booze and drugs to try to regain his creative powers, and brought himself instead to the brink of self-annihilation before turning away from that destructive course at the last minute. (Yes, it was autobiographical.) The day before I was supposed to send in a draft of the script I knew that the endings of two scenes were all wrong. I needed to come up with some better dramatic resolutions before letting the producer and director see what I'd written.

I looked at my watch and saw it was nearly four o'clock in the afternoon—several hours later than I'd imagined. It was one of those times when I'd been staring at the word processor without any result for hours on end. I had a yoga class in Cambridge at five o'clock, and I really wanted to go, but I was afraid of leaving these scene endings unresolved, afraid I wouldn't have time enough to fix them if I took off the two hours it would require to put on my sweatpants, T-shirt and gym shoes, catch the subway to Cambridge, take the class, and return. I sat for another five minutes or so staring blankly at the screen of my computer, feeling stale, numb, and sedentary. Then I suddenly jumped up and grabbed my yoga things, justifying this bolting from duty with the thought, What's the difference? I'm not getting anything done anyway. I hurried off to class.

I put the script and all its problems out of my mind and simply decided to enjoy the yoga experience. While I was doing the shoulder stand—one of the inverted poses—one of the scenes I was having trouble with came to my mind, and the idea for ending it followed immediately, an idea that seemed natural, right, and fitting. I smiled—upside down—and wondered if the key to getting ideas when you were stuck was to stand on your head—or at least your shoulders. Maybe turning the mind upside down had shaken out the right idea!

Later in the class I was doing the "triangle" pose, holding myself as steady as I could at "the edge" of my capacity to stay in the position. When the instructor told us to release, to "come back to center," the ending to the other troublesome scene in the script snapped into my mind, complete, as if freed by the release of the posture.

It felt as if the yoga positions had released the ideas, that stretching my body had somehow stretched open my mind to allow the scene endings to come out. If I had stayed home, glued to the computer screen, I would simply have logged more empty hours and brought myself further frustration—along with rising anxiety—without resolving the questions in the script.

The experience brought clearly to my mind what I'd been living—but not recognizing so specifically—for nearly a decade; namely, that the mind, body, and spirit are inextricably connected, and that what we do to and with our body will influence our mind—including the imagination, and our creative powers.

Ever since I started on the path of bodyspirit in 1980 I have felt far better than I had since high school (waking without a hangover is in itself a plus), and I have enjoyed the actual process of writing more than before. But the direct relationship of the physical with the mental and spiritual—and creative—aspects of life didn't fully hit me until that yoga class.

I don't mean to trivialize the vast and profound significance of yoga in the world by passing it off as a gimmick to get ideas, but rather to suggest what happened in my minor experience was a metaphor that brought home to me some of the connections offered by the "yoke," the tying together, that yoga provides.

To illustrate how rich and varied is the whole concept of yoga, I again call on Nancy Roth, who explains, "Some of these practices concern devotion (bhakti yoga), knowledge (jnana yoga), action (karma yoga), and inner concentration called the 'royal way' (raja yoga). Hatha yoga is a branch of raja yoga and involves postures, meditations, breathing techniques, and concentration exercises, or meditation. The word hatha actually consists of two words, ha, which means 'sun,' and tha, which means 'moon.' The sun represents the expenditure or expression of energy; the moon, the acquiring or conservation of energy. The joining together of these principles through the exercises of hatha yoga creates a balance like that of the cosmic rhythm of the sun and moon.

"Since the human body does not vary according to religion, it is not surprising that exercises which originated in Hinduism can be readily incorporated into another theological context."

YOGA AS PRAYER

Before I had read Nancy Roth's thoughtful concept, in A New Christian Yoga, I found it natural to think of my yoga practice as a spiritual or bodyspirit experience that in no way conflicted with my belief as a member of a Christian church. In fact, I knew the yoga supported and enriched my spiritual life, and, even more dramatically, at a crucial time of darkness was my primary spiritual connection.

Just as I naively was beginning to think I was "getting it all together" in following a spiritual path (always a time to be on guard, I now know), I took a turn in what I thought was good faith that brought pain to another person as well as myself. I made a commitment to a relationship with a woman that I couldn't keep, that I knew almost immediately was impossible for me. It was all the more painful because I had imagined I was doing this out of a spiritual motivation, as part of my own spiritual path. The shock of it turning out to be so clearly and devastatingly a mistake brought down a curtain of darkness in my mind and spirit. Prayers seemed hollow now, and phoney. Weren't these the words I had used to justify this mistake as I was in the process of making it? The words now taunted me, and I couldn't speak them.

At this time, when prayer with words shut down for me, when even going to church was painful to me, the one thing that brought me a sense of peace and interior calm was going to yoga class. I realized this was my prayer now, the one kind I could engage in, because it was wordless. I knew it was no less prayer.

Nor is "Zen sitting" any less a prayer, though it is without words. I have joined others in "sitting" at Zen Mountain Monastery in New York state, near Woodstock, and at the beautiful Zen Center at Green Gulch, outside of San Francisco, where services every Sunday morning begin with forty minutes of silent sitting, followed with a Dharma talk by one of the teachers, questions and discussions from the listeners, and then a community partaking of tea and homemade muffins baked by volunteers in the predawn hours that morning.

RETURN TO THE FORM

Another sustaining concept that came to me, and kept me in the practice of going to church even when it was hard to do, was something I learned from David Zucker in tai chi class. Our classes were held in the beautiful, spacious ballroom of the Boston Center for Adult Education, a former merchant's mansion on Commonwealth Avenue, just off the Boston Public Garden. The setting was wonderful, except that there was a class in wine-tasting in a room next to us, and after our own class began it would inevitably be interrupted by men passing through, carrying cases of wine to the tasters, making a noisy rattling sound as they went, disturbing or breaking our quiet concentration.

My tai chi classmates and I got annoyed and broke our rhythm. David then told us that this interruption was a good thing, something we could make use of, since those kind of unwanted, unexpected interruptions that upset our concentration were part of the experience of daily life. "Let them come," he said. "Don't worry if you break your rhythm or even stop and start over again. The only thing to remember when it happens is: Return to the form."

The words rang deep in my consciousness. "Return to the form." It applied to my going back to church, in the routine I had been in before; it applied to going back to work on a book or a script or an essay or article when something had interrupted it, or taken me completely away from it. There was no use lamenting whatever it was that broke my concentration or yanked me physically or mentally or emotionally or spiritually out of a project. Just center again. Just take a deep breath and remember where you are. Return to the form.

The words have become a guide to me, and come to mind in all different situations, giving me a way back. They are a way of dealing with interruptions, upsets, the million large and small crises that tug and tear at us through the course of a day, a year, a career, a lifetime. *Return to the form.*

ATHLETES LEARN FROM THE EAST

In tai chi or yoga or any other such discipline the action of the body is not just exercise but meditation or prayer, a way of centering, calming, becoming aware. It is a powerful way of emptying, clearing the mind and the body at the same time, making them more alert and effective. The body and mind, working together in these disciplines, act as a living metaphor and expression of spirit, a manifestation of bodyspirit.

In the West we tend to think mainly of women engaged in these disciplines, and most yoga classes in America, as well as tai chi, are made up largely of women. Yet recently, prominent male athletes have made public their use of such disciplines to improve their own skills in professional sports—which also, not incidentally, require enormous creativity. An athlete, in performing, reacts, must "see" the field or court, becomes part of the flow of a game, and even directs the flow. Kareem Abdul-Jabbar is a student of yoga, and Robert "The Chief" Parish of the Charlotte Hornets started taking tai chi at age thirty to make himself more effective on the court.

One does not, however, need to be an athlete to engage in such practices, or get the full benefit of them creatively and spiritually. As athletes can use tai chi and yoga for their development, I can use it to support and enhance my creative life as a writer. The effects of such disciplines are not confined to the hours of actually doing them, or the space where one takes a class or performs the routine. Continuous practice affects other areas of life, as in the experience of tai chi teacher David Zucker who is also an actor, mime, director, and playwright, and finds that "the form" inspires and informs all his creative work. For anyone who practices, the strengthening of the spiritual is a natural and inseparable part of the activity, the integration of bodyspirit.

Tilden Edwards of the Shalem Institute has written, "Our bodies are gifts and vehicles of God, integral to our being. Much attention is paid to the body in contemporary western culture. However, both in and out of the church the body tends to be approached in terms of physical fitness and beauty apart from a direct relation to God. One of the gifts of our greater knowledge of Asian religious practices in the last few decades has been the introduction of hatha yoga, with all its care in revealing the integrality of body and spirit."

I don't mean to proclaim that since physical well-being and care of the body create conditions for the fuller flowering of creativity, that one needs to become a body-built paragon of muscle like Arnold Schwarzenegger or an Olympic sprinter like Jackie Joyner-Kersee in order to create. If that were the case, I'd still be stuck on my last script, much less would I have gone on to produce the books, essays, and articles that followed it. Attention to the body, respect for it, the exercise of it to keep it in good working order, is one of the keys that can help unlock the creative as well as spiritual powers within us.

I take a class now in a form of yoga called "ashtanga," which emphasizes continuous movement during the session so that the pulse runs higher, as in aerobic exercise. The goal of "keeping the body heat up" (which is aided by turning up the room temperature) enables the muscles to move more freely, so we're able to stretch it into more positions. One of the results of the class is a lot of sweat, more sweat than I can ever remember pouring out of my body in any other form of exercise—*pools* of sweat, forming on the floor beneath me. This releases the toxins in the body, according to the teachers. At the end of the class I certainly feel cleaned out.

I originally assumed that at the end of such a rigorous class I'd be dead tired and starving. Instead, I am energized, and not very hungry at all. I think this phenomenon is another aspect of the unexpected rewards of emptying. By using our body till it seems empty of strength, we get new strength; by sweating profusely, the body not only eliminates toxins, but also eliminates the need for stuffing itself with food. It's almost as if by emptying, we are fed—or filled up, as in "made whole" again.

Emptying is part of the process of nature—the leaves fall, flowers wilt, the skins of animals molt, and new buds, blooms, and pelts are grown in due season. The day is emptied of light, so night can come down, and out of the empty dark a new dawn rises. In the ageless lines of Ecclesiastes, "The sun also riseth and setteth in the west, and the rivers return from whence they have come."

Emptying.

Filling.

The process can sometimes be painful. Many people have recorded through the ages that part of the beginning of a spiritual journey is a stripping away of the old person before a new one can be born, the emptying before the filling. When you are being stripped, or emptied, you don't know if you'll ever be full again—in fact, it's hard to believe. In this weakened and frightening state you feel naked, alone, barren. Anyone who tries to reassure you at such a time that "things will get better" sounds like a phoney, a Pollyanna, speaking the platitudes of Job's friends. You snarl back, like a cornered animal.

I did, anyway. In that 1980 flight from Hollywood, the year my parents died and my relationship split apart and I was broke and sick, someone called to tell me that a raunchy movie had been made, using—or partially using—the title of my most successful book, the novel *Going All the Way*. This trashy exploitation film was called *Goin' All the Way*, evidently trying to protect against any complaints of mine that it wasn't exactly the *same* title by replacing the "g" in "Going" with an apostrophe. It seemed like the last straw. The movie played at a Boston theater near where I lived. I passed it on the way to church. Friends asked if it was mine. Ads ran in the local papers. I called my agent from a pay phone at LaGuardia Airport and was told there was nothing I could do about it.

"I feel like I'm being *stripped*," I wailed.

There were tears in my eyes. I really felt stripped. At the time, I didn't know that the very words I used—"being stripped"—were part of any transformative process, spiritual or otherwise. I barked at anyone who told me things would get better. I was empty. Now I know I had to experience that, to be filled in a new kind of way. Now I see that emptying leaves you available for such a transformation. Then, I only knew I was empty.

I'd never have believed what follows: fullness.

Chapter 8

FILLING UP

To each of us, when it comes, the feeling of emptiness seems the darkest of pits, the worst that anyone ever endured. Yet in most cases—certainly mine—our own "stripping" is peanuts compared to that of people who were stripped by accident or nature in some permanent way, and yet use the opportunity to "fill" with a different, greater power. Sometimes the kind of restrictions Rabbi Kushner speaks about, that bring greater discipline and command, are imposed by physical handicaps or ailments. A person may be "emptied" of some function, or many functions, by genetics, disease, or happenstance—yet the discipline required to overcome the losses may increase other powers, especially the creative.

Told in graduate school that he had Lou Gehrig's disease, a crippling illness, physicist Stephen Hawking went into a two-year depression (his own time of emptying). He holed up in his room playing Wagner records, reading science fiction, and "drinking a fair amount," letting his studies and his dissertation fall by the wayside.

In *Stephen Hawking's Universe*, John Boslough tells us that when Hawking's condition temporarily stabilized he realized it would not affect his mind, and since it took no physical ability to do physics, he decided to start working again (filling up). He returned to writing his dissertation, got married, fathered two children, earned his doctorate, and began working on a formidable challenge—nothing less than the mathematical proof of the beginning of time.

Confined to a wheelchair, unable to speak except through a voice box, Hawking has led the way as one of the most important scientists of our time, illuminating black holes, the "big bang" theory and the "unified field" theory of what makes the universe tick. He provides a miraculous living example of the creative spirit working through a severely handicapped body, with incredible discipline.

Audiences all over the world have been inspired by Christy Brown, the Irish writer/hero of the book and movie *My Left Foot*, who managed to create against seemingly impossible odds, finding through heroic discipline a way to use his mostly disabled body to create. Such people also exemplify bodyspirit to me, and illustrate through their lives and work how the creative spirit can triumph against all odds.

Sometimes the odds are physical, as in a paralyzed body. Sometimes people lack opportunities because of their socioeconomic status in a given society; yet, that very deprivation, or emptiness, stirs them to find new ways to create.

I think of a marvelous documentary called *Style Wars* about minority kids from the blighted slum areas of New York City who painted what the world, or at any rate the city government, described and outlawed as "graffiti" on the sides of subways. I had thought graffiti meant scatological words and ugly scrawlings on bathroom walls. These paintings on the subways were bright, colorful, murallike art done with spray paint by young people who stole into the yards where the cars were kept to express their yearning to create beauty in a grim, blasted world. They refer to one another as "painters," and call one of the masters of their form a "Picasso."

When you see one of the subway cars come up from underground in the film, and move into the shattered, broken world through which it passes, brightly alive with colorful scenes, faces and flowers and swirls of suns, stars and planets of the imagination, it's like seeing the spirit break out. It's like a painted cry saying, "We're here—look at us, look at what we see, what we create, look at the beauty of it, you can't stomp us out, we will rise again some other way!"

The spray-painted subway cars reminded me of paintings I had seen from South America, shown by theologian Harvey Cox in a talk on liberation theology. From countries emptied of hope by despotic, dictatorial suppression, where any sign of spirit was stamped out, there were paintings of Jesus lying on the ground with holes in his body, like bullet holes—and growing up through the holes were flowers, bursting toward the sun. They were saying, without words, "You can't stamp us out; you can kill us but we will rise again, this spirit will rise again, through the holes of your bullets it will bloom, and nothing can destroy it, for it is the life force, the spirit."

No more powerful testimony to the spirit exists than the drawings and paintings done in the concentration camps. In *Spiritual Resistance: Art from the Concentration Camps* we see the work smuggled out of Nazi death camps, done by prisoners trapped in the ultimate hell of this century. We learn that "the artists of the camps defied Nazi regulations on canvas, paper, tissue—in pen, or ink, or color wrung from tattered clothing—to demonstrate their transcendence of the horror of the moment. While many of these artists never stepped from the camps, the strength of their will survives." The artists drew portraits of their fellow inmates, and scenes of camp life, hiding their drawings in double walls, or burying them. Some traded bread for paper or paint, and used flour sacks and burlap bags as their canvases. On the doorstep of death, in affirmation of life, they created.

NEW WARRIORS

There is a concept around now, used in the dialogue of the New Age or personal growth or human potential movement, of the "warrior," originating perhaps from Carlos Castenada in his Don Juan books. It doesn't mean the warrior as soldier in the traditional sense of a military man with a gun on a political mission for a nation-state, but rather an individual who has developed his own powers of bodyspirit through tremendous discipline; has developed himself and his senses to be able to perform at his peak or beyond it—not in service to some military aggressor but to the spirit, the life force of the universe. This kind of "warrior" is exemplified in the practice of tai chi, in which no blow is struck, yet a foe is deflected. David Zucker tells how this works, in one of the most illuminating explanations of the power of emptying:

"The basic premise is that you understand your own body's energy completely first, and then you understand the other person's, so if someone is aiming a blow, you're so totally not there you empty yourself completely, which is the meditative aspect, the religious aspect. You empty yourself so you have no ego about it, no fear of life or death, so you kind of become the other person. If I were trying to punch my own hand, I couldn't do it because I know exactly when I'm going to do it—so if I was in tune with you as you are yourself, you couldn't hit me because I would be able to sense that energy coming and just move. That's really the self-defense aspect."

I think of the disciplines of tai chi and yoga as practices to strengthen us to be that kind of warrior, to create, to serve as convey-ors of the spirit. The kind of warrior I am speaking of may use her dis-ciplined power not only for evading injury and deflecting anger, but in the service of healing, in all its manifold forms. Such warriors are in the tradition of the "Flower Soldiers" of the Native Americans, an an-cient discipline of teachers and Medicine Men and Women described by Hyemeyohsts Storm in his wisdom-fiction narrative *Lightningbolt*.

Contemporary healing can come through the laying on of hands. This does not promise an instant cure but brings about an easing of pain and eventual recovery through the practiced, educated use of bodywork techniques. One who employs such methods in such a spirit is Elizabeth Valentine, a masseuse in Boston, who explained she had worked with pregnant women in France, and with clients of a doctor who treated survivors of sexual abuse. "The idea of massage was to help heal the split between body and mind," she told me.

Other kinds of healing come through practice of the arts and shar-ing one's art with others. Singer Judy Collins speaks of healing through music: "I've said that performing is healing, and so is writing, absolutely. I was just talking to my friend Erica Jong about our work, how it heals. It reaches me when the only thing that helps me is writing. I've always been a great believer in the self-healing qualities of creativity."

Healing ourselves is one way we act as what creation theologian Matthew Fox calls cocreators with God—a theology in which we are not helpless pawns who must plead our case to a distant deity, but rather serve as responsible partners in creating our lives and the world we live in. An early, inspirational cocreator was the visionary medieval nun Hildegarde of Bingen who "saw herself as the mouthpiece of the Lord, merely conveying his messages to her hearers and readers," according to biographer Sabina Flanagan in *Hildegarde of Bingen: A Visionary Life*. That might be a way to explain her prodigious output—three massive works of theology, books on plants, animals, medicine and healing, seventy songs, cycles of poetry, a musical play, more than three hundred letters—at the same time she was also a traveling preacher, abbess of a monastery, healer, exorcist, advisor, prophet, and seer.

THE VOICE THAT SAYS, "GET UP!"

Learning the myths about alcohol, drugs, and creativity helps empty our mind of some of the dangerous misconceptions and distortions about the subject. There are also many other negative myths we need to rid ourselves of to reach our full creative potential: the myth of low self-esteem ("I'm not good enough"), fear of failure ("Now there's proof I'm no good!") or of success ("I don't deserve it"). Getting rid of these deep-seated personal myths can be a continuing process, but one that must be engaged in to reach more of our potential as creators and human beings.

Another powerful and debilitating myth is that we can "save" someone else. Many use that as an excuse to continue destructive relationships that for years on end drag us down. I have watched this painful process with a friend who lives with an alcoholic who has "bottomed out" many times. This drinker has been put in jail, lost the love and support of family, been fired from job after job, been taken to hospitals by the police after threatening suicide and/or murder—yet, has never once made the decision to give up the bottle. During all this the partner has lost not only work and income but physical health, with a disease brought on by stress. Both deny that they need outside help, which would be a sign of weakness!

We all have negative voices in our consciousness, and cleaning them out is a lifelong process. Figure skater Nancy Kerrigan sums it up in a Nike ad, which shows her falling down and then getting up to skate again, saying there are always the voices that tell her to give up; the only voice she listens to is the one that says, "Get up!"

But what new voices or ideas do we put in place of the old ones after we have "cleaned house"? Emptiness is only a temporary condition; Spinoza reminds us that nature abhors a vacuum. Jesus tells a parable about a man who cleans his house of demons, and seven worse ones come to take up residence. An empty house is an invitation to intruders, demons who want to take over the place.

Some of those "demons" are fear of the new, fear of change, voices that, sirenlike, try to lure us back to our familiar old pain so we don't have to deal with the unknown. The emptiness that comes after giving up destructive old habits can be frightening, and in our panic we may turn to other ways of numbing ourselves.

I experienced this when I first gave up drinking. So terrified was I of the prospect of full consciousness that I began to smoke marijuana to replace the numbing sensation of alcohol. I rationalized that the marijuana was healthier because I didn't have hangovers, and besides, it wasn't damaging my liver. In a little over a year I realized I was smoking dope regularly—the dependence had crept up on me. This seemed especially ludicrous because I had also begun to go to church regularly and attend classes in Bible study. When I woke up to what I was doing I felt schizophrenic, and worse, hypocritical.

Realizing I couldn't go in both directions at once, I threw out my stash of marijuana and all the paraphernalia that went with smoking it. Of course, I was able to give it up, to rid myself of this very seductive and subtle demon of distraction, because I had something else to replace it with—the spiritual nurturing and prayer and church community that had become a significant part of my life. I am certain that without that sustenance I could never have given up the grass.

That's why I bristle at the simpleminded slogan, "Just say no to drugs!" You can't say no to something that powerful without having something powerful to replace it. I think that's what Jesus was warning us about when he spoke of the demons entering the empty house. I don't mean you have to run out and adopt a particular religious faith if you don't have one; I mean that trying to move in a spiritual direction is important, because the processes of that path are nurturing and strengthening, and the path going the other way leads toward numbing and oblivion.

Another popular route is the path of least resistance, which is not only boring and dull, but dangerous, for it can easily veer off into the direction of oblivion. Laziness and fear prompt us to take this path—or nonpath—for we don't have to think and act, we just sit back and let things happen to us. When you go against your own principles because it's easier to give in to friends than to argue or explain your position—or because you don't want to risk their disapproval, or worse, their ridicule—then you're following the path of no resistance. It's the dark way, the blind way, that's probably led by the spiritually blind.

SPIRIT WARRIORS

Creators need to be warriors—not of violence, but of the spirit. We need discipline, clarity, strength of will, and attention, the mindfulness of being aware of what we're doing and being present in the moment we're doing it. Creators I talk with in every field speak of the agony as well as the ecstasy of creation, the dark as well as the bright side of the process.

To go through the challenges of creation, to fit ourselves for the times when we seem to go dry, when the "boulders" in the path of our creation—as the eloquent theologian Elaine Pagels calls them—seem too enormous to move or get around, we must not give up, but accept the challenge of their stolid resistance, go through or over or around them on our way to realizing the dream, the image, and inspiration that was given us to create. To do that, to realize our capacities as creators, we need to be at our fullest, most integrated state of being, and to keep growing and creating. When we are knocked down and battered and distracted and defeated, as we will be along the way, day after day, we need to be able to call on all our resources in order to take up the challenge again, to pull ourselves up off the floor or out of the pit and—in that wonderfully simple, profound instruction of tai chi—return to the form.

I have said in workshops on creativity that writing is a form of meditation, in the sense that you are concentrating on only one thing, attempting to stop the usual jangle of distracting ideas, thoughts, fears, and hopes, and focusing on your breath or a mantra or a simple way of counting. In the actual act of writing you can focus only on the words you are putting down in sequence on the page, and those words, like an ongoing mantra, are filling up your mind. You can't be thinking of other things.

Taking that analogy a step further, I said in a seminar recently that "writing is prayer," in the sense that it is an act of devotion, of discipline of spirit in the act of creation. A professional writer who was present, who is also a very devout man of prayer, challenged me, saying quite adamantly, "Writing isn't prayer—it's hard work!"

"Well," I said, "Sometimes prayer is hard work, too."

That same afternoon I happened to be at a used bookstore, and I saw on a bargain table a biography of Kafka by his writer friend Max Brod. I hadn't read any Kafka since shortly after graduating from college, yet I felt drawn to this book. Justifying it as a bargain, I bought it. The book was absorbing, presenting a side of Kafka I never knew about—one who enjoyed laughing, talking, taking outings in the country, going boating, meeting pretty barmaids. Brod also reported that Kafka wrote, in one of his journals: "Writing is prayer." I smiled, feeling affirmed; at least I wasn't the only writer who'd had the thought.

I do believe that writing, like any creative act done from the heart, whether it is a painting or a piece of music, a sculpture or dance or a homemade pie, a newly designed dress or a scientific discovery, is its own prayer, its own affirmation of the "animating or vital principal," the spirit in us all. Creation is prayer; to create is to pray.

IN THE ZONE

If we are clear enough and open enough to let it come through, to be a vessel and channel of that creative force, it fills us up. That is the great paradox and irony; to be full, we must first be empty. We all know the great moments when we are "taken out of ourselves," when we are so absorbed in what we are doing—those trancelike times in skiing or writing, dancing or cooking, playing a piece of music or solving a problem in math or chemistry—it's as if we are not even present! It's as if we *are* the music, or the dance, or the mathematical equation; or that those things are "in place of us." We are so filled up by them we become them. Those are the transcendent moments, the "peak experiences" of life that we strive for and long for.

Athletes call it being "in the zone." Michael Jordan spoke about it after a game against the Portland Trail Blazers, game one of the NBA Finals in 1992, when he scored thirty-nine points, including six three-pointers.

Boston Globe columnist Michael Madden reported: "Every athlete knows this feel. For a few precious moments, everything goes perfectly. No athlete knows how to summon this feel, except to mumble about 'zone,' as if this special feeling hibernates in some extraterrestrial zone, drops in once a year or so for a tease, then heads back to its 'zone' for a rest. While the athlete tries his and her all to summon this feel back from its zone, it's never on call. It just shows up—well, when it wishes to show up.

" 'Whenever this feel comes,' said Michael, 'you just cherish it. What it feels like is you're out there by yourself. When I got in that rhythm, it was like a . . . a . . . force.' "

Madden went on, "Jordan had a smile wider and warmer than his usual one this day. He knew he had been touched by a force, and that was enough. He is now mature enough to know that the force calls its own recipients, rather than vice versa.

" 'It's not something you go out and search for,' said Jordan. 'You don't come into the game and say "I want to get myself into that zone." You just relax and you just coax yourself into it. You let the zone come to you. Then, when you're in that zone, you know it. And the next time that zone comes to me, I'm going to ride it as far as I can.' "

Jordan said he had tried to summon the feeling during a three-point shooting contest at an All-Star game once, but it didn't work, and he felt embarrassed by his performance.

Robert Parish, the veteran center of the Boston Celtics and student of tai chi, told me of his own experience with the zone: "It's like trying to find a good relationship. You can't go out looking for it, it just has to happen."

What is known as a "peak experience" or transcendence or inspiration—when some other force seems to take over—comes to all kinds of creators, from athletes to architects. The prize-winning architect Evans Woollen told me that when he's working on the design of a building, "You know the solution exists somewhere—in some collective unconscious, and it's up to you to find it. Ridding the mind of other things—finding solutions—it's rather mysterious.

"It's coming through you, only—it's not knowing where it's coming from. It's a kind of spiritual thing—part of why I think solutions have their own life—they were born entering here, in me."

Many musicians speak of the experience of being empty and at the same time filled, of being an instrument used by a higher power in the act of creation. Judy Collins told me, "I feel I'm an instrument in writing—at the piano, I tape everything—the minute something starts I feel I'm 'taking dictation.' "

Singer and songwriter Nancy Wilson says, "There are those magical times when it seems to pour right through you. That's the most incredible feeling I can imagine as far as songwriting. You're like the vessel or the instrument itself that somebody's playing—somebody or something. I don't have a specific name for it; there's a lot of names: Buddha, God, inspiration."

Singer Patti Smith said of such experiences, "I've had those moments when I do feel the voice coming through me, and I know it's coming from out there. . . . It's really special and it's not of me. . . . I get out of the way and it comes out fast and painlessly."

Biographer Sharon O'Brien described in an essay in the *New York Times Book Review* how at a certain point in writing *Willa Cather: The Emerging Voice*, "I experienced for the first time the process of writing as Cather described it—a submission to a creative force that seems to use the writer as an instrument. I had planned to write only a page or two, but the words kept streaming out, almost as if someone else were producing them. Writing became such a process of discovery that I couldn't wait to get to work in the morning: I wanted to find out what I was going to say."

A STORY IS GIVEN

I've experienced that same sensation in writing, most powerfully when I was living in a house by a pond in New Hampshire. After a decade in New York City I had wanted to live in the country, empty myself of the soot and noise and furor of city life, and experience fresh, clean air, and quiet. I had saved up enough money to work exclusively on writing fiction, and had spent the summer months toiling away at a long story that only a week before I had sent to my agent. I didn't yet have a new story in mind when I came into the living room one brilliant autumn afternoon and felt a surge of well-being and life and—well, creation—welling up in me.

I put my typewriter on a round table in the living room, pulled it over by the window where I could see the pond and the trees, and sat down to write. I had no idea what I was going to write, I just sat down and started writing. First the season came, and then a scene in the halls of my high school, and the feelings of that time and a girl—I wrote, as if the story were already written and I was typing it out, and a little less than three hours later I stopped because I had come to the end and I read the story over and cried. I cried because I had just "de-livered" this story, I had emptied myself out in the most complete way—and I was full. I was full of joy and life and love and the sort of feeling Jesus described when he said he offered us life, more abundant, pressed down and overflowing.

That story was sent by my agent to *Redbook* magazine and they bought it and published it a few months later. The following year it was included in *The Best American Stories of 1966*. Looking back, I can see that in many ways I had prepared myself to be open to that story. I had made a hard and conscious move away from the city, which I felt was overwhelming me then, and into the countryside for the first time, taking many risks to try to follow a healthier path, to find a setting that might allow me to create the kind of stories I longed to write. That one was simply given to me, and I think I was able to receive the gift because I was in a place—in my life as well as geographically—that enabled me to receive it.

Oregon professor Robert Grudin observes that these experiences we call "inspiration" can't be made to happen by our own design; yet, "even if we cannot specify or command inspiration, we *can*, I think, practice deserving it. The lives of people who are inspired or inventive possess a number of characteristics in common. Many of these charac-teristics are less inborn virtues (though seen together they look like 'talent' or 'genius') than plain habits, difficult to cultivate perhaps, but nonetheless far from superhuman. Collectively, these habits might be called an ethos of inspiration—not a birthright but a demanding and integral code."

The key, says Grudin, is "identifying fully with one's work and see-ing it as an expression of one's own character. Such passion, which is generally more characteristic of artists and the self-employed than it is of salaried workers, can nonetheless be cultivated in any work that carries a high degree of responsibility."

You may not be able to go looking for it, but you have to be pre-pared for the zone of transcendence. You have to do the hard, nitty-gritty work of disciplined practice (emptying), as athletes like Jordan and Parish have done, so that when the zone comes to you, you can respond to it, you can move with it, be a good enough instrument of the force to let it move through you and with you. There is no use having the zone come to you if you are out of shape, hungover, or fuzzy from dope or lack of sleep. It would be wasted on you, if it came to you at all.

The zone is possible for all of us, no matter what creative work we do. But just as Michael Jordan and Robert Parish practice the basics of their game and hone their skills to make themselves ready, so must all of us who wish to be creative, no matter what our field. Odette Bery, a chef who is also a teacher, points out, "If you're a musician, or a painter, the technical skills required before you can use your own creativity are phenomenal. It's the same with a chef. A chef is more creative once the technical skills are there, and an understanding of basic food chemistry. It's easier for me to be creative than when I started out—the technical skills have to be there to back you up."

Commitment to and preparation for creativity are crucial. The sort of thing I'm talking about was stated perhaps best of all by Abraham Lincoln, when he wrote—with a vision of something larger than a basketball court or a short story: "I will study, and get ready, and maybe the chance will come."

Had he not done the preparation—including all that reading by the light of an oil lamp as a boy—the chance would not have come, and even if it had, he would not have been equal to the task. We can't just be bystanders waiting for lightning to strike and give us great moments of transcendence. We need to carry out our part of the process; in other words, we need to be cocreators with the force, or spirit, or God.

THE FREEDOM TO SAY NO

The idea that less is more, of emptying being a way to fill up, is described by Rabbi Kushner in *To Life!*: "So many of the rules and rituals of the Jewish way of life are spiritual calisthenics, designed to teach us to control the most basic instincts of our lives—hunger, sex, anger, acquisitiveness, and so on. We are not directed to deny or stifle them, but to control them, to rule them rather than letting them rule us, and to sanctify them by dedicating our living of them to God's purposes. The freedom the Torah offers us is the freedom to say no to appetite."

This philosophy may underlie the phenomenon of the traditionally small number of Jewish alcoholics. A religious Jew, like Rabbi Kushner, "fills" himself with faith and personal power by depriving himself of the indulgences proscribed by the law of the Torah.

How powerful this faith can be is demonstrated by Rabbi Kushner's reaction to the tragedy of his son's painful and early death. He
did not lose his faith but turned to it, and rather than the easy numbing of pain that many people would seek in drugs or alcohol, he wrote
out of his own wrenching experience a book that would help millions
of others around the world, of all faiths, deal with tragedy and loss in
their own life, by being able to survive those times: *When Bad Things
Happen To Good People*. From his loss, he filled others with courage
and spirit.

Filling up, like emptying, has a different meaning on the spiritual
path than on the other possible paths of life—like the path of least resistance, or the path to oblivion. On those paths, filling up would mean
drinking till you're drunk, eating till you're sick, gorging yourself with
whatever sensations pleased you at the first experience of them, without regard to consequences.

Most of the kinds of filling up I've described—from tasting food to
meditation, silence, yoga, tai chi, and prayer—also involve emptying.
Emptying and filling up are really parts of the same process—you can't
separate them and have them make any sense; you can't, in fact, "have
them" at all. There is no filling up without emptying first; there is no
emptying without being full. I remember a Good Friday sermon of
Reverand Scovel when he said that without the Crucifixion there is
no Resurrection; the two events are finally one and the same event,
different sides of the same story.

Sometimes "empty-full" depends on who is seeing it, and how.
Gretel Ehrlich, author of *The Solace of Open Spaces*, points out that
"the emptiness of the West was for others a geography of possibility."
After a personal tragedy, Ehrlich left her city life and went to live in
vast Wyoming, learning that "loss constitutes an odd kind of fullness;
despair empties out into an unquenchable appetite for life."

Emptying and filling, we grow and create.

Part Four

Creation in Action

Chapter 9

CREATING

How do we get access to our own creativity?

When the myth about alcohol and drugs as stimulants to creativity was exploded for me, it was clear that other substances and addictive behavior were just as useless and even destructive in trying to evoke the muse. If having a shot of bourbon or a hit of coke didn't spark a story, it was obvious that gobbling a chocolate cake, having sex with a stranger, or starting a new relationship cycle was not going to call forth the spirit of creation.

The emptying of the myth left a question, a space in my mind, and I felt the impulse to fill it, to explore the mystery of how to summon our creative powers. Over the years, I had tried all the tricks I could think of in my own pursuit of the muse, from bourbon drinking to pencil sharpening, from gnawing a pipe stem to rubbing a worry stone someone gave me. Along the way I'd even stumbled on some useful techniques, easily passed along, but I had no idea what use they'd be to others (who probably knew them all and had even better ones). I sensed I wasn't going to learn much more by sitting in my room and staring at my word processor.

Community came to mind. Since I'd finished writing my book *Returning: A Spiritual Journey* in 1986, I'd been leading workshops in Spiritual Autobiography at adult education centers, churches, and retreat houses throughout the country, from the Episcopal monastery of the Cowley Fathers in Cambridge to the Esalen Institute in Big Sur, California. I'd been surprised and delighted at the quality and substance of the stories people wrote about their own journeys. The writing in these workshops was far and away more interesting than what I had read in creative writing classes at colleges, graduate programs, and writers conferences. I'd learned that writing "from the spirit," asking people to look at their experiences from a spiritual perspective, was enlivening and productive, and had the effect of creating a kind of community among the participants.

I decided I'd try to create a new kind of workshop, with exercises designed to evoke people's creativity, and see what I could find out about accessing the creative spirit, not just for people who were writers, or wanted to be, but everyone who was interested in exploring this mystery of creativity in their lives from a spiritual perspective (as opposed to the sort of workshop promising millions by writing bestsellers in your spare time, or "creating" fortunes in the stock market).

I designed a series of simple exercises for a workshop I called Creating from the Spirit. I've led it now in small and large groups around the country and found it fun as well as enlightening, and always fascinating in the creative work it evokes. I have not yet come across anyone who can't draw and write in response to the simple exercises; and in fact, the drawings and stories people have created are so rich and interesting, I think they'll inspire others to create, too.

The work certainly testifies to what people can create in a circumscribed period of time. I limited all written exercises to twenty minutes, which I now think is itself an aid to creativity. When you have all the time in the world—when you take an assignment home and work on it for hours, you find it hard to get started. Then once you begin, all the internal editors emerge and start telling you to do it a different way, and you start second-guessing yourself, wondering what other people will think if you say such a thing—and by the time you finish (if indeed you ever finish) you may have watered down the work to the point where it has lost its original vitality.

I invite you as readers to now become participants, and follow the same basic rules as the people whose work you will read in the following pages. Set an alarm clock or an oven timer for twenty minutes at each exercise, and follow it strictly. When the buzzer goes off, if you aren't finished, take one more minute (no more than that!) and then, if you still aren't through, end by making three dots, to indicate you have more to say but for now you have to stop.

Ask a friend to join you.

It's more enjoyable—and I think produces better creative results— if you do these exercises with at least one other person, or some friends, members of a church or a Twelve Step group, a writers group, or any other group of people you know who might enjoy exploring their creativity. All you need is a supply of plain white paper (ordinary 8½ by 11 inch typing or copying paper will do just fine), a box of crayons for drawing, and a pen or pencil and notebook to write in.

THIS IS NOT A CONTEST

Whether you do the exercises alone, with one or two friends, or in a group, stop for a moment before beginning and remember that this is not a contest or a guide to How to Succeed in the Arts Without Really Trying. This is not a religious program, in the sense of being limited to any one belief or faith, but it is based on the conviction that true creativity is born of the spirit, in the broad and varied ways I've defined and looked at that concept throughout this book so far. If you are in a faith community, by all means draw on its sustenance and experiences whenever they come to you. If you are not, don't feel left out. We all have a wealth of material, treasures of the spirit we simply don't bother to look for or cultivate.

Before beginning this exercise, take time to empty yourself of other concerns, of the mechanics of getting the paper and crayons or pencils or other supplies you need, or getting yourself to a comfortable place to draw and write. Let go of your fears or expectations, your past experience with creativity, your hopes for what you may "get out of this." Inhale deeply, then breathe out all such concerns.

Now fill up by taking a few minutes to think about what "spirit" means to you, and how creativity relates to, and is part of, your own spiritual path. Take a few more deep breaths and close your eyes for a moment. Enjoy the wordless pause, the rest, the cessation of effort, and feel yourself filled with peace. If you have a short prayer you like, repeat it in your mind. I don't mean a prayer of petition. Don't pray "for" anything, like inspiration, or creative power, or a masterpiece flowing from your pen, simply put yourself in an attitude of prayer, of gratitude for being part of creation.

I like the way Rabbi Harold Kushner talks about the kind of attitude of prayer I'm suggesting in his book *To Life! A Celebration of Jewish Being and Thinking*: "We have learned to think of prayer as bribing God, pleading with God, or educating God." Prayer in the Jewish tradition, Rabbi Kushner explains, "is not 'talking to God' so much as it is using words and music to come into the presence of God in the hope that we will be changed by doing so."

If you don't believe in God or the concept of prayer, simply meditate on a quotation of some kind that inspires you, perhaps one relating to creativity or creation. If you know any lines of poetry you find inspiring, think of those. If nothing comes to your mind, simply think of the spirit, the breath of life, and concentrate on your own breath, being grateful for the gift of it, the gift of life.

Now take up your crayons and paper, with the freedom and pleasure they gave you when you first took them up in kindergarten. You will not be given a grade.

Enjoy.

EXERCISE 1
THE CREATION ROOM

Take twenty minutes to draw a picture—either as a drawing or floor plan, whichever allows you to put in the greatest amount of details—of the room in which you first created something you liked. It may be your room at home or a room at school or an office or an attic; it may be a kitchen or garage or basketball court. You may have written a poem or song or story, or painted a picture, or perhaps you most enjoyed baking a cake or coming up with a new recipe for a tuna casserole; you may have built a model airplane or fixed a car or executed a new play in basketball or a new kind of shot. It doesn't matter what the object or act is as long as you created it, and had a sense of satisfaction in the creation.

Take your time. Think back to the place where this creation occurred. Remember what the room was like, what furniture was in it, what pictures were on the walls. Was it cold in the room or hot? Was there a window, and could you see outside? What was the weather like? Was there any music playing, or could you hear anyone talking? What did it feel like to be in that room? What was it like creating something? Where did you get the idea? What materials did you use?

After you've taken twenty minutes to draw the room, and remember all you can about it, share it with another person, and let them share their room with you. Each person should take ten minutes to explain as much as possible about the room and what you created in it and what that was like.

After you have shared the room, take twenty minutes to write about the experience you had of creating something—or doing something creative—in that room. Tell as much as you can about it.

Here are some of the things people wrote about the room in which they created something:

BEWITCHED

This room was the basement of our house, the orange thing to the right is a curtain dividing the basement in half—my father's workshop was on the right and the playroom (shown) was on the left.

My brother and sister and I spent countless hours playing and watching TV down here. I have many memories of creative occurrences in this room. The view is from the stairs—how I often saw it as I squatted down and peered under the ceiling into the room.

Right below the stairs, out of view from this picture, was a sewing machine. My mother made most of our clothes (as well as the ugly orange curtain—a color fashionable in the '60s. What it was doing in a room with green tiles on the floor, I will never know). I often took scrap bits of cloth and made clothes for my dolls. I designed and sewed them. Nothing fancy, but it made me feel proud when they came out well.

Another thing I did with my Barbie dolls was make them appear and disappear. My siblings and I were fascinated by magic. "Bewitched" was our favorite show, and we wanted to be magic too. So I rigged up a system with thread, tying one end to the railing on the stairs and the other end somewhere at the far end of the room. I attached Barbie to the thread and positioned my brother with her at the top of the stairs. Then, feigning ignorance of his presence, I said out loud, "Gosh! I wish I had a Barbie doll!" Then I wiggled my nose and whoosh! There she came—flying through space into my outstretched hand. Magic!

We were also big into skits and puppet shows. Whenever cousins, or kids whose parents were friends of my parents came to visit, we would recruit them for our shows. Since I usually was the oldest, I was writer, director and costume designer. Then at the end of the visit, after the adults had quit gabbing, we would perform the show. All of the creation and practicing was done in the basement.

This room was the setting for much of my childhood imagination.

—*Stephanie Chase*

Papa's Studio

No place was more exciting. Papa's studio was in a corner of the basement of his house. There was always music in the room either from an old brown radio with its arch-shaped top or from Papa's violin. I loved this space. I particularly loved the different jars of colored water that were always on the counter next to where Papa worked.

Papa was a sweet and gentle person who loved it when I came to his studio. He would always put one of his old white shirts on me. He called it a work shirt. It would keep my clothes from getting paint on them.

I would sit at the counter next to Papa and watch him letter and paint. I never got tired of this.

Papa would offer me a box of brushes. He'd tell me to take any one I wanted. He'd give me paper and I would pick the colors of paint that I'd want to use. He'd always explain that when I used a color I would need to clean my brush in the jar of water that matched the color I was using.

I loved this experience. I loved watching the color in the water become a little darker each time I washed my brush.

The colors were beautiful. The colors in the water jars were as wonderful as the experience of my painting.

I don't remember any of my final products. Those weren't in any way as important as selecting the colors or cleaning my brush.

My favorite part of watching Papa paint was seeing him put one hand under the hand he painted with. He told me he did this so as to keep the paint from smearing and to steady his hand.

I can remember the thick smell of tempura paint and the smell of Papa's cigars.

One of my favorite parts of watching was when he'd take his violin from its old case and play "Turkey in the Straw." He'd play for me after he painted. He'd always put a handkerchief under his chin before he'd begin. His chin moved up and down and his mouth made shapes it never did when he talked to me. I always wanted him to play more and more.

It wasn't only the act of painting that I liked, it was the experience of being in this tiny room and watching Papa do his work. He would leave the room from time to time to clean the water that was on the counter beside him. Cleaning the brushes was very important to him.

Sometimes I'd watch him draw a picture first. It would be a sketch. He wouldn't press hard. Sometimes he'd erase with a soft tan eraser that he'd call an art gum. He would make little crumbs as he used it and he would brush these on the floor.

There was an old dark green rug under the stool where he sat. His stool was wooden. It could turn all the way around and had a back for him to lean on. There were some round holes in the seat and the back. The stool where I sat didn't have a back. When I first sat on it he would put phone books on it to make it high enough for me. Mine couldn't turn.

We would listen mostly to opera as we painted. I loved to come here.

When I went away to camp there would be days that I'd receive letters from Papa. There were pictures that he'd painted for me in his studio.

—Marika Geoghegan

FIRST STEPS

It was my birthday. There were two rooms in my grandfather's house involved in the earliest instance of remembered creativity. I was in one, which was in shadows because the light had been turned off. The door to the kitchen was open and the light was on, which bathed the middle of the living room with a yellowish glow and cast fuzzy shadows.

In the darkness of the living room, I could see a couch with a pillow on the right, where I had been sleeping. On the other side were two chairs and a floor lamp in between. Because it was dark I cannot remember the color. The room was dark because I had been left there to take a nap, and it was now after dark.

My parents and grandfather were in the next room; my mother was preparing dinner. I could watch them through the door, almost like watching through a window. They were talking and had their backs to me.

The kitchen had two windows at the far side of the room that I could see—it was dark outside the windows—4 chairs next to the stove on the left. It was dark above the windows. The sink, stove and refrigerator were all on the right. There were cupboards on the sink and counter top. There were dishes on the table, and pans were out for the food on the kitchen counter. The walls were white and the floor was a light-colored linoleum.

The kitchen was lit by a ceiling light that had a yellowish hue, probably from the bulb. There was a large pillar between the two rooms that almost filled the doorway.

Everything was very fuzzy because I am very near-sighted. This event occurred when I was about a year old. I woke up feeling a little groggy from the sleep and a little lost. We did not go to my grandfather's often, so the room was strange to me, especially in the dark.

I eventually realized that my parents were in the next room and I wanted to see my mother. I felt that she would come get me. When she didn't, I decided that she didn't know I was awake because the three adults were very engrossed in what they were doing and saying. I started to crawl across the rug, but was interrupted by the pillow.

I had been learning to walk, I felt that I could walk. But I did not know how. I decided to try. After a false start or two I realized that I had to counterbalance my weight in the place where I started to fall. I toddled off into the next room, past the pillow, and no one noticed me at first.

My dad saw me first, then my grandfather. My mother turned when Dad said, "Don's walking." She screamed and scared me. I fell. My parents tell me I did not walk again for six months.

—Don Mitchell

FURTHER EXERCISES: GOING TO NEW ROOMS

It turns out that everyone has an early memory of being in a room where they created something—though I know of no such memory earlier than Don Mitchell's recalling the rooms where he took those first steps when he was a year old!

Drawing the "creation room" and telling someone else about what happened there helps release that memory, and writing about it becomes a fascinating story, one that affirms our own creative powers. It also affirms that the source of creation is not alcohol or drugs. The story coming out of this process is itself an affirmation of the creativity we have access to right now, without any outside stimulants.

There is not only one "creation room." If you wish to draw more on your own creative history, draw other rooms in which you created something—in high school, or college, or your first apartment, or at camp, or a friend's house, or whatever place you remember as being a site of your own creativity.

Don't limit yourself to the type of creative activity you do most often. If you're a writer, think of other things you've created besides stories or poems; if you're a painter, recall creative acts that have nothing to do with paintings or art. Look at your creative experience in a larger way than the one that usually comes to mind. Think of meals you've created, trips you've planned, friendships you've formed, ideas or projects you've created in your community. Discover how much creating you do in the normal course of your life.

Draw the room where each of these creations had its origin or its completion. Each room will provide a picture and a story, as well as a new affirmation of your creative power.

How can you relate this exercise to your current creative activity? Think about the room where you now write or paint, keep a journal, meditate, or whatever creative activity you are practicing—or want to practice. Many creators find that going to the same place to create every day is helpful in evoking the aura of creativity. If you live in one room, as I have on different occasions, create a space in a corner of the room that is the focus of your creative activity. If you can, put up a screen to give it a sense of specialness, of spiritual privacy.

Once I was living in Greenwich Village and trying to write a novel at the same time that I was writing magazine articles to make a living. I felt stifled in trying to do both kinds of creating in the same room. The novel notes and pages got mixed up with notes and pages for articles. When I started to work on the novel, I'd begin to think about the article I was also working on. I couldn't shake my mind from one kind of writing to the other. I felt that the solution was to work in two different rooms, but I had no other room, nor did I have the money to rent one.

Then it occurred to me that a teacher friend was out of her apartment every weekday from eight in the morning until five in the afternoon. She might let me use it to work on my novel. She agreed, and we created a schedule. I worked on my magazine articles at home in the morning, and at noon walked six blocks to my friend's apartment, picking up a sandwich along the way, had lunch, and worked on my novel at her dining room table until she returned, then talked with her over a cup of coffee, and went back to my place.

It's as if a new physical space allows for another space in your own consciousness. I have heard that John Updike uses different rooms in his house north of Boston for the different varieties of writing he does—there's a room for novels, another for short stories, another for book reviews, etc. I admire Updike's creativity in setting up his house that way, but, of course, most people don't have the luxury of a room for each of our creative endeavors.

I am living in a one-room, or "studio" apartment in the Village as I write this, and I have designated one wall for my word processor and "writing space." When I was working on a novel last spring, I had my most creative period when I spent a month in another city doing workshops on the weekend and writing every day during the week. When I return to the novel I plan to use the Writers Room in the Village, where I can rent a cubicle for a nominal fee and have a separate place to work on that book—just as I used the Writers Room in Boston to work on *New York in the Fifties*, while I wrote articles, lectures, and workshop material back at my apartment.

Writers in cities like New York and Boston have joined together to seek grants or corporate sponsorship or donations of space to establish writers rooms with office cubicles and desks for word processors where they can go and work in silence, away from their apartments but in community, surrounded by other writers. The Writers Room in Boston lost its foundation sponsorship in the general economic crunch, but Ivan Gold (who is now president of the Boston Writers Room) organized some of the regular users of the room and they found a new space to work in. It's a project that writers or artists of any kind in any community could create.

PLACES OF POWER

The space where we work is important. I've always had a sense of the places where I could write and where I couldn't write. There is no way to describe it. I have to go into a room and look around, and I know at once. I once went looking for a house to rent with a friend in the summer and one had everything we were looking for except I knew I couldn't write in it. I didn't know why, I just knew it was true, and I knew it wasn't some silly feeling to dismiss. I lost a whole summer once by staying in a place where I felt queasy about working from the first time I went inside. I should have listened to that instinct, and from then on I did.

"I think where you write helps," Rabbi Kushner told me when we talked about creativity. "There are two places in my house where I write, one in summer on the back porch, one in winter in my study. I suspect that being where the creative process worked well before increases the chance that it will again."

For architect Evans Woollen it's important to live for a while in the place where he's going to design a house or building. He has lived with clients, and doesn't put pencil to paper until he knows them. At a school or college he takes a room on campus and talks to as many people as possible.

Creative workers also have found inspiration from what Carlos Castenada calls "places of power." There are some geographic sites in the world that have proved through the centuries to be such places—like Jerusalem, the sacred city of three great religions. There are also places of power for each of us, places that may not affect anyone else in the same way, but somehow touch us, stir our imaginations and our creative sensibilities.

Willa Cather experienced that feeling when she went on a two-week trip to New Mexico. She was so moved by the place, by the very look of the land, that she came back East inspired to write a book about it. She did research on the early settlement of that territory and out of that knowledge, fired by the inspiration that being there had for her, wrote one of the great novels of our literature, *Death Comes for the Archbishop*.

We experience places almost the way we do people—some we immediately love, others make us uncomfortable; sometimes we change our minds (and emotions) about them as we get to know them. Some people inspire us, others put us in a dark mood. It's the same with places. I love Boston, and Beacon Hill, where I had an immediate sense of being home when I first saw it; yet, I've always felt uncomfortable in Cambridge, just across the river. I know people who have the opposite reaction. It's a mysterious, individual matter; just because other people love a place doesn't mean you will, too.

I made a pilgrimage once to the island of Iona, off the coast of Scotland, because I'd heard it was a spiritual place of power. Saint Columba had used it as a base for his missionary work among the Celts in the sixth century and it was thought to be holy. A member of my own church in Boston had experienced great peace and spiritual insight there. I found it to be the most bleak, barren, and depressing spot of land I'd ever seen. I had, in fact, an *anti*-religious experience (I woke in the night to see a mental vision of a wall with the words "There is no God") and I felt such inner turmoil I left there as soon as I could. I was later told that others, too, had had "dark" experiences there, and were relieved to get to the mainland city of Oban—so was I.

There is no way to predict in advance how a place will strike you (any more than a person—think about blind dates!).

British novelist Christopher Isherwood, author of *The Berlin Stories*, on which the musical and movie *Cabaret* was partly based, surprisingly found his place of power in Southern California. I met Isherwood in Hollywood in the late '70s, when he was in his seventies. This joyous, full-of-life man told me he had come to the U.S. in the '40s and, to his amazement, was drawn to the desert landscapes of Southern California. Though he had grown up in rural England, he said that when he saw the desert area south of Los Angeles he felt he was home. He settled in Santa Monica with his longtime partner, artist Don Bacardi, and lived a rich, creatively productive, and successful life in a setting completely foreign to the England of his childhood.

We aren't always able to live where we feel drawn, and each of us has more than one place of power where we feel at peace, enlivened, full. If you think back on your experiences, you'll know at once your places of power. If you have a chance to spend time in one of them to work creatively, do it. If you don't have that opportunity, you still can conjure up the place with memory, journal notes, photographs, pictures, and books about it. These are sources of raw power you can translate into creativity.

Where are your own places of power? Make a list of them. Write a paragraph about each place. See what place you'd like to write further about—or paint or photograph. What kind of music conjures up the place for you?

Spend a few minutes in contemplation about what you've learned and experienced about creativity from this exercise in drawing and writing "the creation room." Contemplation is different from meditation, where you're trying to empty your mind and focus on a single word or mantra or image, or simply concentrate on your breath. In contemplation you just get quiet, and relax, in the same sort of position of comfortable attention you would want for meditation, but then let your mind dwell on a particular subject, in this case, the mystery of creativity.

Now that you've created some drawings and stories, what do you think is the source of your creativity? Was the story you wrote already

in your mind, waiting to be told? Was it somewhere out in the atmosphere, waiting to be drawn in to your own consciousness and written
down? Did it "come through you" or "come out of you?" Are there
stories in you—or "out there"—waiting to be told? How do you find
them? Are they "given" to you? By whom, or what? Why?

There are, of course, no "correct answers" to these questions, as on
a test, but they are fruitful subjects for contemplation.

EXERCISE 2
STORY MUSIC

I have often used music in my own writing, not for evoking ideas, but
for bringing back past scenes, places, people, and situations. When I
was working on my novel *Going All the Way*, which was set in Indianapolis in the 1950s, before writing I would play records I loved from
that era, like Chris Conner's album *Something Cool*, or Chet Baker
playing and singing "My Funny Valentine," or Les Paul and Mary
Ford's rendition of "How High the Moon." When I played that music
and closed my eyes I could summon up the sounds, sights, smells, people,
places and faces I knew back then.

When I wrote *Home Free*, which was set in the late 1960s, I played
the music I loved at that time—Judy Collins's *Wildflowers* and *Who
Knows Where the Times Goes* albums, the Mamas and Papas singing
"Monday, Monday" and "California Dreamin'," Nilsson wailing "Without You." A rush of memories filled my mind with that music, scenes
crowding in on one another—streets of Los Angeles, the beach at
Venice, protest marches on Beacon Street in Boston.

When I started my recent book, *New York in the Fifties*, one album
I played over and over evoked an apartment where I spent a lot of time
in 1957 in Greenwich Village, and brought back the feel, the outlook,
the ambience of my life at that time. It was Miles Davis's *Sketches of
Spain*, which I had played in that apartment and loved. The mood of
that era comes back to me with that musical evocation.

When I decided to play that piece as a musical exercise in evoking
creativity, I did not imagine it would bring back memories of Greenwich Village to anyone else but me, unless by chance someone else

had lived there at the time I did and associated this music with the time and place.

The reason I decided to try it in this exercise was that it seemed especially haunting to me, bittersweet and full of mystery and passion. My idea was to play it without naming its title or author or anything else about it, and simply let people draw whatever scene or colors it brought to mind, then ask questions after they had listened to it for a while, questions that might prompt their own ideas and stories, and see what came out of their own imaginations. It is fascinating to see what completely different and yet imaginative, colorful, and dramatic drawings and stories came out of people who listened to that same piece of music.

The same exercise and the same set of questions can be used playing any piece of music—as long as it doesn't have words. As soon as there are words, they will fill your mind, and your own imagination won't have a chance to respond with its own ideas and images. Select a piece of music of your own—or if you are part of a group, it might be more fun to let one person select a piece of music and put it on without telling you beforehand what it is.

Before playing the music, sit quietly, to empty yourself of other sounds and noises and talk. Think about the power of music, how it can produce moods and feelings of joy, despair, excitement, peace, comradeship, loyalty, love, patriotism, and inspiration, and a sense of the sacred. Imagine what your life would be like without music! Think about the gift that music is in your life, how it adds beauty, harmony, color, and meaning. What is the source of this gift that we take for granted? How does music affect your spirit? How has music played a part in your own spiritual journey, your search for meaning?

When you put on your piece of music for this exercise, imagine the music moving throughout your whole body and mind. Imagine the music "filling you up." Think of the music as being inside you, and you being inside the music.

When you feel the music is part of you, absorbed by you, and you are absorbed by it as well, respond to the following questions. Take your time in answering.

What kind of landscape do you picture with this music? Where would such music be played? What sort of scene and scenery does it evoke in your mind?

What sort of house or building would be in this setting? A log hut, a castle, a skyscraper, a tent, an apartment house? Or some other kind of dwelling altogether?

Who is in this building? What kind of people would be in a room in this place? What does the room look like? What do the people look like? Are they old or young, rich or poor, tired or exuberant?

What are these people saying to each other?

This is what some people wrote after listening to Miles Davis's album *Sketches of Spain*, without knowing the title or the musician, simply responding to the sound as they answered my questions:

REMEMBERING

When my father died the priest said prayers at the funeral home one of the prayers asked for Robert to gather the pieces of himself together that phrase stayed with me tagging along like a baby sister I listened to the music and landscape appeared large grey rocks nothing green no grass or trees I heard a funeral dirge but the notes were twisting the ends of sadness like pieces of lemon and lime brighten a drink long flat notes became all the pieces of Robert lying under those gray stones but the notes climbing a staircase were lifting the stones halfway up suddenly snake charmer music coaxing the pieces of Robert out from under the climbing twisting notes singing it can be done until the music turned low slow trying for the last time to draw Robert out crying at the end I could almost hear bells the mood new I could see Robert all dandied up pushing open saloon doors and telling an off-color joke then three long notes death knells wailing I know I know I know

—*E. J. Miller Laino*

HONG KONG LOUNGE

When Ruth left him after twenty years of marriage, Dirk thought that he would make a new start, far away from his familiar life in Miller's Falls, Idaho, but Hong Kong was not what he'd hoped it would be. It had been three years now and, though he had managed to land a clerk's job in the Kowloon office of the Cathay International Bank, Dirk was more alone than ever.

"Ah, Mr. Dirk, you're late tonight," said Sam Wah, the small, wiry bartender at Hong Kong's Forty-Second Street Lounge.

"Yea, Sam, gotta pay the rent," Dirk replied, straddling the stool at the center of the long, dark, teakwood bar.

Outside, the warm spring rain dissolved the smells of roasted meat, spices, and brown eggs preserved in mud and horse urine into the soupy mix that was Hong Kong. Here, inside the Forty-Second Street Lounge, the only smells were whiskey and stale beer. The place was dark and nearly empty except for a few couples leaning toward each other over small tables against the wall, whispering words of love or plotting to separate some poor fool from his money.

A melancholy tune washed over the desolate floor littered with matchbooks and napkins, carelessly dropped by earlier patrons. The droning, mellow horn emphasized Dirk's loneliness in another empty night.

—Alan Bodnar

OUTLAWS

Place
  Southwestern
  deserty terrain
  dry
  flat
  You can see a long way off

Room
  Movie theater (belongs with a film)

People
  Swarthy Mexicans w/bullets criss-crossed across self
  hardened cowboys
  loose frontier women

Bittersweet mood—success, but at what cost?

A movie.

The old West. New sheriff and his sidekick come to town to rid the area of lawless bandits. They are met with resistance from the incumbent authorities who are working in cahoots with the outlaws.

Not your usual shoot-em-up movie, but a conflict of wills and values. More subtle, covert action. In addition, good and bad guys are not clear. There is a bittersweet tone to the setting. Is what the sheriff doing truly good? Are the "outlaws" truly bad?

The sheriff and his deputy prevail. They win. Perhaps they even shoot and kill the bandits. But at what cost? The music plays as they ride off into the sunset, leaving the audience with the unsettled feeling that there was no winner.

Be still my friend.

These great trees are prayers.

—*Stephanie Chase*

FURTHER EXERCISES: LISTENING FOR IDEAS

It always amazes and moves me after listening to the music and then hearing what people write—the scenes, stories, plots, characters that weren't there fifteen or twenty minutes before. Where did they come from? Did they come from the music? But how did the music create such different places and faces and words? How did these people hear the same piece of music and create from listening to it stories of Hong Kong, the Wild West, the desert, lovers and sheriffs and farmers and fires, sunsets and marshes and wakes and spirits and trees?

Where did it come from?

What an unexpected, incredible, colorful, dramatic well of stories and sights and places we all possess! What is the source of it? Is the music we hear instilled in us? Does it become part of us—our mind, our consciousness, our unconscious? Does it become part of our soul, our spirit? There is a category of sacred, or spiritual, music, but beyond that, is all music spiritual, or "of the spirit"?

Listen to more music. Try the exercise with different types of music. Here are some ideas of some of the kinds of music you could listen to while "writing out of" the music: symphonies, cantatas, sonatas, etudes, jazz, rock, heavy metal, country and western, sacred music (hymns without words). Listen to music of different ethnic backgrounds, nationalities, and cultures, and write "out of them." The only music that I think doesn't work for this process are songs with lyrics, rap, and opera, because they have words, which create their own scenes and messages.

Invite a friend to do the exercise with you and bring his or her own piece of music; in a group, take turns in letting each person supply the piece of music which everyone uses to "write from."

Summon new landscapes, people, stories. They are there for the playing of each new piece of music.

You will never run out.

If, like me, you're not trained in music, speak to a friend who plays a musical instrument about how they create as musicians. While writing prose seems to almost come naturally to me, the whole concept of writing music is one of the deepest mysteries I can imagine. I was fascinated to read about the creative process of Maria Schneider, a jazz composer, arranger, and band leader. She has written for the Woody Herman Orchestra and was an assistant orchestrator and arranger for Gil Evans (the title piece of her debut album, *Evanascence*, is dedicated to him).

Schneider told *New York Times* reporter Sheila Rule, "If I have one idea, I try to put down all sorts of possibilities that the idea could be manipulated into. Then I draw arrows to things, what fits on top of what. Then it becomes like a puzzle. I may come up with contrasting ideas that intuitively fit, but I have to intellectually try to see why. When it all comes together, when I listen to my pieces at the end, it's like they did exist before but I had to find them."

Ask yourself how this process relates to your own creative work. How could you apply it to your own creative work?

MUSIC AS PRAYER

Here's another exercise to use with music.

Pick out a piece of music that to you is "of the spirit." It need not be what anyone else defines as spiritual, it only matters that it evokes that kind of response in you.

Play the music, and as in the first exercise, let the music come inside you, and try to feel yourself inside the music.

Think about the idea of music as prayer.

While listening to your piece of spiritual music, and letting it fill you up, write your own prayer, a prayer that comes out of the music, as the story you wrote came out of the music. It doesn't need to be a prayer of petition, it may simply be a prayer of thanks, or appreciation, or joy, rejoicing, praise. It could be a prayer of participation in the universe, as a cocreator of life, at least of your own life and of those whose lives you touch and are touched by, twine and are intertwined with. Let the music "pray in you" and for you, and let your prayer come out of it. Just listen, and when you begin to fill up, let the words of your prayer flow out on the paper. Whatever comes is your prayer.

EXERCISE 3
LOOKING CLOSE

"Miracles . . . seem to me to rest not so much upon faces or voices or healing power coming suddenly near to us from afar off, but upon our own perception being made finer, so that for a moment our eyes can see and our ears can hear what is there about us always."
—Willa Cather

For most of us, nature is background. In fact, most of life is background. We buzz by it, in cars or planes or just walking swiftly to work or a party or dinner or whatever destination, not noticing who or what we see, paying little or no attention to the world we live in.

Nature is part of the world's creation, just as we are. Though we may pay it homage culturally or politically—we're dedicated to preserving the rain forest, warding off the greenhouse effect, stopping the pollution of lakes, rivers and streams—we don't bother to look at any of it except for a glance, if that.

Nothing is more creative than nature, more evocative of creation and the creative process, more a living metaphor of creativity. If we want to learn, it is there to teach. But first we have to learn to look. One of the most powerful exercises I know is to go out and actually "look close" at an object in nature—a leaf, a twig, a flower, a rock.

Writers think they know how to look; in fact, they pride themselves on their ability to see—especially reporters, whose job it is to notice details. Many aspiring novelists first work as reporters for the very reason that they hope to hone their ability to observe, to see and record what is in a particular scene, place, event. Sometimes, though, I think we writers get lazy and sloppy in our looking. We assume we are looking when in fact we are letting our eyes slide by and over and through the details that may hold the key to the importance or understanding of the story.

I have come to think that scientists are better at looking for the telling detail, the key to the mystery. Their own work is dependent on it. Without looking, scientists would not be able to do their job. The expertise and power that a scientist brings to bear in "looking close" was brought home to me, thanks to a man who took one of my workshops at the Rancho La Puerta health spa. He had done this exercise in "looking close" and said it reminded him of the way good scientists are trained to look close. When he got home he thoughtfully sent me a marvelous essay by a scientist about how he was trained in this discipline.

This essay is from a book of memoirs about the great Harvard professor and scientist Louis Agassiz (*Louis Agassiz as a Teacher*, edited by Lane Cooper), written by his former students who themselves became scientists and professors of science. This recollection of Professor Agassiz teaching a student how to look at a fish, describes so powerfully the discipline of looking close, and its rewards, that I now read it in my workshop before sending students out to look closely at something in nature.

THE LESSON OF THE FISH

"Take this fish," said [Professor Agassiz], "and look at it; we call it a haemulon; by and by I will ask you what you have seen."

In ten minutes I had seen all that could be seen in that fish, and started in search of the Professor—who had, however, left the Museum . . . nothing was to be done but to return to a steadfast gaze at my mute companion. Half an hour passed—an hour—another hour; the fish began to look loathsome. I turned it over and around; looked it in the face—ghastly; from behind, beneath, above, sideways, at a three-quarters' view—just as ghastly. I was in despair; at an early hour I concluded that lunch was necessary; so, with infinite relief, the fish was carefully replaced in the jar, and for an hour I was free.

On my return, I learned that Professor Agassiz had been at the Museum, but had gone, and would not return for several hours. . . . Slowly I drew forth that hideous fish, and with a feeling of desperation again looked at it. I might not use a magnifying-glass; instruments of all kinds were interdicted. My two hands, my two eyes, and the fish: it seemed a most limited field. I pushed my finger down its throat to see how sharp its teeth were. I began to count the scales in the different rows, until I was convinced that it was nonsense. At last a happy thought struck me—I would draw the fish; and now with surprise I began to discover new features in the creature. Just then the Professor returned.

"That is right," said he; "a pencil is one of the best of eyes." . . .

He listened attentively to my brief rehearsal of the structure of parts. . . . When I had finished, he waited as if expecting more, and then, with an air of disappointment:

"You have not looked very carefully; why," he continued more earnestly, "you haven't even seen one of the most conspicuous features of the animal, which is as plainly before your eyes as the fish itself; look again, look again," and he left me to my misery.

I was piqued; I was mortified. Still more of that wretched fish! But now I set myself to my task with a will, and discovered one new thing after another, until I saw how just the Professor's criticism had been. The afternoon passed quickly; and when, toward its close, the Professor inquired:

"Do you see it yet?"

"No," I replied, "I am certain I do not, but I see how little I saw before."

"That is next best," said he, earnestly, "but I won't hear you now; put away your fish and go home; perhaps you will be ready with a better answer in the morning. I will examine you before you look at the fish."

This was disconcerting. Not only must I think of my fish all night, studying, without the object before me, what this unknown but mostly visible feature might be; but also, without reviewing my discoveries, I must give an exact account of them the next day. . . .

"Do you perhaps mean," I asked [the next day], "that the fish has symmetrical sides with paired organs?"

His thoroughly pleased "Of course! Of course!" repaid the wakeful hours of the previous night. . . . I ventured to ask what I should do next.

"Oh, look at our fish!" he said, and left me again to my own devices. In a little more than an hour he returned, and heard my new catalogue.

"That is good, that is good!" he repeated, "but that is not all, go on"; and so for three long days he placed that fish before my eyes, forbidding me to look at anything else, or to use any artificial aid. "Look, look, look" was his repeated injunction.

This was the best entomological lesson I ever had—a lesson whose influence has extended to the details of every subsequent study; a legacy the Professor has left to me, as he has left it to many others, of inestimable value, which we could not buy, with which we cannot part.

SEE FOR YOURSELF

You can now make your own "scientific" discovery by picking out an object in nature and looking at it to see what you can learn about it, what a period of concentrated observation will reveal to you that you didn't see at all on first glance. Now that you have read of Professor Agassiz's lesson, it will surely not seem unreasonable when I ask you to take at least twenty minutes to observe your natural object. Time after time, though, people will get bored after the first five or ten minutes, assure me there is nothing more to see about this piece of bark, or stone, or pine cone. Like Professor Agassiz, I can only instruct them to look again, to keep looking.

This simple exercise is one way to waken us to the immense possibilities of nature as a stimulant to our own creativity—and to the enrichment of our experience. Before setting out, sit quietly, and empty yourself of your preconceptions about familiar natural objects and what they look like. Tell yourself you are going to look with fresh eyes, as if you have never before seen a tree, a leaf, a fallen branch, the bloom of a rose or a violet. Think about Professor Agassiz's lesson, and how the student's continuous looking kept revealing more and more, even though he thought he had seen everything there was to see. Read again the quote by Willa Cather on "Miracles."

Set out with a pencil and notebook to search for an object in nature to bring under your gaze. You can find it in your own backyard, or any field or vacant lot or city park. If you can't do this, use for your study a piece of fruit or a vegetable—a stalk of broccoli, the sections of an orange, a bunch of grapes.

Look at it up close, steadily, for at least twenty minutes. As you do this, try to forget about yourself and concentrate your full consciousness on the object you're examining.

Elissa Mintz, a technical writer in Boston, explained her use of this process in a paper she wrote in my creativity workshop: "When I need to accomplish something, complete something, I can only do it by looking outward—by losing as much of my sense of self as I can and looking at the thing itself, the thing as *it* is."

Take notes on everything you can observe about it—color, texture, smell, taste, how many leaves or seeds or sections it has, how it is divided, markings on it, everything you can discover about it.

Pretend you are taking these notes so you can describe this object to a person from another planet who has never seen such a thing before and doesn't know what it is, or what it does, or is—or is not—used for. Discover it for yourself for the first time. After you think you have noted everything there is to know about it, look some more, see if there is anything further you can learn about it.

After you have studied the object for at least twenty minutes (take more time if you wish), jot down answers to the following questions about it:

What else does it remind you of? Does it remind you of anything in your own life—any experience you've had, any emotion, or idea? Does it remind you of anything else you have heard or read about? What kind of character would your object be if it were in a story?

Now draw the object, and see what more you can learn from the new "eye" provided by the pencil! If you are doing this with someone else, or in a group, show the picture of the object you have drawn to the other person or another person, and tell them what you learned about it.

Take twenty minutes and write about the object you have drawn. Write either a description of what you saw and learned, or a story, inspired by what the object reminded you of, or what you discovered from it.

Another way of writing about it is to imagine you are speaking for the object. Write its own story—if that grape, or leaf, or stone could speak, what story would it tell?

These are some of the things people wrote about their experience of looking close:

FEEDER OF NATIONS

I chose to approach this exercise from the perspective of trying to describe a common fruit or vegetable to someone from another planet.

I feed nations
Yet I began life underground
A small swelling on a hairlike strand of root
One of a thousand hairlike strands of root
The roots of my mother
She stands aboveground
Small and greenleaved
Under a bowl of cool, spring sky
The warming fingers of the spring sun pluck at the winter
    coldness of the earth
I swell into a tiny sphere
Then grow marbleized

Nourished by the dark earth
I swell again
Above my head
My mother opens herself to the sun
And bursts out with blossoms
Small, white and yellow flowers
Among which bees hum
I, however, burrow deeper into the warm, brown earth
And swell
I am a large sphere and solid
An earthworm burrows by
I interrupt her journey, a hard, brown sphere in her path
She inspects me, then
Burrows blindly on in search of another worm
A fat, white grub pushes up and nibbles on me
But I am hard and bitter, and she pushes away
A caterpillar samples a strand of my mother's roots
But it, too, is bitter
The caterpillar propels himself to the surface
Bursting out into the hot hum of summer
There, he attaches himself to the underside of one of my
     mother's leaves
Rolls himself up and encloses himself in a hard shell
And hangs there, secretive and hidden
Beneath him, in the dark, I continue to swell
I have grown a skin
A thin, brown skin enclosing the white meat of my core
Above, the world hums with the sounds of summer
The hard shell of the caterpillar splits
The creature inside heaves and struggles
A leg is thrust out, an antenna unfurls
A thin, fragile wing flops loose
Soon, amidst the hum and heat of summer
The creature spreads his thin and trembling wings
Brilliant orange and black. And, in a while, lifts off
To float and flutter on the hot summer breezes
To browse on the sweetness of the summer flowers

I am alone in the dark
And now, I feel a pull and a stretch
I am losing my roundness and becoming oval
My brown skin thickens
I stretch my oval self and become full of the fat sweet hum of
    summer
Full of the nourishment of the rich brown earth
I lie in the dark, brown earth and rest
Above, my mother is slowly dying
Her leaves brittle and edged with gray
She droops
And then, with the first cool wind of autumn
I am pulled violently from my resting place
The hands of a small child grasp me
Wrench me from the umbilical cord that has attached me to
    my mother all summer
Above me curves the bowl of a deep, blue sky
The air no longer hums
Its summer work done, it has become quiet
Waiting and resting before the challenge of winter
The child carries me away
I am washed
The rich, brown earth scrubbed from my skin
I lie glistening on a table
Rich with the nourishment of the deep, brown earth in which
    I formed and grew
One end of me is sliced off
It contains a small knot
And in this small knot is the Essence of my Being
The rest of me is placed in boiling water
Within that moist, hot world, the white meat inside my skin
    softens
I become soft and white
I am broken open and given to the child to eat
I have a gentle taste
Soft and white, with a faint memory of the brown earth in
    which I grew

I release my taste into the mouth of the child
The child is nourished by my soft, white meat
Filled with the nutrients I have drawn from the rich, dark earth

Next spring
The small piece of me set aside will be planted
From the small knot of the Essence of my Being contained
    there
I will push a green tendril up through the dark earth towards
    the warming fingers of the sun
I will sprout leaves
And thrust down into the earth a thousand hairlike roots
I will become the mother

Thus, I do feed nations

                              —Pam Moriarity

TULIP

Vivid red leaves. Inside: flaming yellow; star-shaped at bottom of the red cup. Six little stamens of what I think of when I hear the word, and a paler yellow kind of extension of the stem but a little thicker, exactly in the center. Six vivid red petals, not leaves. Two are torn, dog-eared; did they grow that way? Some stamen dust rests on the yellow cup contrasting magnificently. A little tulip colony. Now there are four flowers. Yesterday I counted 6 bulbs ready to bloom. Looks like one plant was torn from this clump of life and another green stem was clearly ripped from the plant. There are 3 more scraggly-looking pieces of this pie. I don't know if they'll make it to adolescence. Tough neighborhood. Rhododendron tree behind it is looming and messy. And the dreaded tiger lilies are now just a lot of green pointy leaves growing taller by the minute, threatening to bloom. But these tulips. I call them roses. They're glorious and majestic. The 3 shorter flowers are distinctly different from the bigger, bolder, older, more defined flower leading the pack. The soil is moist but doesn't look nourishing. And now I see a stream of ants down there busily circling nothing.

I left the house deciding to choose something to stare at, (for the assignment) maybe while driving in, and these tulips called to me—stopped me in my tracks on my way to the car, thankfully inspiring me and forcing words from the pen and paper, stopping all other thoughts.

There they are, now I'm across the way, in the car. They exist before and after me, without me at all.

No. They were not here before now. Not last year or the other 3 years I've lived here. When the green clump first staked its claim on the patch of dirt by the porch steps I puzzled over how they came to be and suddenly remembered: Nancy. Last year we spent all hours together but went our separate ways and now rarely speak. Seed catalogues last year planted her hope in the world and she planted their seeds. She's moved away but this little package of life was her doing. Maybe she mentioned it to me, and like so many words, rolled off of me, and were trampled underfoot.

They remind me of a poem by Danny Siegel, something like, "my defiant shabbos rose"—maybe black, and something about a buttonhole and rebellion; and of Li Young Lee's poetry book called Rose. And Benjamin Tammuz: ". . . the rosebush next to the bench has opened three red eyes during the night and looked out onto the street, shy and happy." Tulips don't get the press roses get, and maybe it's better for their character. They are the first hearty spring flowers after the crocuses who clear their way through the days where frost is still likely to pounce and stifle tender, young beauty.

If it were a character in a play, it'd be a long-legged woman full of surprises—unnoticed at first but slowly, from the first opening, blooming into a gorgeous, vibrant, and steadfast individual.

Look Again: Tulip 2

The messy clump of green has been one surprise after the next. Each sign of more life made me curious. I have to say I was expecting very little but pleased at the thought of Nancy's work/gift. At first the bulbs were dark red, not promising. And the proximity to each other odd—literally a clump, one on top of the next, as if randomly tossed in my direction by Nancy walking old Scout, tugging at him to stop walking nose in the ground and get on with it.

No these aren't prim and proper Boston tulips, in manicured lawns in a row: yellow-red-yellow-red, arrogant and untouchable. These are flawed and forgiving flowers she planted.

I'm hurt by the senseless destruction of part of their little colony. Trying not to take it too hard, but tension with the downstairs neighbors mounts as the temperatures rise, doors and windows open, and all signs of life are amplified obnoxiously ending the privacy of winter. I'm thankful for the end of that privacy which usually feels like isolation, but when the grass is greener my perspective shifts. I blame it on the neighbors because they bug me and hate me—and they monopolize any outdoors there is in this little urban suburb yard. They make it a dump—tossing cig butts and scattering broken toys and pieces of fence.

The poor clump really looks trampled and torn at. A slightly gaping hole where part of the plant once lived and a broken off stem are evidence of the crime. These are otherworldly gifts of love from a friend and they've been violated, terminated. The pigeon poop piles up and suffocates any attempts at plant life farther down. But this spot was the right one for planting. Nancy's oddly unassuming and humble. You'd never know she's a musician who is asked to perform all over the world. She is not impressed with herself and often seems clumsy and in need of direction—but she's like this tulip—surviving and shining, eager to please.

—Lisa Hurwitz

FURTHER EXERCISES: SEEING MORE

Just as there is no end to the music you can hear, there is no end to the objects in nature you can look at—trees, flowers, twigs, buds, rocks, fruit, vegetables, bulbs, bushes, vines, plants—and we haven't even gotten to bugs and animals! Each time you look close, as you have in this exercise, you will see new connections to your own experience, find new stories, ideas, analogies, metaphors.

There is another fruitful and creative way to look at such objects in nature. I learned this from a nun whom I had sought out for spiritual direction. I went in hopes of learning exotic mysteries about arcane paths to God, keys to spiritual understanding I had never dreamed about as a mere Protestant. I felt that a Roman Catholic nun would have all the answers in this realm, would be an expert in such matters. I was prepared to do whatever she asked me to do, even if it involved such artifacts as beads and incense.

She told me to go look at a tree.

"Look at a tree," she said, "and try to think why God made it, what he had in mind when he created it."

She told me to sit down and meditate this way while looking at the tree for twenty minutes, and to write down all the things that I observed about it. I have to admit, I was a little disappointed, since the assignment seemed so mundane. Look at a tree. Is that all? I thought maybe she gave me such an easy assignment because I was a Unitarian; she figured I wasn't up to much more than a tree.

I dutifully went off to the Boston Public Garden, one of my favorite places of power, and sat down in front of the biggest tree I could find. I closed my eyes, took a deep breath, put in my mind the question of why God would make this tree. With that in my head, I raised my eyes to look at it.

I was overwhelmed. I felt as if I had been pushed backward by the force of the tree. It was so complex, so intricate in design, so hugely various—from the patterns of bark that in themselves seemed like pictures and hidden murals, to the top of the limbs and the panoply of leaves, the pattern of limbs—the whole thing seemed far too huge and complicated for me to begin to perceive in the way the Sister had instructed me.

I decided to look for something simpler, something on a par with my own primitive level of spiritual understanding. After looking around, I settled on grass. A blade of grass. This plain, small object seemed the thing most suited to my own level of perception. Of course, I wasn't sure I could single out the exact same one each time I looked, but I could try; I could stare at the same patch of grass and observe the blades as best I could.

I went back to the same spot every day for two weeks and meditated on the blades of grass for twenty minutes each day. I kept discovering new things all the time—different shades of green, different thicknesses and textures, the way the grass moved in the wind, how blades bent toward and away from one another, the sense of the aliveness of each separate blade. I wrote in my notebook, as Sister had instructed, the words that described the qualities of God as I imagined God was manifested in the grass that she/he created: "tenacious," "resilient," "communicating," "alive," "dancing," "dependent," "surprising," "reaching," "responding."

Originally I had planned at the end of the two weeks to pick a blade of the grass to tape in my notebook. But by that time I felt such a relationship with the grass that I felt its aliveness, and the idea of tearing off a piece of it seemed a cruel and unfeeling thing to do. If, before I had meditated on the grass for two weeks, anyone had told me I'd have such misgivings about tearing off a blade, I'd have thought they were balmy. That's how deeply *looking* at it changed me.

I also began to see other things in a deeper way. After my meditation sessions I would look around at the rest of the garden. One day I looked into the eyes of a squirrel and he looked back directly into mine. I felt a connection, as if we were both *creatures* together, and that I was made of the same "stuff," or material, as he was; and as the grass I was looking at, and the trees, stones, birds, insects, animals. I felt a part of the scene, not just an outsider observing it but an integral part of it, part of the world, the whole *creation*.

You may want, having done the exercise in looking close, to try now looking in a meditative way at an object of nature to see—as the nun instructed me—what God had in mind in creating it. If you don't believe in God, simply contemplate it from a spiritual point of view. Ask yourself why it was created? How? By whom, what, where, when?

What does it have to tell you? Even if you don't believe in God, you can look at a tree or blades of grass or flowers or bushes and think about their place in creation.

Do this for two weeks and write what you learn in your journal every day. What do you see that you didn't see before? At the end of the two weeks, write a letter to a friend, telling about the whole experience. Invite a friend to go with you to a park, garden, field, or wooded area, and pick out an object in nature to study closely for twenty minutes, writing down everything you can see about it. Then tell each other your discoveries. Write about them.

PEACE IN NATURE

One of the benefits of looking close at something in nature is simply the pleasure of being outside in the natural world. Most people find peace and relief there that refreshes them, like business executive Arnold Hiatt, who likes to walk in the woods, the mountains, and sail on the ocean.

We can find peace and refreshment in other places as well. When I gave a workshop in Spiritual Autobiography at Sing Sing prison for a group of men studying for a degree from the New York Theological Seminary, I found a depth of spirit and creativity in a place that would seem to stifle such elements. I went to inspire the men; but with their patience, faith, and striving to create something useful out of their time in confinement, they inspired *me*.

One of the men of this group, Billy J. Griffin, wrote, "The most spiritual incidents that I recall are those surrounding my staring out the window and watching the stars after my nightly prayers. Everything was so peaceful, so tranquil. These times were of great value to me, especially after a troubled or hectic day.

"I'd just sit at the window, watching the goings-on of my neighbors as they wound down their days. They seemed to move slower. Lights went out, the noise of television and radios stopped. . . .

"The night sky was always dark and clear, I'd locate stars and wonder if they were planets or not. I'd look for constellations, especially the big and little dippers. I'd often reflect on how tiny I and the world was. This was usually my point of departure as I would muse over different topics without trying to force the issue. Wherever my mind went, I followed until I was too tired and ready for sleep. And sleep would be so good."

A man in the group who signed his paper "Fred" wrote, "Growing up in South Carolina's rural farm land, daily I would go to one or the other of my two favorite hide-a-ways and meditate. One of those areas was near a brook behind a pasture which ran beneath a line of shade trees. The other was in a patch of woods about a quarter of a mile from my grandfather's house. These two places were special to me, there I could commune with God—who in those moments was nature at her finest."

Another man in the group wrote of going out in a rowboat to the middle of the lake in Prospect Park in Brooklyn and lying back and floating, finding a sense of peace.

LOOKING CLOSE IN YOUR WORK

We don't need to restrict looking close to the wonders of the earth and sky. It's a practice that also helps us be creative in our work, regardless of what it may be.

Architect Evans Woollen tells how his mother pointed out buildings to him as a child, reacted to them with laughter or scorn, and got him interested so that he *looked closer* at them. Looking close is part of Elizabeth Valentine's technique as a body worker, which she developed by learning anatomy through studying sculpture. Chef Odette Bery says the best experience for learning to be a creative cook is watching other people prepare food.

Watch. Be awake and aware, and discoveries will unfold before you.

EXERCISE 4
FINDING INSPIRATION FROM OTHERS' CREATIVE WORKS

When I was eight years old I read a book at the Broad Ripple Branch of the Indianapolis Public Library (my favorite place in the neighborhood, aside from Wally's Grill for hamburgers) called *The Bears of Blue River*. I was so moved by it I wanted to be a pioneer, like the hero,

Bowser Brent, and if I could not go back in time to do that I wanted at least to go on a real canoe trip into the woods and camp out and live on fish I caught myself. I did that twelve years later with my friend Joe "The Fox" Hartley. We went to Great Sand Lake, Ontario, above the Lake of the Woods, and camped for a week without seeing any other human beings, and lived on the Northern pike and muskies we caught. In a sense that whole trip, that marvelous adventure, came out of my reading *The Bears of Blue River*.

All of us have read books that moved us that way, have heard music and seen movies and plays, looked at paintings and sculpture that have influenced our lives. Remembering how we were affected by the creative works of others gets our own creative juices flowing, bringing back memories of what happened and who it happened with, and how we and they changed, or were surprised, or inspired, or illuminated by what we heard or read or saw.

Creation begets creation. Many writers I know have told me that when they're stuck in their own work or feel they've hit a dry period, they turn to books or stories or poems that have inspired them in the past, to tune in to that wavelength of creativity. Even when the creative spirit seems dammed up in us, or gone dry, we can sense it, even sometimes revive it by reading books whose own creative power has moved us on a deep level.

Think back to some of those special creative works that had a special influence on you. Take twenty minutes to write about what it was like when you read that book or heard that song or saw that painting, and were deeply touched. Write about how it felt, and how it affected you.

This is how some people responded to that question:

OPEN SESAME

In San Francisco in 1969, I journeyed through a retrospective show of the work of Van Gogh. At that time I was living in a Yoga Ashram under a discipline of poverty, chastity and obedience; a daily routine not unlike that of the monastery here.

It was a traveling show with a tremendous amount of his work in it. I have met many people who saw this memorable show during the years it went from place to place. Each one of these people shared my wonder at it.

I had some very good art teaching and doing but was not at all thinking of being an artist when I went to this show.

It seems like it was 50 rooms. Each work is quite small, a jewel. The show was arranged chronologically. I began quite early in my parade around the walls to be profoundly affected. Each brush stroke was exquisite; each canvas amazing. If you go close up to a Van Gogh anywhere you will see what I'm talking about. The paint is laid exactly so the bumps of paint are sensuous beyond description and a field of wheat will have been painted with thousands of these precise touches. The color is intense, simple, direct, clear. The drawing of shapes is a harmony of the spheres. To move from painting to painting and from room to room was to take a journey from which there was no returning.

I have studied Van Gogh's work and life and have come to know that he regarded colors as symbols, the background colors of all his portraits are chosen to harmonize with the subject. Did you know he painted at night with a candle on his hat? A barroom scene was painted in garish yellow-green, red to give a hellish aura to it; I find this painting beautiful anyway. His colors are uncomplicated. They support rather than distract. Many great colorists use very obvious, mostly complementary color schemes. This was the first time I fully comprehended the spiritual power of painting.

—Susan Anderson

THE SECRET GARDEN

I read this book when I was perhaps 10–12. I don't even remember the story but I do remember the feeling. I loved that the book took place somewhere else and at a different time. I remember identifying with the little girl even though I can't recall her character totally. But most of all I loved that she has discovered this secret place. A place of beauty and mystery. It had a forbidden quality to it and I loved her courage and curiosity to explore and to continue to go there. This garden was attractive to her in the same way this book had an attraction for me. I just wanted to know more about this place. Perhaps I longed for such a place. But I needed my own space. I know that I was not told to read this book. I was not reading it because I was supposed to. I wanted to and it didn't matter if it won me any approval. That was the same kind of feeling the little girl had for her secret garden. This was important to me because I remember feeling for the first time interested in a book on my own that was a new side of me. I don't think I ever finished the book. But it had captured something in me that had been untouched and today I still feel grateful for this book.

—M. *Whiteford*

RECALLING INSPIRATION

Thinking back to books, songs, stories, sculptures, dances, plays, movies that have moved us never fails to touch a creative spark. It reminds us of the power of creativity, how it not only produces aesthetic pleasure, but also how it acts on our lives, influences our actions, understanding, emotions, intellect, and spirit.

Whenever you are stuck for ideas or inspiration, think back to one of those works of art or literature that altered your own life, and write about what it was, how you experienced it, and what happened as a result. Soon you will be in the realm of creativity—first, the one created by the work that moved you, and then your own, as you create the story of how this work changed (re-created) you.

Creative people use others' creative works for their own inspiration, as well as learning their craft. Author-attorney Alan Nolan felt "released" by reading Salinger's *The Catcher in the Rye* and J. P. Donleavy's *The Ginger Man*, novels that broke rules and gave him the courage to try something original. When therapist and author Claire Douglas feels bogged down in her writing, she reads the work of writers she loves, like the nineteenth-century novelists Edith Wharton and Henry James. Chef Odette Bery sometimes gets inspiration from reading recipe books.

Make a list of some of the books, movies, poems, plays, and other works of art that have inspired you. Think about your actual feelings when you experienced whatever work it was. Remember the emotion, the "spirit" of it.

Pick one of the books you put on your list and read it again; get back in touch with the feelings it evoked in you.

Keep your list and add to it. Note in your journal what events or experiences inspire you as they occur.

Here is a list of some of mine that may help you create your own list. You'll undoubtedly think of examples in each of these categories you like better than mine!

Books:
>   *The Bears of Blue River* by Charles Major
>   *The Red Badge of Courage* by Stephen Crane
>   *Let Us Now Praise Famous Men* by James Agee
>   *The Magician of Lublin* by Isaac Bashevis Singer
>   *Reaching Out* by Henri Nouwen
>   *A Palpable God* by Reynolds Price
>   *Body and Soul* by Frank Conroy

Movies:
>   *Yankee Doodle Dandy*
>   *The Graduate*
>   *The Razor's Edge* (updated version starring Bill Murray)
>   *My Left Foot*
>   *The Commitments*
>   *Carrington*

Opera:
>   *La Bohème*

Symphony:
>   *The New World* by Dvořák

Jazz Works:
>   *No Sun in Venice* by The Modern Jazz Quartet
>   *Straight, No Chaser* by Thelonious Monk
>   *Sketches of Spain* by Miles Davis
>   *A Love Supreme* by John Coltrane

Plays:
>   *Darkness at Noon* by Sidney Kingsley, based on the novel
>   by Arthur Koestler
>   *The Iceman Cometh* by Eugene O'Neill
>   *The Real Thing* by Tom Stoppard

Blown Sideways Through Life by Claudia Shear
Angels in America by Tony Kushner
Songs:
"Suzanne" by Leonard Cohen, sung by Judy Collins
"Just Like Tom Thumb Blues," by Bob Dylan, sung by
       Judy Collins
"Anticipation," sung by Carly Simon
Poems:
"Things of This World" by Richard Wilbur
"Live or Die" by Anne Sexton
"The Key to Everything" by May Swenson

KEEPING A JOURNAL

Are you keeping a journal? It's a good seedbed for creativity. A journal is a place where you can put down anything you want, without any rules. A journal provides the chance to kick off your shoes and not worry about what the neighbors think. It's only for you. If you want to share it or any part of it with any particular person, that's fine. But here's the basic rule for enjoying and getting pleasure and inspiration from your journal: *Don't write for posterity! Or even your best friend, or loved one.*

As soon as you become self-conscious, and worry how your journal is going to sound to others, you might as well forget it. What do you write in it? Thoughts, ideas, scenes, snatches of overheard dialogue, wishes, memories, jokes, poems, recipes, dreams—anything you want, in any style or form you want. Some people write in their journal every morning, or at night before going to bed. Others use it when the spirit moves them. You can make up your own rules about how to use it, as well as what and how to write in it. If you skip a day or a week, don't let this discourage you. *Nobody knows!* Return to it when you feel like it.

I always use a loose-leaf notebook with lined paper, probably because I'm accustomed to writing on lines like I did when I started school. Many people prefer to have a bound book with blank pages, which is easier to draw on. Bill Donaldson, who served as chair of the religious education committee at my church, suggests "a blank unlined book, a pen for writing, a different pen for drawing, such as a wide blue calligraphy felt tip." Many of the people who come to my workshops use many different colored pens or crayons to draw with in their journals.

A journal also is good place to write down quotes you want to remember from books, newspapers, poems—whatever strikes you. These can be a good source of ideas and inspiration, as well as a record of what you were thinking about, what was meaningful to you at a particular day, month, and year.

You might record movies or plays you saw, books you read, outcomes of sporting events you attended, or events you read about or watched on TV that were meaningful to you. What's in the news that you want to remember? Clip out a picture that meant something to you from a magazine and paste it into your journal. Be creative.

A journal is a key creative tool for many people. Author Ivan Gold feels journals are important for getting memories down; he sometimes segues from his journal right into the book or story he is working on. Judy Collins says "the opening line from a journal can be the beginning of a song."

DREAM DOORS

Dreams have always been a part of the human story; they are part of the Bible and sacred books of other religions; Freud and Jung saw in dreams keys to understanding our own nature. There's a renewed interest in dreaming, and what it can tell us—books, workshops, courses, lectures, and theories of dreaming abound. Stephen LaBerge of Stanford University is the exponent of "lucid dreaming"—a technique of becoming conscious in our dreams that we are dreaming. The advantages, he says, are that we can alter the "script" of the dream, have it come out the way we want it. These methods and results are described in his books *Lucid Dreaming*, and *Exploring the World of Lucid Dreaming*.

I've resisted attempting that practice, feeling that interfering with my own dreams isn't a good idea. This is not based on anything more than my own instinct, and has no scientific or spiritual basis. What I do practice is telling myself to remember my dreams when I go to sleep, and this usually works. On waking it's necessary to jot down key phrases or scenes from the dreams, or they quickly evaporate like wisps of smoke.

Judy Collins believes the main access points to her creativity are her journal and her dreams. Therapist Claire Douglas writes down dreams and meditates as a way to get ideas. Chef Odette Bery has dreams with recipes. Architect Evans Woollen had a dream about the form of a monastery he was commissioned to design.

One of my own most powerful dreams had a great influence on my creativity. After my nonfiction publisher had turned down my first attempt at a novel, I was devastated.

I kept on writing fiction secretly, not telling anyone but a few confidants. One morning I woke at dawn and felt exhilarated, because I had just had a dream in the form of a novel. It began with a title page; then came a simple story with a beginning, middle and end, and then a page that said "The End." It was like a signal from my inner self telling me, You have a novel in you. I knew then I would write it—not the story of the dream, but the novel "in me" I wanted to write. It was seven more years until I did, but I always remembered the dream, and the dream helped me believe.

Even if we remember our dreams, how can we use them? Some therapists make creative use of dreams to deepen the dreamer's understanding. I think that even without such aid we often get insights about ourselves, and sometimes about our work, from dreams. If you want to explore that further, look for one of the many workshops on dream analysis or interpretation offered at most adult education centers.

Tibetan lamas have taught "dream yoga" for centuries to help their students develop mindfulness in daytime living, and get a sense of the illusory nature of life. What if our waking life is a dream, too? Or our dream life is actually the "reality"? What if everything is a dream? Fred Alan Wolf, author of The Dreaming Universe, is a quantum physicist who asks the ultimate question these other questions raised by dreaming lead to: If life is a dream, who is the dreamer?

Here are some simple exercises for experimenting with your own dreams as creative possibilities:

Keep a dream journal for a week. Write down everything you can remember about your dreams. Draw with pens or crayons scenes from your dreams, or feelings of dreams. See if there are any stories in the dreams. What do they tell you about yourself? About your relation to the universe? Share your dreams with a friend. Ask about his or her own dreams. Use one of the groups you are in—or form a new one—to read about dreams, and get together to draw, write, and share about dreams.

EXERCISE 5
DRAW A ROAD MAP OF
YOUR CREATIVE JOURNEY

Our whole lives are studded with creative activity—creations of others that have moved us, as well as creations of our own. To get in touch with our continuing creative experience, the way it has moved through our lives and still moves us, take a large piece of paper from a drawing pad and use your crayons to illustrate as colorfully as possible the course of your creative journey.

Before starting to draw, spend a few minutes of quiet. Think of the people and circumstances that led you to this point—of drawing a map that will enable you to look at your life as a creative journey. Think of all the gifts you've been given that have enabled you to make such a journey, to create in so many different ways. Jot down some of the highlights you want to include—times when you were opened up creatively by some other's work, or when your own creativity blossomed; when you acted creatively in your job, or relationship, or family life; creative activities outside of the arts, like creating ways of service to the community or to other individuals. Think in the broadest terms possible of your own creativity, and decorate the map of your journey with the signs and symbols of your creative development and growth, the high (as a mountain peak) or low (as a mine shaft) points of your creative pilgrim's progress.

Let your imagination flow, and don't stint with the crayons; the more color the better.

After drawing the map, share it with someone else. If you are doing these exercises by yourself, show your map to a family member or a friend, and explain what the symbols are. Take them with you along the route of your creative journey.

After drawing the map, and sharing it, take just ten minutes to write about one of the points you drew on your creative journey. Of course, it can't be a whole story, only the beginning. It demonstrates that every point on the map is a story, that each creative act can pro-duce another (the story of the creation).

FURTHER EXERCISES:
MAPPING NEW TERRITORY

Keep the road map of your creative journey. You can look at any point on it at any time and find a story. Each turning point gives you the ideas, emotions, drama, and insight of a creative experience that moved you, turned you, opened you up in some way.

You can write "off of" the map for a long time, remembering and recharging your own creativity.

Start a new map. Draw the new creative experiences that occur during the coming week, and if you aren't aware of any occurring—create some! Look at what and how you created things in the past. Re-vise and retool those creative ideas and experiences you liked, or that seem relevant now.

Don't think of creativity in a narrow, confining way when you draw your maps. Remember how other people play a part in your creativity—and you in theirs. When asked about the factors that helped him break his long creative block, novelist Ivan Gold said, "It's got to do with love, confidence. . . ." His wife Vera, his son Ian, his writer friends, a publisher who believed in him (Seymour Lawrence) and offered that belief in the form of a contract with an advance against royalties for an unfinished manuscript; all were part of the chemistry of his creative rebirth.

Religious historian Elaine Pagels, who tackles the biggest subjects in her books, like *Adam, Eve, and the Serpent*, said of her creative work, "It's lonely—it's important to have people in your life who know what it's all about—I know they're there."

None of us creates in a vacuum. People are part of our creative journey, giving us not only encouragement and support, but ideas we couldn't see ourselves, even though they are right in front of our noses. My publisher Seymour Lawrence wrote me when he read an essay I did on James Baldwin and said, "That should be part of a book on New York in the fifties!" It seemed a natural. Why didn't I think of it? Sometimes it takes others to tell us what's right in front of us.

Editor Andre Schiffrin called radio host and interviewer Studs Terkel when he read some interviews Studs had done with people in South Africa in which they told the story of their village. Schiffrin suggested he do the same thing with "an American village." That's how Studs's first book, *Division Street*, was born.

We could all make a map of where we met the people who helped, inspired, and supported us in our journey!

Think of different kinds of creative maps you could make of your life. A couple who did this workshop with me in Palm Beach, Florida, told me they are making a creative map of their relationship, and are going to continue to draw it, reminding themselves to keep creating it as they live it, and not simply "let it happen" or get boring or fall into a rut.

Here's another exercise for partners: Each person draws a map of the way she or he would like the relationship to look if it were the greatest relationship imaginable! They show their maps to each other, and see how and where the maps could merge into a great relationship for both partners at the same time.

Taking off from that idea, you could make a creative map of your job, your family life, your service to the community, your education, your pursuit of art, music, sculpture, writing, acting, or filmmaking. Map what has occurred up to now; how this part of your life went in the past year, the past week. Then draw a future map, how you would like it to look if you could map it any way possible. What stops you from following that map? Create ideas and methods for making that map unfold in your life the way you design it.

FAILURE AS OPPORTUNITY

Sometimes your attempts at creativity have failed—and others will fail in the future—whether with your work, or art, or relationships. No road map of a creative journey is a series of triumphs. All of us suffer disappointments, frustrations, and downright defeats in our creative life as well as in any other aspect of life.

So has every other creator in the history of the world.

When you are brought down by one of those inevitable defeats, remember the great tradition you are in! James Joyce, like many writers, was a "failure" in his own lifetime. Some creators are fortunate enough to have their rejected work vindicated in their lifetime. When Julia

Child submitted *The Art of French Cooking* to a publisher, she was told that Americans would never be interested in French cooking, and besides, the book was too long. It was bought by another publisher and has sold more copies than the Bible.

Joan Didion's first novel, *Run River*, was turned down by thirteen publishers; Norman Mailer's third novel, *The Deer Park*, was turned down by five publishers, even though his first, *The Naked and the Dead*, had been a bestseller. Kurt Vonnegut's first bestseller, *Slaughterhouse-Five*, was turned down by two of his previous publishers before being accepted by a new one.

As I read through the interviews I did with creators, it struck me how many of them mentioned some failure or other, which usually opened a new door, though it wasn't visible at the time.

Elaine Pagels wrote poetry as a teenager and now describes herself as a "failed poet," but the world knows her as an outstanding writer of religious history. Odette Bery was turned down for a teaching job by Garland Junior College, but later, as a well-known chef, taught cooking there. Yoga teacher Danielle Levi-Alvares worked on a novel for a while but felt better when she gave it up, deciding she was more creative in her life than in her writing. She later got to translate one of Thich Nhat Hanh's books into French.

Sometimes failure persists, we bottom out, and the world gives up on us. But always there are those who rise again—who hear that voice that says, "Get up!" John Frankenheimer, the director of some of the most commercially and artistically successful films of the 1960s— *The Manchurian Candidate*, *Bird Man of Alcatraz*, and *Days of Wine and Roses*—found himself at sixty-four in 1994 "trying to pick up the pieces of a career that went awry," according to a *New York Times* article by Bernard Weinraub.

The occasion of the interview was Frankenheimer's return to television (considered "Hollywood's bottom rung"), where he had started out in the '50s. Weinraub reported that "personal difficulties, including alcoholism, left [Frankenheimer] tormented for years and plagued his career." Talking about it with what Weinraub called "unusual candor and without a trace of bitterness," the director said, "I have to rediscover myself, reinvent myself." Frankenheimer said he'd had a drinking problem but "straightened out in 1981" and "from that day on I haven't had a drink."

"The 1980s were spent putting my life back together," the veteran director said. "But look, I don't want to cast myself as a victim in any way because I'm not. I've had a terrific career and a long run. And if you keep stepping up to the plate, sooner or later you get a hit. And sooner or later you get a home run. The important thing is to be resilient enough to keep stepping up to the plate. And I'm stepping up to the plate."

It reminded me of Henry James's injunction to himself in his journal after his own big failure: "Produce; produce again; produce again better than ever and all will be well."

Every turning point, whether of success or defeat, creates new openings—new opportunities to create.

How do we bring the creativity we've now experienced into our daily lives? How do people use their creativity in their work, not only in the arts, but in all fields?

Let's listen now to creators telling how they do it.

Chapter 10

CREATORS TALKING

We learn to create from other creators—not only from those in our own field or specialty, but perhaps most from those who use their creativity in other ways and other areas of life than we do. Listen now to the voices and experiences of people of different creative backgrounds and interests. Some are well known to the world, or within their field; some are not in the kind of work that brings public renown. Some are established, some are starting out. All are creative and share more than I would have imagined.

Listen to their stories, look for what relates these seemingly disparate kinds of creators to each other, and see what they do that could enliven your own creativity. As Baudelaire found "correspondences" in the arts, so can we find new correspondences in fields not usually thought of as part of that realm.

JUDY COLLINS
Singer and songwriter, author of Trust Your Heart, *an autobiography, and* Shameless, *a novel*

I became a fan of Judy Collins when I was a guest lecturer at the University of Illinois Journalism School in the spring semester of 1968. A student thrust on me her album *Wildflowers* and insisted, "Listen to this!" That summer while I lived at the beach in Venice, California, and started working (again) on my first novel, I got all her other albums. I played them over and over, listening to her clear, lyrical voice singing "In My Life," "Just Like Tom Thumb Blues," "Since You Asked," "Suzanne," "Who Knows Where the Time Goes." My friends were listening to her songs the way I was—not just for entertainment, but for inspiration. I think we found in her music a kind of spiritual nourishment (though we wouldn't have called it that back then), a sense of connection with the beauty and mystery of life.

I met her in 1991 in New York City at a gathering of people who were interested in talking about the spiritual or religious dimensions of life. When I started to interview people whose work I admire about their own experience in creating, she was one of the first who came to mind. I went to her apartment on the West Side of Manhattan to hear her thoughts about it. We talked in a room with a grand piano, where she writes the lyrics and composes the music to her songs.

As you read this, look for what different kinds of obstacles she had to overcome to create her work. Have you had any similar obstacles?

ACCESS FROM DREAMS*

There are two access points to my work. The first is a dialogue between the waking and dreaming worlds. I'm always writing dreams down—writing songs comes straight out of dreams, or they provide the emotional environment for songs. The melody follows. When I write a poem there's a rhythmic dictation of the melody. I don't think lyrics should stand as poetry—they're married to a melody.

I'm working on a collection of my own material now. As a singer, I must be aware of where my musical patterns are taking me, and what's going on internally. If I'm looking for material to sing, I'll find the piece that reflects what's going on with me at the time.

My access points are my dreams and my journal. Those are consistent threads. The most crucial point is consistent discipline—to write down my dreams, and to keep the journal on a regular basis. The opening line from a journal can prompt the beginning of a song.

*This material is copyright © Judy Collins 1991.

Sometimes writers say they worry that they might "spend themselves" on their journals. I know what they mean, because my journal-keeping has diminished since I've been writing a novel. That concern is more to the point for me when I'm writing prose, as I have been these last three or four years while working on a novel. As a poet I kept more in the journals, now I do less there as a prose writer.

I do this writing in order to experience my life completely. It's not processed unless I write about it. That's the burden and journey of creativity, or of being a writer.

My father was an interpreter of songs—he didn't write much. I was taught to emulate doing the best interpretations—my ideal was Horowitz, who played Rachmaninoff. I wasn't trained to create the music, my models were people who played Chopin, singers who sang Rodgers and Hart. I heard what the best sounds like. In studying music, I wanted to play and sing well. That gave me longevity—people sing and conduct till they're ninety years old.

I wrote lots in high school till this woman stopped me—a teacher—she accused me of plagiarism. It was a horrible action. Extremely damaging. I was very frightened off of writing. I was studying the craft of singing, not the writing.

I started writing my own songs because of meeting writers who put me at ease—Joni Mitchell and Leonard Cohen. They were different—what they wrote was more accessible to me. Cohen read my journals and said, "You're doing something different in your journals—you shifted into songs."

CREATING CLEAN

When I started writing again the difficulty was not to drink and take drugs. I stopped drinking in '78 and the writing started to flourish and take hold in the disciplined way I wanted. "The Blizzard," which I wrote at that time, was my most sustained piece of writing, most effective. With healthy tools, an impact on how I focused and where to go, I was able to think in produc-tive terms. In my twenties and thirties it might take years to write songs. I wrote the song "Che," it took me four or five years. At least I didn't give it up. I could have called it a writing block.

I think the use of any kind of stimulants—alcohol or drugs—has a short-term impact on ideas—but the long-term use is very destructive to the spark of intuition. Otherwise you're so involved in the physical battle of the body—*I got sick and everything stopped—that you can't deal with the creative aspects.*

Through all this I always kept journals, always wrote down dreams. Then I overcame that period to get further than journals and dreams.

I went to a creative writing workshop with Ira Progoff. That was an inspirational breakthrough point for me. I read his book The Practice of Process Meditation. *I went to Ira's workshop, not really expecting much. At four in the afternoon of the first day I got a pain in my lower stomach—I don't have stomach pains. I broke out in sweat and said I had to leave. I got in a cab and thought I would pass out. The next day I spoke to Ira—I started writing—songwriting came back. I saw that it was physical, as well as mental, emotional, and spiritual.*

FEELING LIKE AN INSTRUMENT

The first song I wrote was "Since You Asked," then I was off and running. I started writing every day. I had a breakthrough from the perspective of discipline. I practice the piano—at the piano I'm in touch with songs—melodies come to me. Now I'm writing a novel, and I'm trying to do three or four hours of writing a day. When I'm really tearing into it, I work around the clock. When I'm finishing the novel, I'll work every possible minute. This is my fourth full edit of the novel, I think it's got the right shape now. I'm going to sit down and finish next summer.

I feel I'm an instrument in writing—at the piano, I tape everything—the minute something starts, I feel I'm taking dictation. The novel popped out of the blue—a character with quirks and ideas and problems came to me full-blown and began to have her own voice—a funny voice. In the purest sense, I was taking dictation.

My difficulty as an artist is, I don't have a well-honed commercial sense. I have tremendous riches, but I don't know much about how to sell myself. I see my work as maintaining creative fertility and staying alive out there. I have to keep my attitude good and positive and be consistent and optimistic—choose people who are in spiritual synch with me.

Yes, I think writing and music are spiritual disciplines. Absolutely. It's a very important entering point. I realized this many years ago. I'm a devotee of Yogananda. For thirteen years I've meditated consistently—for the past eight or nine years once a day, and for the past three or four years twice a day. It's part of continuity, all part of the same thing. It's essential to keep in the flow of that.

TECHNIQUES TO CENTER

I use self-reaffirming work—like my yoga routine. I'm indebted to my teachers. Dr. [Antonio] Brico, my piano teacher, introduced me to Yogananda's work—I read his autobiography in '78 [The Autobiography of a Yogi, *by Paramahansa Yogananda].* I *was very profoundly moved—it's one of the most well written autobiographies of all times. I also loved Merton,* The Seven Storey Mountain, *and William James,* The Varieties of Religious Experience.

I use exercise and breathing to center and clear my head. I like to run and swim—I believe those are the Western forms of Zen. I've worked out now for about twenty-three, twenty-four years—it's very much a habit, a pattern.

Place is not important to me, in the sense of needing to be in beautiful or compatible physical surroundings. My memories are more important than wherever I am at the moment. But at a certain phase I need to go away from New York City. I work well in New York, I need the stimulation of the city, and I wouldn't want to live anywhere else—but a time comes when I need no calls, and I cancel dinner dates. This is a difficult physical location to be in to finish work. It takes focus, and it's hard to maintain in this environment. There's so much going on, so many people—I can turn off the phone, but it's very nice to be in a place where you can be focused and wander in a daze.

It's amazing to me how we know internally where we're supposed to be. If we only gave ourselves time to see into ourselves. You can tap into the inside of you in finding a master, a teacher. You may need a teacher on the outside to help you with discipline—but the voice is inside each person. The discipline and struggle are to illuminate from within what that voice is—that illuminates itself and is a healing power.

Creativity is very fertile. I know artists in different fields. It's very important to be around those with an artistic vision—they can be weavers, potters, painters, artisans, filmmakers. I'm interested in the spectrum—it's all the same thing. Creativity is all similar—it doesn't matter what outlet you choose. Talent is very important, but the desire to see it unfold is more important. People with only a small talent can go very deep. Other people have tremendous trouble and great talent and can't get off the dime—it's very mysterious. I know a gifted person, a painter, whose work stands up to every classic model—but he can't put it over the edge.

LOOKING FOR MENTORS

I like success on the outer level, of course, everyone does. But the success inside is the the one that lets you sleep at night and keep moving creatively. I've had both—I speak from my own relative point of view on both levels.

It's very important to look for mentors, teachers. Learn the techniques of teachers. I like dialoguing with mentors, living and dead. I wrote a dialogue once with Socrates. We have all this information inside us. I've done dialogues with people on paper, bringing it into consciousness, from reading about mentors. You read other artists' works—we model ourselves on others we admire. Picasso did it, painted "in the method of" until he learned his own style, found his voice. You need to learn from the greatest in the fields you're interested in.

The most profound mentoring for me is in the printed word and the recorded sound of great performances of music. Reading about people's lives is fascinating—I love biographies and histories. I can't listen to bad singing—if I'm in a restaurant and I don't like the music I ask them to turn it down. We can get bad pollution in our sound environment. Also, there are some people who aren't healthy for us. If people don't make me happy, if they're not a healthy influence, I have a built-in exit line. You have to be very careful with your environment.

DANIELLE LEVI-ALVARES
Yoga teacher

I went to the Kripalu Center in Lenox, Massachusetts, for a weekend of intensive yoga, and I liked their approach to it so much that when I got back to Boston I looked for a list of Kripalu yoga teachers. The one closest to me was Danielle Levi-Alvares, who taught classes in the basement of a church in Cambridge. I went to the classes, and not only did I enjoy Danielle's teaching, I became fascinated by this French woman with a sharp wit and a wide-ranging interest in people, literature, politics, health, and transformation.

Over coffee one day after class, Danielle told me she had studied yoga as a teenager growing up in Paris, but did not take it up again until a friend sent her for a week at the Kripalu Center. She liked the experience so much she went back to take their three-week yoga teacher training program, and started holding her own classes in Cambridge, where she lives with her husband Randy, a doctor and medical researcher.

Danielle said that when she first went to Kripalu she was smoking and drinking, and feeling dissatisfied. After the week there of vegetarian food, yoga, and no tobacco or alcohol, she felt so good she decided to continue that lifestyle and become a teacher of yoga.

I had imagined that Danielle was born teaching yoga and had been a model of health and fitness all her life. When she said she had only taken that route five years before, I was impressed by the powers of human transformation—the way people can create a new life for themselves, and then help others get out of their own ruts and find more satisfying ways of being. In addition to her other work, Danielle recently translated into French a book by the Vietnamese Buddhist monk Thich Naht Hanh, the author of *The Miracle of Mindfulness* and *Being Peace*.

I asked Danielle to speak about creativity in her own life and work.

Look for the way she refreshed herself as a teacher. Is there any way you could refresh your work through a similar approach?

LET'S EXPERIMENT

In my yoga classes, I consider what I do patchworking—I take pieces from different traditions and make a quilt.

I wrote part of a novel but I don't consider writing my creative work— the way I put together my life is my creativity, the way I invent it as I go along. Ask yourself questions—what do I do next?

I'm more creative in my life than when I write a book—I felt a compulsion to write a book—I didn't feel creative. I don't like it, I'm not happy with it. I feel better since I stopped writing—for me it wasn't creative. If I fight with my son and I keep creating the same pattern, and then I stop and say, Let's experiment, and see a way to behave differently—that's creative. Or if I am stuck with a sexual problem, I say, Let's try something else. If a problem arises I go solve it.

As a child I was creative in resisting oppression. I had tuberculosis and was sent to a sanitorium with nuns, Catholic. I was Protestant, and we were made to say Catholic prayers, so I twisted the words into slang, turned the prayer upside down. In the '50s, that way of forcing was the style, but I resisted it creatively.

I was reactively creative as a child, it was my rebellion. I survived creatively.

Kripalu re-empowered me to do things I wanted to do—to play with my life. I was teaching French at Boston College then, just because I was French, and it seemed the thing to do, but I hated it. After I went to Kripalu I realized I didn't have to do it. I could teach yoga and if it didn't work, so what? I could try something else. At Kripalu I learned your life is your life, you can do whatever you want. For me creativity is to take a fresh look at life, play with it.

I'm one of the people who's creating a course with Jon Kabat-Zinn, the author of Full Catastrophe Living. We're creating a course for stress reduction in the inner-city section of Worcester, a Hispanic community that's not schooled in yoga. So this is a challenge, to get these people to reduce stress by meditation and yoga, which they aren't familiar with. We want them to actively look at what happens and get things transformed instead of being passive.

MAKING IT FRESH

We believe meditation is very intellectual and these people are not very intellectual, so we're going to start with more yoga first, it's an easier way to access stillness—through the body rather than through the mind, so we'll do more yoga at first.

Teaching has its ups and downs. When I want to be more creative in my teaching, I stimulate myself through other people in the same field. I rent a yoga video to see how others do it differently—or I sit with my boredom, see what's behind it, what it's able to teach me. I try to be patient with it, and use meditation to come up with ideas.

For a while my yoga workshop seemed stale, so I wanted to know how to make it fresh. The answer was simple—it was more fresh for me if I was in touch with myself. I decided to take the students outside. I said, "Let's get our feet in the mud, don't worry what the neighbors think, let's do a walking meditation in my yard. Let's take a little risk, let's be silly."

My last workshop was very creative. I had given everyone a schedule and I was feeling confined by it, like I had to get everything done that I'd *promised. I had a dream that all the clocks and watches broke, so I told it to my students, and we threw out the schedule. I felt exhilarated—this was a message. We forgot about time, I had them put their watches away, and the whole quality of the workshop was much better. I enjoyed it.*

RABBI HAROLD KUSHNER
Author of When Bad Things Happen to Good People

My old Columbia friend Ivan Gold told me he had met Harold Kushner at a book publication party in Boston, and it turned out the famous rabbi and author was a fellow alumnus of our college and a member of my own class of '55. Ivan got the three of us together for coffee at his apartment in the spring of '88. I learned that in college Kushner had published some stories in the *Columbia Jester*, the humor magazine, but in spite of his youthful interest in writing, had decided to become a rabbi. That happy choice enabled him later in life to combine his writing talent with his learning and experience as a rabbi, to become the most successful and influential spiritual author who had gone to Columbia since Thomas Merton!

I enjoyed Harold's quiet, wry humor and his unassuming manner that combined with a real sense of centeredness and inner strength. I went to one of his services at Temple Israel in Natick, and was impressed with his deft skill as a teacher. He taught his congregation by questioning them, engaging in a kind of spiritual seminar that was entertaining as well as enlightening. Since then, we have met for coffee and dinner, and I was honored to be invited to the ceremony marking his retirement as Rabbi of Temple Israel and honoring his new title— not of Rabbi Emeritus, as would ordinarily be the case, but more befitting his accomplishment and his continuing work, Rabbi Laureate.

I consider him a friend, and his generosity extends to inviting me every summer to join him for Red Sox games in his excellent seats behind third base as a season ticket holder. It was before a Red Sox game that we met to have coffee and talk about creativity. I told him about Michael Jordan's theory about "the zone," the athlete's experience of being able to "do it all," almost to score at will, to feel completely in the flow of the game.

Notice how Rabbi Kushner's faith plays a part in his creative work.

LOCATION HELPS

Getting access to creativity is partly like what Michael Jordan said about the zone, that you have to let it come to you. It's like being hit by lightning, you can't just go out and summon it.

There's a rabbinic commentary on the Psalms that says when the title is "A Psalm of David," it means David had a great idea and he sat down and wrote the psalm. When it says "To David a Psalm," it means he didn't have an idea but he just started writing. That is my experience. There are times when I've written very pedestrian material, then had a really creative thought that I'd never have thought of if I hadn't disciplined myself to sit down at my desk and start writing.

When I was a rabbi I'd do difficult writing in the morning. If I didn't get it by ten-thirty or eleven it wouldn't get done. I'd do that early and do administrative or pastoral work later in the day. I started at nine or nine-thirty, after morning prayers and breakfast.

If I get stuck, I read something else, someone else's work. Getting involved in other people's thought processes will trigger something in my own. It doesn't matter what is is, whatever book is on my shelf at the time.

Yes, I think creativity is spiritual. Absolutely. Creativity is a synonym for inspiration. One of the most profound religious experiences I have is to find myself in possession of an idea and not know where it came from. I'll be trying to convey some difficult material in my writing and suddenly it comes clear to me what I need to say and how to say it. I feel awe when this happens, it's an inspiring experience. I don't know where it comes from—I'm tempted to say it comes from God. For me this is an experience of divine self-disclosure—it's the intellectual version of a person having to do something that's very hard and suddenly finding she has the qualities of soul to enable her to do it that she never had before.

CHARITY AS PRAYER

Suzette [Rabbi Kushner's wife] noticed I do something I hadn't been aware of. Before I write a new chapter I write a check to a charitable organization. I thought I was just clearing my desk, clearing another piece of paper off my desk before I started writing, but when Suzette pointed it out, I realized it was a kind of prayer. I saw Suzette was right.

Now that I'm retired from the active rabbinate it's much easier to write.

Even when I was working part-time as a rabbi, that work was an investment of emotion, energy, and imagination that left less for writing. The only advantage of being a rabbi was to have more people sharing their life experiences and giving me raw material—that kept my books from being abstract intellectualism. When I retired I took thirty years of experience with me, so I'm still mining that vein.

In Hebrew, creativity, or inspiration, means the Holy Spirit—not as in Christianity where it may mean the third part of the Trinity. It's referred to hundreds of times in the Talmud. Probably always the Holy Spirit takes the initiative. I don't know any case of a person invoking the Holy Spirit. It comes on its own schedule, not yours. There are all sorts of disciplines for invoking a sense of mystical insight—how do you make this appear? I'm uncomfortable with that. It's something like Sir James Frazer's distinction between magic and religion—magic is using God, religion is serving God. That's my objection to astrology, necromancy. Theologically, I don't think you can see the future. Traditional Judaism sees that as arrogance—it's like picking God's pocket.

CREATIVE COUNSELING

You use creativity as a rabbi—I used it on counseling my congregation. In my book Who Needs God? I describe how, aside from fixed times in liturgy and prayer, the time I really pray is when I open the door of my office to a member of the congregation. I ask God to show me how I can help her. She's come thinking I can help her, and there are plenty of times I feel stumped, then suddenly I come up with an insight of what she really needs to be told and needs to do. It's the same feeling, the same process as in writing, when that inspiration comes.

In my new book [To Life!] I write how Martin Buber said that insight can come out of meeting with no words—there are times when you meet someone and if you're open you get the message without anything being spoken. You can meet someone with an illness and know what it feels like, or know how to appreciate your own health and physical condition; a father can look at a newborn child and know what it means to be a father. Buber says the Revelation on Sinai was like that—God didn't have to shout. That meeting was what opened up the Israelites' souls to understand what they'd never understood before.

At five A.M., in that state between half sleeping and half waking, the *title and first sentence of my first book came to me. After that, I essentially wrote the book.*

MARY BETH COUDAL
Stand-up comic, writer

Mary Beth Coudal took a Spiritual Autobiography workshop I gave at Auburn Theological Seminary, and we got to be buddies. I've watched her do stand-up in basements of obscure clubs and basement hangouts around New York, getting funnier and more confident and original, moving up to aboveground performing at Caroline's Comedy Club, the New York Comedy Club, Stand-Up New York, Crazy Nanny's, and CBGB's Improv Group, while she works by day as a consultant for the Women's Division of the Methodist Church. She produced and hosted forty half hours of a talk show she created on Manhattan Public Access Television called "Mary Beth and Friends" that I'd put up against anything on the networks.

IS MENTAL ILLNESS CREATIVE?

When I was a kid, my Norwegian grandmother told me, "Oh, you can't be an actress, it will lead to divorce and an unstable life." But my mother signed me up for drama classes at a summer drama camp in Park Ridge, Illinois, when I was nine. That's where I met my best friend Colette Hawley, who's a singer. Every assignment we ever got—from our fifth grade science project on houseplants to our social studies report on Louis XVI—we turned into a singing and dancing extravaganza. Colette and I were always compulsively creative.

When "Sesame Street" and "Electric Company" came out, I learned all the songs. I loved singing Oscar's song "I Love Trash" really loud. In school when all the other kids were just singing the song timidly, I belted it out, and I got a lot of attention. And I liked it.

In junior high, I got a lot of attention when I was the first girl president of the student council. That's when women's lib started, too, and I was into it. Then in high school, I was on the student council again and the school paper, and in all the plays and musicals. With friends, I wrote comedy skits and song parodies. "The hills are alive with the sound of mucus—huck tooey." That kind of thing.

In high school we partied, too. All of us drama freaks shared a subculture from the movie Animal House. We had toga parties and called drinking parties "benders." People tried smoking pot, too. I tried smoking pot in eighth grade—to no effect. In high school, it was the suburban thing to do when someone's parents were out of town—to go to their house and have a bender.

In college, a lot of my friends were doing a lot of creative stuff—making movies, writing plays and poetry. And a lot of people had problems, too—eating disorders, heavy drinking, and sleeping all day. We all slept a lot, too—we slept and read.

Mental illness was common, and I did associate that with creativity. I had a friend who was supposed to be psychotic. It was interesting to have a playwright friend who lived on the edge. He was wild and fun; he used K-Y Jelly to gel his hair. Then he tried to commit suicide, and we realized how messed up he really was. Eventually, it became a lot of work and worry. After his third attempt to kill himself, we were just so scared, upset, and exhausted! After psychoactive drugs and psychotherapy, he got a girlfriend and stopped writing. But maybe writing and having friends had helped cure him, too. In my personal mythology, now that he's "normal"—he's a successful businessman—he's not really as creative anymore. We glamorized his mental illness; he seemed so cool, living the tragic artist's persona, a Tennessee Williams–like playwright with a tormented soul. But it wasn't cool. It was just awful. Especially for him.

If playwrights could lose control, filmmakers couldn't. A lot of my friends were in film school, and I acted (or overacted) in their films. Some people idolized Steven Spielberg because he was young and had all this power. The image of the true artist was someone who didn't give up control of the movie or artistic project. I graduated from NYU in '84.

I'd heard since high school that drinking loosened you up, freed you in ways to get to the unconscious. But the myth doesn't ring true for me, though I do have guy friends who still romanticize the power of drinking as a way to get in touch with the muse. In comedy clubs, you'll still hear men comics brag about drinking and then having the best gig of their lives. I'm like, "Yeah, right. What have you been smoking?"

I've met some of my artist friends in New York at Twelve Step meetings.

A lot of the entertainment industry's into self-help stuff. It's a great source for material—you have to change the names, of course. So many writers and actors—and well-known ones—get help from Twelve Step meetings and spiritual programs, but you rarely hear about that in the media. But artists do need a lot of support. Anywhere you can find help, you should get it. The real world just doesn't support you the way meetings do.

I belong to Marble Collegiate Church and church's great, too. There's an artists' meeting at Marble every Monday night. Sometimes a hundred people come. There are Bible studies, discussions, sharing of common problems, ways of envisioning success for yourself and then doing it. Exercises like writing down what you want to be doing in five years and then putting it in a prayer box. If you're performing, you announce it, so people can come. For my last gig at Crazy Nanny's, I sent ARTS an announcement that was listed in their newsletter. A lot of people came. People like helping each other. People there have booked me for gigs, too—recently one at a supper club in Soho. It's easier to take creative risks if you know you have a community of artists behind you. I've never taken a risk creatively that didn't pay off in some way.

I work sometimes with Emmy Gay, a fellow comic. We met in this multiracial improv group. And even though we're from diverse backgrounds—she's Caribbean African American—we share a common feminist sense of humor. It's great to work with Emmy; we've gotten each other loads of work. We help each other set goals. Like Emmy had a goal once of writing thirty jokes a day for a week. It helps to have a buddy to report your progress and read your stuff to.

Lately, I find it easier to do stand-up than write a novel. With fiction you don't know if what you write will ever see the light of day. I like the instant gratification of comedy. And yeah, the attention. It's like in your Spiritual Autobiography workshop, where you write and then you read aloud—you know you've got an audience. You know your voice is gonna be heard.

I have a prayer I read before writing and performing. I pray to God to make me an instrument—help me let go of my ego and surrender to the creative process.

The first time I was booked to do stand-up in a club—instead of just an open mike night—I said this passage from the Upanishads over and over as I was walking to the comedy club. It was something like, "God walks before me, God walks beside me, God walks behind me, God walks above me, God walks below me"—so it's like you're never alone.

Maybe it's God—a creative and creator God—who works through friends, support groups, and even comedy to make a person Godlike—creative and creator, too. And unlike what Grandma told me, life as a performer doesn't make you unstable.

MARK MATOUSEK

Journalist, editor, columnist for Common Boundary *magazine, author of the memoir* Sex Death Enlightenment

Mark Matousek stepped off the fast track of New York celebrity journalism as a bright young editor of Andy Warhol's *Interview* magazine in the mid-1980s, and turned to a spiritual path in order to discover a new way of living and writing. When I came down from Boston to live in New York for a while, our mutual friend, journalist and playwright Barbara Graham, introduced me to Mark. As a fellow writer and Greenwich Village neighbor he welcomed me and offered to help me get a desk in the Writers Room here. We met for breakfast at a Hudson Street coffeehouse to talk about creativity.

THE BEAUTIFUL, FAMOUS, AND RICH

I always wrote, but I wasn't serious about it till my junior year in college, at Berkeley. I didn't fall into the myth about drinking or drugs leading to creativity, simply because I've never been able to do anything stoned or drunk. My mythology revolved around poverty—to be an artist you had to take a vow of destitution. The underlying belief was, you couldn't make a living writing what you really wanted to write.

I started as a beginning editor at Newsweek, *and I lasted six months. It was a corporate atmosphere, you couldn't progress according to talent, you had to wait your turn on the corporate ladder, and I never had the patience. I freelanced for Reuters, was their theater critic for a while, then I joined* Interview *and worked there from '84 to '86. I started as a staff writer, became a senior editor. I could meet and interview anyone I wanted, if they fell into one of the following categories—they had to be famous, beautiful, rich, or notorious. I've never been a groupie, but it was fun to be able to meet whoever I wanted to meet. Andy was still alive and the magazine had real cachet. It was a powerful feeling for a kid—I was only twenty-six. I interviewed writers I admired, like Gore Vidal, Kurt Vonnegut, Lawrence Durrell.*

I was working twelve hours a day, and climbing the masthead. I wasn't doing much creative writing then—first I needed to know what it felt like to have a job with some authority.

One day, I happened to interview Andrew Harvey [author of the spiritual classics Journey in Ladakh *and* Hidden Journey*] and he told me I was wasting my life. I had this great job, but creatively I was nowhere. I was lost between needing to earn a living and being dazzled by my own success. I don't regret that time. I learned a lot, but it was "off the path" for me.*

I'm a "fallen Jew," from an agnostic Jewish family. I had a bar mitzvah, but it was only a ploy to make money. At the time I met Andrew I was an atheist. I felt deeply unhappy, lost, with no interior life. I was hungry but I didn't know what I was hungry for. After meeting Andrew I quit my job and went with him to India. First we stopped in Germany to see an Indian teacher named Mother Meera. Meeting Mother initiated a process in me that's still going on. The experience of being in holy company for the first time was even more powerful than the three months we spent in India.

When I came back to the States I started exploring different practices— yoga, Buddhist meditation, chants, contemplation, meeting various masters. Before I could really claim Mother Meera as a focal teacher, I needed to do this wandering for five or six years. It is not Mother's way to tell the people who visit her what they should do. There is no ashram, and practice consists of a few minutes of silent meditation per day. Mother says if you can sit silently five minutes a day your life can change. It's a matter of starting small, then integrating simple practices into your life in a realistic way.

I do yoga and meditation as often as I can manage. I'm not trying to be a "super yogi." Reading is a big part of my practice—wisdom literature of all kinds. If I don't sit for half an hour in the morning doing this kind of reading, it affects my state of mind. I need the dharma to ground me.

Spiritual practice has challenged me to look at what I think about love— to think of places where I was closed, where my body wasn't attached to my heart. It's a gradual process of bringing them together.

GENET AS A MODEL

I haven't been discriminated against for being gay. It's always been to my advantage. I've never found a job through a résumé. The man who hired me at Interview was a friend of my lover at the time. My models as writers were Genet, Beckett, Vidal. Genet more than anyone. He combined homosexuality and poetry, graphic sex, and lyricism. He could write about the eros of men loving men. He showed me that you could be gay and a criminal and be a great artist.

I had been in jail three times before I was eighteen. I grew up in the San Fernando Valley. They found some pot in my locker in high school—just a few joints—and the police came into my history classroom while I was taking a test, put handcuffs on me, and took me away. I assaulted a policeman at sixteen, and I also was arrested for drunk driving. I was a mess. There were three years there when I could have gone off the deep end.

When I hit twenty I stopped doing drugs. I had done every recreational drug—never heroin—and I just got sick of it. Occasionally I smoked pot over the years, but nothing more.

I've gotten over my myth about the vow of poverty. I'm finally making some money. There's a certain amount of paying your dues that one must do as a writer finding his own voice. I certainly needed to go out on a limb, go for broke. I felt there wasn't any other way. I think all of us go through a period of doing without, unless you have a personal income. But the myth of impoverishment was not one I cared to live with forever.

I write every day from seven till about noon or one o'clock. If I can get in four good hours of writing a day I'm doing great. I never work after lunch. What do I do the rest of the day? My life! I like a balance. I get up, make a cup of coffee, and start. If I'm stuck, I let it rest till the next day. You learn to have a sense of whether you're "full" or not. If I feel drained, I walk away from it. But I show up every day. I used to sit and beat my head against the wall if nothing was coming, but now I walk away. When I force it, eke it out, it tends to be pretty bad anyway.

I have a community of support, a lot of writer friends. Now I'm learning to let people read things. I used to be so anal about my work, no one saw it before I thought it was perfect. Now I let two or three people read the stuff in progress and talk to them on a regular basis. I need the encouragement of my friends.

CLAIRE DOUGLAS

Jungian therapist, author of Woman in the Mirror:
Analytical Psychology and the Feminine, *and*
Translating this Darkness: The Life of Christiana Morgan

A friend in New York spoke highly about a Jungian analyst she knew who was in Cambridge for a year on a Bunting Fellowship at Radcliffe, researching and writing a book on a woman who had been a disciple of Jung. I met Claire Douglas, and found her as interesting and winning as the introduction to her first book, in which she tells of two dreams that helped her write it when at first she was stymied. She recounts the two dreams, gives her interpretation of them, and explains that she learned from their message that in the writing, "I have to be alert to the tone, to recognize what maims creativity and self-esteem, what hurts a woman's soul and needs to be changed in light of present social and cultural conditions."

I wanted to hear how someone so sensitive to tone, and to the value of creativity, used them in her own work as an analyst and a writer.

Watch for the methods she uses to access her own creativity.

THERAPY AS MUSIC

Being a therapist is like playing a musical instrument—with training, and a gift, an hour with a patient can be like an incredible musical composition. It's interesting, there's a very delicate attunement.

No, I don't play a musical instrument—but yes, I do see patients.

There's an art to it—it requires a creative sensibility of some sort. It's like playing one's soul, and with another person's soul—it's a duet.

My idea of creativity is tied up with Jung's four functions. People are either extrovert or introvert—either go out towards or let it resonate. There are thinking people who say the whole meaning is in thinking, sensitive people who are intuitive. Feeling people see possibilities—is it good, bad, right, wrong? For me, for most people, one of these functions is predominant. For me, it's thinking.

I'm a thinking type, and also intuitive. My creativity lies in my feeling function—it's primitive, uneducated, awkward. It's the undeveloped part that didn't get squelched in childhood.

WRITING DOWN DREAMS

When I want to get access to my own creativity, I write down dreams, and meditate. I don't meditate for that purpose, but during meditation it happens, ideas come. When I want to get unstuck I read people I love—late-nineteenth-century writers, Edith Wharton and Henry James. When writing is hard I read them, and I read poetry.

In therapy you pay great attention, relaxed attention, like you do in writing. You're open to many different things at once—what the patient is saying, how their body looks, and you're asking yourself questions. What is transference? Is it projection? Also, you're just being patiently aware, in a meditative state, and at the same time—not trying!

IVAN GOLD

Novelist, teacher, author of Nickel Miseries,
Sick Friends, *and* Sams in a Dry Season

I met Ivan Gold in Mark Van Doren's class in The Narrative Art when we both were students at Columbia in 1953. I have been a friend and a fan of Ivan's since Columbia days. Several years ago we worked in cubicles across the aisle from one another in the Writers Room in Boston, where one day I asked him to take a break and talk about his own experience with the muse of creativity. I began by asking how he had ended a twenty-year drought that followed the publication of his first novel.

Look for what role community plays in Ivan's return to writing. How does he use other people's writing as inspiration?

ONE IS NOT ALONE

Starting to write again after you've been stuck for a long time has got to do with love, confidence—affirmation from the world that you're not barking up the wrong tree. Everyone is creative, but a commitment of that size— writing a novel—is hard to make in a vacuum. The sense that one is not alone is needed. Also, the love of literature has to survive one's inability to produce it.

I just found a new novelist—I mean discovered her for myself. I'd never heard of Ellen Gilchrist—then I read her book The Anna Papers, *and I* was floored. Your own creative sense is affirmed when you find prose that can move you. Rereading King Lear and Don Quixote do it, too.

My son Ian brings home poems from his classes at UMass Boston— Bishop, Dickinson, Keats. Suddenly I want to read them, to fill the well again.

The sense that you might be creative starts early—it was implanted by my mother when I was really small—and then there is always the opposite— the world is always correcting you. It depends on which message is in ascendance in any given week, and whether I get any work done.

I keep a journal; even in the lean years I kept it. Even when the book is going well I keep it. I segue from the events of my day to the aesthetic task. Since I write autobiographically anyway, I make entries to get the memory down. Also, I like to stop work when it's going well—it's like stopping eating while you're still hungry—sort of like Hemingway is said to have stopped work every day in the middle of a sentence. Of course, that can be a ruse at times, an excuse to walk away, so when I'm in the Writers Room I don't just go home when I hit that point, I wander around. This is a good place for wandering, as you know. Sometimes I get in a few more lines.

In the lean years, when I wasn't publishing fiction, I was still writing. I made false starts, filled pages, but nothing went anywhere. To keep the world apprised of my existence, until the gift returned, if it was meant to, I wrote book reviews. It was a strategy.

In '85 I started writing anonymous pieces—I wanted to say something about my experience in AA to define my relationship to it. It was important to them that I use a pseudonym. Anonymity—it's Alcoholics Anonymous after all—was significant. I wrote a piece about AA's fiftieth anniversary celebration in Montreal in 1985 for the Boston Globe Sunday Magazine. They said I'd have to use my real name—they only granted anonymity to creative mafioso. I was going to withdraw the piece, but they had a change of heart. Later, in Sams in a Dry Season, I gave myself permission to write fiction about AA and use my own name.

I envy fluency—people who write easily, and often, and well. Not deathless prose, perhaps, but something useful frequently gets said.

THE PANIC STOPS

At some point I gave up panic. If I was meant to write again, I would, if not, not. Through it all friends, many of them writers, were affirming and *kind. It also helped enormously, during the lean years, to have a working wife—it's a great boon to dormant creativity.*

Raising a son may be the most creative thing I've ever done. Of course, I plan one day to write about it—life-as-possible-material sustains the writer through the darkest times. On the other hand, if I'd been less tolerant of indolence, I like to think I "coulda been a contender"—maybe you should mention that.

ELAINE PAGELS
Theologian, professor of religion at Princeton University, and author of The Gnostic Gospels; Adam, Eve, and the Serpent; *and* The Origin of Satan

I had admired Elaine Pagels's books for their clarity and grace as well as their theological—and human—insight, and I was pleased to meet her a year ago at an informal dinner in New York of people interested in discussing religious and spiritual subjects. I was even more pleased to be invited to talk to the students in her religion seminar at Princeton, and lead them in one of the exercises from my workshop, Spiritual Autobiography. We had lunch before the class, and I asked her to tell me about her own experience of creativity in writing her remarkable books.

See how a historian of religion deals with her own fear.

BOULDERS IN A STREAM

When I was writing The Gnostic Gospels *I realized I didn't have to write the book. What I had to say was already present, in my relationship to the material, but it was difficult to allow it to break free. I felt as if I had to move huge boulders from a stream. The difficulty in writing the book was not in making it up—the difficulty was in letting it out. Writing clarifies our relationship with a subject. I don't know why doing it is so difficult. It's very hard for me to write. I write every sentence several times; to make it conscious is very hard work.*

I take my fear in my hands, sit down and deal with the resistance to it, which is sometimes enormous—and I'm resolved I'm going to sit there two to four hours and struggle, whether anything comes or not. The resistance is

quite intense—but the resistance gets less as I continue the work. I'm work-
ing on it in dreams. Sometimes it emerges there.

    I wanted to be a poet—I started writing at thirteen, fourteen, fifteen.
I'm a failed poet.

    It's lonely—it's important to have people in your life who know what
it's all about—I know they're there.

EVANS WOOLLEN
Architect

I've known Evans Woollen and his family since I was in high school,
and admired them all. Evans Junior, known as "Chub," the oldest of
three children of Lydia and the late Evans Woollen, graduated from
the Hotchkiss School, received his B.A. at Yale, and his master's degree from the Yale University School of Architecture. He apprenticed
with architect Philip Johnson in New Canaan, Connecticut, where he
subsequently practiced before returning to Indianapolis and establish-
ing his own office in 1955. His firm of Woollen, Molzan and Partners
today specializes in housing, libraries, buildings for the performing and
fine arts, and academic structures.

    Through the years, in visits to my hometown of Indianapolis, I
have heard people speak with pride of Evans Woollen and his work—
work that is known and praised outside of Indiana. His award-winning
works range from the Benedictine monastery of St. Meinrad's in
southern Indiana, to Clowes Hall for the Performing Arts at Butler
University in Indianapolis, to the Hotchkiss School in Lakeville, Connecticut.

    On a visit to Indianapolis I called Evans and asked if I could stop
by his house and ask him about what inspires a person to become an
architect, and how creativity plays a part in that profession. On a later
visit to Indianapolis, I had lunch with Evans and heard about a trip he
was planning. He had won a frequent flyer award for a free round-trip
ticket to any destination in the world—but he had to use the ticket
within the month. He decided he would turn his work schedule upside
down and take out two weeks to go to a place he had never been but
always wanted to go—Japan. He would take only what he could fit

into his backpack, and stay in Buddhist monasteries. He was leaving in a few days on what I knew would be a marvelous journey of discovery.

As you read this interview, look for the ways in which an architect uses creativity like a writer or painter.

BUILDING SAND CASTLES

My mother was the stimulus for my interest in architecture. I got an interest in form from her—I got nothing of that order from my father. We usually don't stop to think about where that stimulus comes from. My mother was always talking about buildings. From the earliest time I can remember she pointed out buildings, what their age was, whether they were funny, or awesome, or awkward—she looked for the impact or meaning of a building. Sometimes she'd laugh, or even pout, in response to a particular building. That interested me very much, and I'd look still closer. My practice as an architect began in the sandpile. When we went to the beach, if I was missing, my parents knew where I was. And I got reinforcement. People would peer down at my sand castles and say, "Oh, he's going to be an architect!" And I went on to model airplanes. At one point, when it became clear this was really what I was going to do, my father, a banker, said very gravely, "If you have to be an architect, you had better be a good one." I think he felt it was the sort of profession in which you might just have a bank account, but it was questionable.

In terms of getting access to creativity, it's very important for me to clear the deck mentally—to be able to direct energy toward just the problem or subject at hand—not to be loaded with relationships or material things. The more I can get those things away from me, the more fun I'll have working out the problem. It's a matter of flow—of removing blocks of any kind. Maybe people think drinking is a way of removing the blocks—I never got into that.

Synonymous with creativity in architecture is the unfolding meaning—it didn't have meaning before, it needs something said. It takes a lot of dream time. If you're dealing with places and spirit of place, you have to immerse yourself in it—summon up things from the past, see what's on sight now. You hope your building says something that has continuity—that wraps it up again. Guy Davenport, the literary critic and professor of English at the University of Kentucky, has a book called Every Force Evolves a Form.

It's true in literature, maybe in all the arts—every great thing is based on something that preceded it. It's a new view of an old theme. Many architects in the modern era lost sight of that—they thought things could be done cut off from the past.

Architecture is a creative act—leaving yourself free enough from the business of the world to summon up what buildings evoke from the distant past—even Stonehenge—it's part of the collective conversation of people's vision of standing forms.

We used to be taught to be embarrassed by predecessors—a childish re-action, like "You copied." It was downright ridiculous.

THE NEED TO BE ALONE

When I'm working I have a schizophrenic need to be away from every-body—and then alternately to be back with the people I'm working with. I'm stimulated by the reaction of others—but then I have to have complete isolation.

When you put up ideas for a building to an audience of five people, some-thing wonderful happens. I'm suddenly mentally putting myself in their shoes, seeing the building from their eyes. I'm no longer myself, I'm everybody else in the room. Interesting things pop out at me I hadn't seen by myself.

Architecture is a much more social act than writing—you have to win over the client. There are extremely talented people who withered in the profession because they weren't outgoing enough to win clients. The actual creation in architecture—the creative time—is, proportionately, seemingly minuscule. But it's what you live for, it's why you do the other things. Ten percent of our time is golden time—we envy painters because it's just them and the canvas. In architecture you have to make others part of the creative process, make them feel it is indeed theirs.

You know the solution exists somewhere—in some collective unconscious, and it's up to you to find it. Ridding the mind of other things—finding solu-tions—it's rather mysterious.

It's coming through you, only—it's not knowing where it's coming from. It's a kind of spiritual thing—part of why I think good solutions have their own life—they were born entering here, in me.

I've gone to clients and lived with them—I don't put pencil to paper until I know them. At a school or college I say, "Give me a room on campus, ac-cess to talk to as many people as possible." I'm much better prepared to draw—and draw on—living people and their mind-sets. I have a feeling about environment. Sometimes institutions don't like that, they don't want you to talk to people, they'd like your inspiration to come from only one or two people.

St. Meinrads, on the Ohio River, is the second-largest Benedictine congregation. They gave me a cell, let me live their life. I got up at four A.M. and went to the offices, and in between I talked to the monks, went to meals—I couldn't have begun without that experience. What would I have based it on otherwise, a country club? Not being a Roman Catholic, I had to immerse myself in that, too.

While I was living there I had a dream about the form of the monastery. I later told the monks that dream, and I found a receptive audience. Some clients would never have wanted to hear about my dreams. The dream in this instance revealed the form—I saw the monastery as the island. The natural landscape of hills around it forms an island, although there is no water. The form of the monastery later came out of that—the dream was ancestor of the result. St. Meinrad's was a wonderful experience.

A SON'S PRODDING

It was also a wonderful experience at Hotchkiss, the school my father and I went to. My boys went to it, too. I had cut off my feelings from the place, having come back from the East to Indiana. My son Ian wanted to go there. He saw it on a tour with a boys choir. In '72 he had been in school at Hotchkiss a year, and he told me the school was going to go co-ed and they were going to build new buildings and I should try to get the job of designing them. I explained to him I was unknown to them, and there were many good architects available in Connecticut, throughout New England, but he insisted I call the headmaster and ask for an interview.

The headmaster said, "We're really through with our interviews, but if you want to come in, we'll see you." I went to the school three hours early and went to the library. Ian had told me there was a certain shelf with committee reports on co-education, and he told me to read them all. I did, and it was wonderful. After reading them I sailed into the interview with an "insider" feeling. I wasn't going to get it, so I would just have fun—be loose as a goose.

The headmaster said, "Which of the new buildings do you want to be considered for?" I said, "All of them." I told him, "I don't want to work

*here unless I live here first and make a master plan and see how the buildings
impinge on me. Give me a room in the Infirmary—I'll do a master plan over
a two-month period." No one had said that before—he had interviewed
five people. They chose us. I worked from '72 to '85—continually working
on some building. It was very satisfying, it was like fortifying the whole,
knitting it together.*

*You can't produce a photo of the Parthenon and say, Here's what hap-
pened—you have to live there. So place is more important than the individual structure. The whole assemblage is a kind of place—I don't think there's
any analogy in literature.*

*My son pushed me into the Hotchkiss experience. He has an "any-
thing's possible" attitude.*

ALAN NOLAN
Attorney, novelist, and Civil War historian, author of As
Sounding Brass, The Iron Brigade, *and* Lee Considered

I met Alan Nolan in 1967 when I went to my old high school in Indianapolis to talk to young people about the Vietnam War, as part of a
whole issue of the *Atlantic Monthly* I was writing called *Supernation at
Peace and War*. I interviewed his son Pat, who was president of the
student council, and he told me I ought to meet his dad, who was also
a writer, as well as a lawyer and a great guy. It was the first time I'd
heard a young man of that era say his father was a great guy. I was intrigued, and went home with Pat to meet his dad, Alan Nolan.

I decided Alan was not only a great guy but one of the few people
I'd ever met who might live up to the title of Renaissance Man. As
well as being a successful lawyer—he became chairman of the biggest
law firm in Indianapolis—he was a founding member of the Indiana
chapter of the American Civil Liberties Union, which was a radical
act in the Indianapolis of the 1950s, when Senator McCarthy was
spearheading the "Red Scare" of the era. The group was barred from
meeting in the Indiana War Memorial because of allegations it was
"pinko," and the ruckus brought Edward R. Murrow to the city to tape
a program on the controversy.

Nolan is a practicing and parish-active Roman Catholic, and

father of eight children. He and his family stayed in the house they lived in when the neighborhood was becoming integrated and many families with children in school fled to the all-white suburbs. Nolan was proud that his children continued to go to Shortridge High School when it became fully integrated. One of his sons was in the last class to graduate before the school was closed as part of a local school board consolidation and later converted to a junior high. The Nolan house was a center for kids during those years—girls and boys, black and white, enjoying a continuous welcome inside and out, where a basketball game always seemed to be in progress at the backboard in the driveway. (One of Nolan's daughters played varsity basketball in college.)

Somehow, between fathering and lawyering, Alan found time to write not only a very good novel called *As Sounding Brass*, but also a prize-winning book of Civil War history, *The Iron Brigade*. Several years after the death of his wife Betty in 1967, Alan married Jane DeVoe, a young widow who had three children of her own, and the families, (including Alan's five children) were joined together in the same house. Even with this increase in the domestic population, and attendant responsibilities, Alan somehow managed to write another highly acclaimed book on the Civil War, *Lee Considered*. It drew rave reviews, as well as angry reactions from Lee partisans, one of whom sent a letter to Civil War buffs urging them not to buy the book, and if they already had, to burn it!

In spite of such Confederate criticism, Nolan has also become a distinguished lecturer on the Civil War at universities and history clubs around the country. The last time I was in Indianapolis I asked him what I've wondered for years: How does he find time to do all he does, and do it so well, and where does he get the creative energy for all of it?

Look for how Nolan's different professions nurture each other rather than detract from his creativity.

WRITING AS ESCAPE

My mother [Jeannette Covert Nolan] was a writer—she wrote over fifty books. There's a whole shelf of them up there. She used to say that only 2 percent of writers do only writing—the others are teachers, lawyers, doctors, whatever. She was one of the 2 percent.

Writing has been an escape for me—retrospectively I can see that through writing I've escaped a lot of contentiousness, of having to deal with people. People spark conflict—writing is something to look forward to that detaches you from the conflict of life.

When I'm working as a lawyer I'm talking to a client about a problem—but there's another track going in my head all the time. I'm really thinking about other stuff, and I'm incorporating his character—the client— what he says or how he says it—into the ongoing process.

With historical writing I've got a thesis and I'm ready to start writing again. I start reading a lot. I took on Lee as a mythological figure—he was an expression of the whole myth of the Civil War. Now I want to write a whole book on the mythology of the Civil War. There are things like this that get ahold of you and that's what you think about. Though you're dealing with unrelated, mundane things, you can take a legal pad after a meeting with clients and put down some good ideas on whatever it is you're writing, and stick it in your pocket.

I started out as a "battles and leaders" man—now I'm not interested in retelling a well-known story, now I'm interested in going behind what everyone thinks happened. If it did happen that way, fine, and if not, it piques my interest—it's the revisionist approach to history. I get interested—feverish, almost—in digging it out, finding the story.

BREAKING THE RULES

The more you read, the more you're motivated to write. I remember being released by reading The Catcher in the Rye, realizing you don't have to follow all the rules imposed by an educational process. It gives you the courage to try something of your own. Reading J. P. Donleavy's The Ginger Man, I realized you didn't have to have a subject and a predicate. In legal writing I've been something of a novelist and gotten away with it. I don't follow the "whereas" forms, I just tell the story.

I started as a kid to read Civil War stuff—my great-grandfather was in the Civil War. My dad had a strong sense of the family escaping the famine in Ireland and making it to the U.S. My dad was patriotic. He took me to Gettysburg and Antietam when I was in the eighth grade. So I got interested in the Civil War right off the bat.

Finding time to write is different with young children at home. With children you do the best you can—it may be weeks that you don't touch your writing. In wintertime, there are days on weekends when you can get four to six hours. And you've got evenings, when small kids are at home. Now that the kids are gone, I can put in four hours a night.

Of course, you're driven to do it, and everything else falls away. You become not a good citizen—there's a tension between "real life" and the drive to do this thing. Writing is an enormous ego trip—the charm of it is you're doing it yourself.

There's a detachment—almost like the writing comes unconsciously. It's a flow—there are times when it goes, and sometimes you're dead.

When it's dead, when things are not going, I'm an outliner. I say, what the hell do I want to do? I get out a yellow pad and start Roman numeraling what's next. That pushes me back into approaching it. Lots of it, you abandon. You never know how much is baloney or is useful, you just get it down.

STUDS TERKEL
Radio host, author of Division Street, Hard Times, The Good War, Race

I met Studs Terkel when he interviewed me on his radio program in Chicago in 1968. I was amazed that he had not only read my recent book, he had underlined passages, as if studying for an exam. He was the most thorough interviewer I ever met, and the most congenial host, not only at the station, but in his home, where he invited me to come after the interview and have a chicken dinner with him and his wife Ida. I have always looked forward to being on his show when I've been on a book tour. Studs continues to be as creative a radio journalist as he is a writer and popular historian. When I went on his show to talk about Returning: A Spiritual Journey, he had found a record of the old hymn "What a Friend I Have in Jesus" to play as introduction, and asked me how I had felt about the hymn when I was a young atheist, and how I felt about it now as a Christian who had returned to church. Now, that's creative interviewing!

Look for the themes that spark Studs Terkel's creative impulse.

"WHAT IT WAS LIKE"

Andre Shiffrin, my editor, plays a big role in my creativity—in my books. That's how I began—Andre called up. He'd read some interviews I did on South Africa, and he said he liked them—something hit him. He said, "How about doing interviews about an American village—Chicago—how it's changed—by interviewing people, telling their stories?" And I did Division Street.

Then Andre called one day and he brought up the Depression. He said, "Kids today don't know about the Depression—they have no sense of the past, of what it was like to be alive at certain times." That haunted me—it was oral, connected to my work on radio. I talk to people—I realized kids had no idea what it was like. They read in history books about the New Deal, or how war broke out—but it's not told like: "When father came home at two o'clock with his toolbox on his shoulder," or what it was like when the strikes began, when the CIO was organized. That became Hard Times.

Race—the black and white—that was my own idea—getting ordinary black and white people to tell the truth, to say, "What do you really think?" Through all these books it's getting to what it was like to live at a time, what it felt like.

I do it haphazardly, the interviews, then finally when I'm near the end, I take three months off, I don't get out of my pajamas. I play the tapes here, listen again, go over them. I'm like a gold prospector—that's me. I hear about a person, I go see them—that's my strike. Like a gold prospector, I come up with rough ore—that's the sixty or so pages—that's like tons. Now the prospector starts sifting. That's a dangerous moment, how you edit—the idea is to highlight what's said—to get the gold dust. How you edit comes down to maybe eight pages of gold dust. Now comes the molding of the gold. I rearrange to make it flow more, but I never alter the words, and I only use my own words in the introduction.

ODETTE BERY
Chef, Another Season *Restaurant, Beacon Hill, Boston; author of* Another Season Cookbook

Odette Bery's restaurant Another Season was one of the attractions of the Beacon Hill neighborhood I lived in during the '80s and into the

'90s. Odette's cookbook also drew rave reviews, and one of the notices called her "an outstanding cooking teacher and a sophisticated creator." I knew she was a good teacher because I took one of her courses in French cooking at the Boston Center for Adult Education, in which she proved as entertaining as she was instructive. I knew she was a true creator because not only was the food she cooked for her restaurant first-rate, she created a new menu every month.

I thought about what kind of imagination it must take to come up with original recipes for a whole new menu every month. I decided to stop by Another Season and talk to Odette about her work.

See how cooking is like the other creative arts, in the way a chef thinks about her work.

SKILLS COME FIRST

I grew up in London, and I was interested in art and theater from an early age. I attended drama school during vacation times. I wanted to go to art school. My father thought it was in my best interest to attend the Cordon Bleu. He didn't see me pursuing a career—he thought the Cordon Bleu made me a better wife candidate. I attended the Questers Theatre School in the evenings while going to the Cordon Bleu.

Cordon Bleu was a one-year course. Then I went to Maxime's Academy—cooking in the morning, taking history at Versailles, wine tasting, different lessons throughout Paris. We visited French legal courts; they took us to designer workshops like Dior to see the way clothes are crafted, and to Cartier to watch goldsmiths at work. It was like a finishing school, but much more than that, very creative, very eclectic. I had a wonderful teacher who knew I loved the impressionists and took me to gallery openings, and also introduced me to Duchamp.

When it comes to food, I'm not of the artistic school, though. I see my food as more earthy, not a lot of garnishes. To me, a beautiful loaf of bread or a rustic stew looks great. I have a chef, Bryan, who is more interested in colors and artistic presentation. He balances what I'm not so interested in and we work well together. We did a catering Friday and he arranged a plate in seconds—for color and balance—he's a painter as a matter of fact.

One of our teachers was the niece of the president of South Africa. She left South Africa for political reasons. When I was offered a job in South Africa, I took it because she had instilled in me a great interest in the country.

After eighteen months I went back to England to look for a job, but I didn't find anything right off. I had lots of American friends, and I thought about going to America. What cinched it—this may sound funny, but it was a book that really got me to come to America. It was On the Road, by Jack Kerouac. When I finished reading it I was elated, excited. I wanted to come here. I thought I'd work for a year and then go back home to England.

At first I worked as a cook for families in the North Shore—it was very difficult even though they were quite nice to me. Then I was offered a job at Polaroid, a very exciting environment, and I was there for eighteen months. I took some time off then and took a drive-away car—a beaten up Chevrolet—from Boston to L.A. It was a wonderful experience, I took the long route. Then I took another drive-away car from San Francisco to Boston, and I took six weeks. That was in 1968 and I'm still here.

I wanted to teach, was turned down by Garland Junior College. Then I got a job there—I taught an introductory cooking course, quantity cooking, and a new course—cultural aspects of food and nutrition. Then I opened the Turtle Cafe in Cambridge with Joyce Scardino and was there from '70 till '77. In '77 I opened Another Season.

WATCHING OTHERS

The best experience for getting to be creative in cooking is watching other people and seeing how they approach food. Some understand the balance of flavor and texture and can put a recipe together—others can't do that.

There were a couple of breaking points for me—feeling at ease with what I wanted to do. At Cordon Bleu the teaching was very strict and classical, with great teachers and an emphasis on technique. I went to a small cooking store owned by Elizabeth David, and I read cookbooks she'd written on Provençal and Mediterranean food. I bought the Provençal book and read it from cover to cover in a few days. It was a great release from the structure of the Cordon Bleu. Reading this book, you were suddenly in the hills, picking fresh thyme off the mountainside, covering a leg of lamb—it was more earthy, a more intuitive way of looking at food and cooking.

That was what freed me up. The next freeing up was from Joyce Scardino, whom I worked with at the Turtle Cafe in Cambridge. She had a wonderful, gutsy feeling for flavor—she found me much too confining, narrow in my approach. She's Italian. She'd just cook, she showed me how to bring out more flavor, use the best herbs, be more daring.

We did an entirely new menu each month at Another Season. I got ideas for it by reading recipes from different regions. One year I did extensive research on the Nordic countries, and Russia, Poland, and Czechoslovakia—they have wonderful winter foods. I'd see something, take ingredients, then produce the dish—not going by the method, but doing it stewed instead of boiled, or using a different flavor—I'd find a new dish, but then cook it to order.

An example of doing this is with sauerbraten—it's a pot roast. You make a great stock, you take the ingredients, but then instead of a roast you get tenderloin tips and sauté them—it's lighter, but you get a depth of flavor. Some people say, "She's 'nouvelling' the dish." But I have a problem with that term, that concept—it's too froufrou. No, that's not fair—but for instance, I like a stew to have gutsiness, nouvelle is more delicate.

FLAVOR IS CRUCIAL

Part of knowing flavor is born in us—it comes from smell. Unless you have a good sense of smell, you can't know flavor well—that's part of the tasting process.

Flavor and texture are crucial. When we eat food we should have texture. It wouldn't do to serve a mousse of salmon with mashed potatoes. It's all too soft. A mousse of salmon would go well with a puff pastry whose shell was very crisp.

Of course, I get stuck. There are times when putting a menu together is a nightmare. Sometimes I'm blocked. I sit home, go through book after book of recipes looking for inspiration. I also get inspired and unstuck by seeing the other chefs working in the kitchen. I encourage them to be part of the menu planning. We change the menu every month because I personally can't cook the same item for a month. As difficult as the first day of doing a new menu is, by the end of the month we're ready to change. A chef who worked for me said that one of pleasures of working here is you leave with five hundred ideas.

If as chefs we had a set menu through the year, we'd end up just schlepping food—then we might as well be a steak house. That's perfectly fine if it's what you want—nothing wrong with a steak house. But this is more challenging.

Ninety percent of what we do is manual labor—it's just the last few seconds on the sauce that's the creative part. Watch us some evening.

*We'll show you how quickly a sauce can break, and how to create the fla-
vor. The last few minutes are the most critical. The sauce can be too heavy
if you reduce it too much, or too insipid if you don't reduce it enough. Ap-
plication of heat to food is in my view the biggest challenge in creating a
dish—where every component of the dish should be cooked to the correct
done-ness.*

GROUP INSPIRATION

*When we're on the line in the kitchen we talk of food. In December we did a
wonderful sauce of dried apricots in a sauce of beef reduction and whiskey
with freshly cracked walnuts. It has the Christmas spirit without being sweet.
Someone said, "Whose idea was this?" and none of us could remember. It
came from all of us. We tend to work as a group, so it's not uncommon to
say, "Whose idea was it?"*

*It's great creating like that. It's not just what I come up with—Richard
came up with a wonderful sauce for beef last summer. Creating new recipes
is a wonderful feeling. Last summer I was reading in an Asian cookbook
about a soup with yams, many other vegetables, and fish and ginger. It's
difficult to cook such a variety of vegetables—they have to be added at different times so some are not overcooked. It's a wonderful flavor for summer, and it was exciting when it tasted wonderful and people would say, "I
love that new soup!"*

*Sometimes I get ideas from dreams. I had one last week for yam salsa
with fresh corn. Two years ago, I dreamed three dishes—all in the same
week—but I didn't write them down, and when I got to the kitchen I'd forgotten them. This time I wrote down the recipe when I woke up. I didn't see
it as words, I saw pictures—chunks of yams, and corn.*

*I want to write a book on how people perceive food. What I want to
share with readers is to approach food more in terms of the flavor, texture. A
lot of people go to wine tastings today but they know little about the flavor of
food. If we brought in three cartons of milk and put them in pitchers and
tasted, you'd see there was a difference. The average person in America has
never tasted a fresh nut—they're mostly rancid. I was at a friend's house
and we did a buffet luncheon—I pulled out a bottle of walnut oil, and it was
rancid. If I'd used the rancid oil no one would have known the difference—
we're more discriminating with wine than food.*

If you bring up children at an early age and introduce them to the flavor of healthy foods, they'll love that all their life. Teach them when a peach is really ripe, not just to eat it because it's there—or to smell a tomato. Do that sort of thing at an early age, as people grow up, and they'll be more demanding in terms of the quality of food they buy.

At Bread and Circus in Cambridge the parking lot is full seven days a week. They have a phenomenal array of fresh vegetables. Also they have the best variety of cheeses.

I come from an Anglo-Indian family, and I had Indian cooking at an early age. When I was twelve an Indian aunt came to England, and we had the most wonderful home-cooked Indian foods—very different from restaurant Indian food. In my first boarding school was a Chinese student whose father owned three restaurants in London. I had great Chinese food at an early age—growing up in England this was unusual.

FRESH FOOD FOR CHILDREN

Children are hungry for fresh food. I taught a special needs class in Cambridge—children from sad, difficult backgrounds—they'd had lots of McDonald's, Hostess cupcakes. For the first class I brought in big baskets of fresh vegetables—it was a class in slicing food—and we cooked the vegetables and everything was eaten. Children love fresh fruit, too—they have an appetite for these things if they're available.

Some people say Bread and Circus and stores like that are just for the elite, but I go there and see lots of Jamaicans, Haitians—they know it's where you go to get mangoes, collard greens, good beans. The immigrants preserve their taste. Maybe they'll preserve our taste in America.

ARNOLD HIATT
Former chairman of the Stride Rite Corporation,
now director of the Stride Rite Charitable Foundation

Both the New York Times and Boston Globe ran front-page stories when Arnold Hiatt resigned as chairman of the Stride Rite shoe company to devote his efforts full-time to its philanthropic foundation. In the past few years I had heard several friends in Boston speak highly of Mr. Hiatt and his work, but until the newspaper stories I didn't realize how innovative he had been as a business and community leader. I learned from the articles that he had in 1971 opened a day care center for children of the depressed Roxbury section of Boston where his manufacturing plant was located (as well as for children of employees), opened another at his new headquarters in Cambridge, and turned it into an intergenerational center for both young and old five years ago; banned smoking from the company in '86, and opened a fitness center for employees.

Hiatt had managed to make such changes with the approval of his board because the company's return on investment has earned it a spot among the top one percent of companies whose stock is traded on the New York Exchange, and it has grown from a market value of $36 million in 1968 to $1.5 billion in 1992. The president of another footwear company credited Hiatt with anticipating the three major changes in the footwear business in the past two decades, with acquisitions of a company that produced work boots in the hippie era, Sperry Top-Siders in the Yuppie era, and Keds sneakers for the "back to basics" trend.

Hiatt seemed creative not only in his business dealings but in his philanthropic innovations, and I asked a mutual friend to introduce us. We talked about creativity over lunch at the Legal Seafood restaurant, which prompted him to speak of his love of food and cooking and the creative challenge of being a chef.

Notice how crucial the art of noticing is to Mr. Hiatt.

HEARING SILENCE

When I was a student at Harvard I was torn about what I was going to do. I was in premed and studying to be a doctor like my brother, but it wasn't what I wanted to do. It was a time of turbulence in my life. One afternoon I was walking along the Charles River—I often walked along the bank of the river—and I noticed the monastery of the Cowley Fathers [The Society of St. John the Evangelist, an Episcopal Order] there on Memorial Drive. I went in, and I sat down, and it was very peaceful and calm. It was like hearing silence. I decided I wasn't going to pursue this course I was on, that I really didn't want to do it. I went out very relieved. After that visit to the monastery—after realizing I didn't want to go to medical school—I dropped out of college. Coming from a Jewish family, who set a high store on education, that elicited quite a response from my father. He did everything but say a prayer for the dead—that's what happens sometimes when a Jew marries a non-Jew; what I'd done was almost worse than intermarriage.

I joined the Merchant Marine and came back to Harvard afterward. I decided to major in what had always interested me—history and literature. I thought I'd teach. But when I got out, and I was engaged to be married to a young woman from Vassar, I felt I wasn't going to be able to support a family on a teacher's salary. By a process of elimination of what I might do to earn a living I joined the executive training program at Filene's department store.

In those days they'd admit a large number of people—MBAs, who were very aggressive, climbing up the corporate ladder. The ladder got narrower and after a year I didn't feel I was in my element. The people in the program were much more aggressive than I, and I knew I wasn't going to make it in a department store.

BUYING A SMALL COMPANY

I'd heard about a small company in Lawrence, Massachusetts, that was going into bankruptcy, the Blue Star shoe company. It was one of those companies that sprang up after World War II, but then, in a time of declining demand, fell by the wayside. I borrowed money from my father and the Bank of Boston, and I found myself an entrepreneur at the age of twenty-four. Suddenly I was having my attention focused—the way it is when you suddenly are faced with survival.

LISTENING FOR MESSAGES

I didn't have a vision, I wasn't a visionary. I knew I couldn't be a sharp businessman. If the company was to succeed with me at the helm, it would have to succeed in a different way. We had to be responsive to the consumer. You learn to listen carefully—your hearing becomes acute. You learn to pick up messages out there—in the market—and in the workplace. I learned that at this small company which I started. No one was looking for products from this small, start-up company. I was very young, and I tried to find my way. I had to do something that was not being done. I had debts and the will to survive. At that time there were no quality brand shoes for children that were affordable. There were brands like Stride Rite and Buster Brown and others, all in the higher price brackets. I knew everyone in the country wasn't rich. The next tier down were mass merchandisers like Sears or JCPenney or Thom McAn. I was developing my own sense of the market.

In 1967, Stride Rite, a New York Stock Exchange company, acquired Blue Star, the small company I had built. I left the company shortly thereafter to become the national treasurer for the antiwar candidacy of Gene McCarthy. When I came back, six months later, I became president of the company. I thought it made sense to do something for the community in which we were located, in Roxbury, an inner city of Boston. We are credited with opening the first corporate day care center in America. Actually, it was for children who lived in this blighted community. Six months later the head of the union said if you're spending money for these street kids, why not spend it on higher wages. I said wages were a separate issue, but if any of the workers had children and would like to use the day care center they were welcome to do so. Because it was free, I think some of them overcame their fear of having their children mingling with black and minority children. So the center became half community children and half employee children.

This initiative did raise some eyebrows, in contrast to starting the fitness center for employees.

When I worked as national treasurer for Eugene McCarthy's campaign, I noticed that young people were wearing work boots and heavy shoes and camping-type gear. When I returned to Stride Rite we acquired the Herman shoe company, a manufacturer of work boots and outdoor shoes, and of course those caught on.

Then there was a company in Naugatuck, Connecticut, called Uni-Royal that owned 60 percent of the sneaker market in 1977. They owned Keds. They had diversified—they had tires, chemicals, other divisions. It was fashionable to be a conglomerate. You were supposed to diversify in the name of "synergy."

I CAN TURN IT AROUND

I learned that UniRoyal was losing lots of money in footwear. I called their chairman of the board and said I'd like to meet him. I drove to his elegant office in Oxford, Connecticut. They were losing $22 million a year in their footwear division. He asked what I wanted to see him about, and I said I could be helpful—I could improve their earnings by $22 million a year because I knew I could turn the Keds division around. I said, "I'll take the footwear division off your hands, and you won't have an ongoing loss." He suggested we meet again.

This time his office called to say they were sending one of their corporate jets to Hanscom Field to pick me up. I was impressed. There was a beautiful DeHaviland twin jet waiting for me and a pilot and a copilot and a refrigerator full of cold drinks and snacks. I went to Connecticut and landed at UniRoyal field. There was a limo waiting for me on the tarmac, and it took me to their plush executive offices. It was very pleasant. But there was one thing missing. There was no one on the plane, there was no one on the tarmac. When I travel I look at children's feet, I look at women's feet. And I learn. But here I was, traveling by corporate jet and limo, and that's how their executives were traveling; they couldn't see what people were wearing.

Sperry, the company that made Top-Siders, was also a division of UniRoyal. Mr. Sperry was a man who noticed things—he noticed that dogs didn't slip on wet decks of sailboats even when boats were pitching in a rough sea. So he looked at the paws of dogs and saw how they were serrated, and he serrated a piece of rubber soling material and patented it, and that was the beginning of Sperry Top-Siders. He did this for sailors—UniRoyal sold Top-Siders only in the marinas. But I was aware that they had a cachet at colleges—worn by kids who sailed in the summer. I didn't sail myself back then, but if you were in the clubs at Harvard or Princeton, you noticed that those shoes were worn like a badge of honor. But you could only buy them at marinas. That was the business of UniRoyal that I really wanted, because I knew Top-Siders would do even better in stores outside of marinas. Six months after we acquired Sperry Top-Siders, we opened up this new channel of distribution. The business exploded and imitators came in. I didn't anticipate Sperry would be generic in this marketplace.

Two years later we acquired Keds. We struggled at first. But we stopped the losses—$22 million a year. We eliminated performance shoes, because UniRoyal had missed the running shoe trend. No one jogs on the tarmac. Nike and Adidas moved into this vacuum, and UniRoyal had missed its chance at this market. So we focused on casual shoes—we concentrated on sneakers, in the style of the '40s and '50s. They had clean, classic lines, without the bells and whistles of the new jogging and running shoes, and a whole new group of consumers liked our product. Our timing was good.

IN THE UPPER 99TH PERCENTILE

Getting into the social initiatives was a form of stimulation for me. I was engaged by it, and it gave meaning to what I was doing. Business was a natural base to launch social programs that wouldn't have the same meaning if developed by a private citizen.

I had going for me the popular conception that businessmen are narrow and parochial at best, Neanderthal at worst—so people paid attention to what we were doing. Fortunately, the company continued to be successful. If the company had stumbled, some of the board would have said "This happens when you don't pay attention to the bottom line." But we couldn't be dismissed summarily—since we were in the upper 99th percentile of all corporations in financial performance. Over time a few people said, "Hey, maybe there's a correlation between profits and good treatment of employees." However, the economic rationale for investing in the community still eludes people.

I haven't had time for a lot of relaxation—this is a highly competitive business with an 82 percent mortality rate, so staying around requires my full attention. I love to travel, though, and play tennis, ski, take short vacations; and I like to cook. I'm a great soup maker.

DAFFODILS IN THE SNOW

I started cooking fifteen years ago. I also love to work with flowers and grow things. We built a small greenhouse, and in the winter I enjoy defeating the elements and forcing bulbs like daffodils and anemones into bloom while the snow is falling outside. My other passion is helping people get started in the political process. Since working for Gene McCarthy, I've been a soft touch for any decent person who wants to run for public office. This afternoon I'm cohosting a fund-raiser for a friend who used to be an advance man for us in Gene McCarthy's presidential campaign, Jim Moody. He got hooked on politics and public service by being in that campaign—now he's a congressman running for the Senate.

As a boy I went to services during the High Holy Days. I listened to the services, and what was said, and the words seemed at such variance with the conduct of the congregation. There seemed to be no correlation between what was said and what was practiced. At any rate, I felt that way. It led me to be skeptical of religion, and the people in the business community who weren't as generous as they were pious.

I like to walk in the woods, and up in the mountains—Aspen is very quiet. It's quiet out at sea. I finally took to the ocean five years ago; I learned how to navigate. It's a quiet place and the world looks very different out there than on land. Next week I'm going to Wales, to walk in Wales, along the river Wye.

KAREN MONTI LINDO
Telephone receptionist and administrative assistant

When my book *Returning* was published an excerpt appeared in *New Age Journal*, a national magazine whose offices are in a suburb of Boston. I never went to the office, but I called on a number of occasions to speak to editors. I always looked forward to calling because the phone was answered by a warm, musical voice that made the name of the magazine sound like a song: "New Age *Jour*-nal," with the last two syllables rising in a lilt. I couldn't help smiling every time I heard this songlike answer. "Who is this person who answers your phone?" I asked one of the editors. "Is she a singer? Is she happy all the time? What's the story?" I was told that Karen Monti Lindo was as good as she sounded, and everyone loved having her in the office. I decided I wanted to interview her, for she had done the most challenging creative act of all—she had made answering the office telephone an art form. In the way she sang-spoke the name of the magazine, she altered the moods of callers, and at least in my case, created a smile. Karen lives in Watertown, Massachusetts.

Look for the underlying assumptions (or attitudes) that enable Karen to be creative.

"I BURST INTO SONG"

I'm a very happy person. Every day offers me a new opportunity to enjoy myself. In an office, people look at me as if: "I'm happy to see you." So I pick up the phone, and I'm being open. If people walk down the street with a smile, you wouldn't mind approaching them and saying hello. I've never been in a choral group, but I love to sing, and at home I burst into song. A lot of time I get feedback from my phone answering, people say it's pleasant or, "I like your voice." So they're giving back something that I'm giving them, they're giving something to me.

My family has always loved me—I'm an only child, and I'm very close to my parents. My grandparents lived downstairs, we were a nuclear family. I could draw a picture of us—grandfather, grandmother, and two aunts, all of us under the same roof. My father's sister and my mother's sister, they're wonderful ladies and I was their special niece. They showed me not to take anything too seriously in life. On holidays people were always welcome, and we didn't need any entertainment, we entertained ourselves. I played the piano, someone danced, someone read tea leaves.

A STRONG FAMILY LIFE

My father worked for the post office. I had a good home life, a strong family life. I think my father is the most wonderful father in the world and my mother the most wonderful mother. I have people who love me enough to say, "We want you to be happy."

We had Bradshaw on the cover of the magazine when he said 96 percent of people in America come from dysfunctional families, and I'd say, "I don't know about that, I'm one of the 4 percent." I don't know where John is coming from.

I like to make gifts for people—blankets when a baby is born—and I like to decorate, make packages and gifts. I afghan blankets.

When I was fourteen I had been in a rigid school system and I transferred to a new school—no more uniforms, no more of them telling you what to do. I saw what it was like to be in a harsh environment and then in a happy environment. I had been at a parochial school that was very strict on discipline, very rigid, little opportunity to express yourself. You wear a uniform as a sign of uniformity, as if everyone there is the same—and I think we're all different.

It gave me a feeling I had to be an individual—to make a personality. You had to find a way—for me, it was to be exuberant, friendly, happy.

I come from New York, the Bronx, and I went to a community college the first two years, then my next two I went to a Catholic college. There was not as much activity, and that made me create activity. When people say, "I'm in a stagnant environment," it's their responsibility to make it less stagnant.

I'd been temping and was offered jobs but I always turned them down. When NAJ asked me, I thought, I like this environment, and they want me to contribute. I've been there since 1988, four years now. I answer the phone, do the mail, Xeroxing, that's about it. My desk is right in the lobby, so I'm the first person you see when you come in. We just started a social committee and I volunteered. We're going to plan activities for the people who work there—about twenty-five people. We all like each other, outside the office, too. We're planning a New Age Summer Solstice Soiree—a day's outing at a state park. A memo went out, we'll have a picnic, we want to do something like that every month. When Halloween comes I'll wear a costume to work. At Christmas I wear red, I really get into those things. Halloween and Valentine's Day are my favorite holidays. Last Halloween I came to work as Spider Woman, I wore a black cape and red fishnet sockings.

Working at New Age Journal, I've been more aware of issues. I never knew animals were used in testing cosmetics till we had a story on it. I learn all the time—it's been a great experience.

THE POWER OF PRAYER

I'm a Catholic, I never lapsed. Catholicism is important to me, it influences my decisions. There's only two of us in the office and we're pro-life, while the others are pro-choice. We respect each other's opinions, we can feel relaxed about it.

I feel strongly about the power of prayer. I thank God every day for the life I have. I say, "Thank you for allowing me to have a happy life." People say, "What are you so happy about?" I say, "Why not?"

ELIZABETH VALENTINE
Masseuse, president of the Massachusetts
Professional Body Workers Association

In 1986 I had a massage at a place in Boston called the Aqua Center (specializing in flotation tanks for relaxation, as well as acupuncture and other healing processes). I came away from it feeling so relaxed and nurtured that I went back for more. Over the ensuing months I got to know the masseuse, Elizabeth Valentine, a quiet, sensitive woman of great skill in her work and a real dedication to learning more and making a difference in people's lives.

In the course of writing my book *Returning*, I got into a routine of weekly massages with Elizabeth, which I felt was part of the supportive process of the writing itself. I justified the expense of a weekly massage in my always precarious budget by rationalizing that I didn't drink any more, and I used to spend at least that amount of money on booze every week! There was no doubt in my mind that the massage was a better bargain for the well-being of bodyspirit than alcohol. With Elizabeth, who is a naturally nurturing human being as well as a fine massage therapist, the experience was part of the overall structure of support for my own creative process. I recommend it highly.

See how the creative process works in the physical realm.

TRANSFORMED BY MASSAGE

I was a modern dancer at the American Dance Festival at Connecticut College in 1977, just after I graduated from high school. I had my first massage there from a Danish man. I felt transformed and elated, felt I was "inhabiting" my whole body. It was a wonderful experience, a spiritual experience.

As a result of that experience I took a massage class, to learn how to do that kind of Danish deep muscle massage. I was amazed by the power of it.

I went to Boston University as an anthropology student, interested in cross-cultural types of healing. A massage course wasn't offered at BU so I searched Cambridge and Boston, and I found a polarity class. It was my introduction to energy work. I found it through a Whole Life Times *ad on the bulletin board at BU. The class was hands-on experience, using light pressure, with thumbs and fingers and holding polar points to bring balance. The whole concept of polarity is bringing you to balance. It gave me exposure to a subtle form of contact with people. I liked it, it was a new layer of experience with the body, having to do with energy.*

I graduated from BU with an anthropology degree. I was trying to decide whether to do research at the Harvard Education School or go to Nepal with the Peace Corps, when I had an opportunity to go to Paris and take over a family friend's massage practice. My father was in the Air Force in France and I had been born in Paris, and lived there till I was two and a half years old. I studied French in public school starting in the sixth grade. I took over this woman's eight clients in Paris and started out.

SOMETHING TO OFFER

I'd been getting hands-on experience whenever I could, and I'd studied anatomy and physiology at the American Dance Festival. I had done that polarity course and given massages to graduate students and musicians at a house where I boarded. I realized I had something to offer. First I just did it free, I loved seeing the results. Then someone said they should pay and they gave me ten dollars. I knew my limitations and I was not promising clients to fix anything. I was interested in making people feel relaxed, feel good. You'd be amazed at the transformation you go through when you receive purely, as you do in massage, and I enjoy giving that.

In Paris the woman who gave me her clients also put me in touch with a gynecologist and a Jungian therapist who would recommend clients, and she gave me lists of dance classes. I stepped into the whole arena and tried to make as much contact as I could. People felt the work I did was spiritual and took them to deep places. They associated the sort of work I did with California—maybe because it made them feel good!

I found that, although the French are supposed to be earthy, they have an intellectual, cerebral headiness. There's a certain focus on cognac and cigarettes. Holistic health didn't really exist there then, and the whole body-mind connection was just coming together there.

HOLISTIC WORK TAKING OFF

I worked in Paris for a year and a half and then came back to Cambridge, where I saw that holistic work was beginning to take off. I decided I needed more intensive training, so I went to the most intensive massage school I could find, the National Holistic Institute in Oakland, California, in 1983.

After that three-month intensive course in California I worked at the Women's European Skin Care Center on Newbury Street in Boston and Room to Stretch on Newbury Street, then the Aqua Retreat Center in Brighton, and now I have my own private practice in Watertown, Massachusetts, in a group called Body Mind Associates. At first I made house calls, traipsed my table around everywhere. My clientele varied from wealthy businessmen and their wives in the Prudential Center apartments, *who thought of massage as a service, to the Cambridge crowd—educated, academic women involved with Radcliffe, who saw massage as a means of personal and spiritual growth—and also dancers and musicians.*

HEALING THE BODY-MIND SPLIT

I had worked with pregnant women in France and developed that work back here, too. I also worked with clients of a doctor who treated survivors of sexual abuse. The idea of massage was to help heal the split between body and mind, for those people who feel they can't inhabit their own bodies. This drew me into more training in body-centered psychotherapy and I took seminars in Hakomi. It's a Japanese word for "bringing into balance." The work was to access feeling by holding and supporting and taking resistance away from someone's body so they have room to feel. It's a subtle form of bioenergetics. It allows people to feel through their pain. Then I was introduced to a doctor who was head orthopedic surgeon at Mass General, who came as a client. We developed some research on lower back pain, and he referred clients to me for muscular therapy.

The kind of work I do is based completely on the person, relying on my visual ability, which I developed by learning anatomy through sculpting with an artist from New York. I had taken courses, but the sculpting enabled me to understand it best. I experienced kinesthetic learning, which developed my eye to see someone's body structurally.

Hakomi helped me see character types—how people hold themselves, what it means. Is the chest concave or is it puffed out like a rooster? Are the shoulders stooped, are the feet strong and wide or narrow and collapsed? Then I get information from what people tell me about their history and how they feel at the time; it gives me a sense of how best to support them.

With sexually abused people, their eyes dart around. I ask what would make them feel safe, maybe I just hold their head or their feet. I try to be present to each individual's needs and not come in with an agenda. What I feel in the body is physical tension or openness and then I sense how I can best continue to open them up physically.

HONORING THE EARTH

Before a massage my own orientation is to get myself physically grounded, get my body in alignment and go through this series—first visually attaching my feet to the earth, and honoring the earth—I ask the earth for support. I got this from studying Native American meditation. After attaching to the earth I bring my energy up and ask for God's support; then I ask for a kind of thin membrane of protection that will allow me to stay receptive but filter out negativity and energy that's not mine. That's a challenge, because I absorb from people. I make a prayer, thanking God for his presence and that he may lead me through the process basically to continue the right path, that I can support the person on their path and bring them to the right alignment. Sometimes I do it quietly and sometimes I make a prayer with this person I'm about to massage. I wash with water after every session, all the way up my arms—cold water, then hot, then cold—if I don't do that I gain weight, I get injuries, and headaches. It's psychic as well as for cleanliness. And then I stretch and shake my arms out. If someone was especially uptight I do another prayer, or stamp my feet around to make contact with the earth.

SPIRITUAL BODY WORK

Most clients experience a profound depth from massage that is spiritual. I don't know how many acknowledge it. But it shows in their faces. People know me as a spiritual body worker.

My practice evolved in a creative way, and I attribute it to trust and listening to myself, my own instinct, which my mother taught me to develop. I've had a sense of trust and protection, I feel blessed to be in this profession, and I've spiritually and emotionally evolved in it. There's been an exchange of energy with various people who have enlightened me.

Mother said when I was ten that I should be a massage therapist and I took it as an insult. I come from an intellectual family and being a masseuse wasn't intellectual enough. Ironically, the profession has brought me into my intellect. I have studied scientific aspects of the body, and I always want to work through Western medicine. I see myself as a bridge. My mentors were my grandmother, Lucy Valentine, my father's mother, a writer and architect; and also Elizabeth Cless, who's on the board of trustees of Radcliffe, and started continuing education at Claremont College in California, an artist and designer who's interested in Tibetan and Nepalese art. She was a client and became a friend. She pushed me and challenged me to strive as a woman, encouraged me to continue my studies.

THE REVEREND CARL SCOVEL
Minister of King's Chapel, a Unitarian Universalist
Christian church in Boston

One of the reasons I was drawn to King's Chapel was the sermons Carl gave, which impressed me as a writer because they all seemed like wonderfully crafted short stories. They didn't ramble, like many sermons I have heard, but had a beginning, middle, and end—a point and a lesson! I always look forward to Carl's sermons, not only for their spiritual insight but for their pure storytelling joy. I respect Carl for that kind of creation, as well as the hundreds of other ways he creates in his calling as a minister to counsel, advise, organize, administer, lead, inspire, officiate, fund-raise, cook, dishwash, and perform almost every other activity conceivable, always in a creative way. In fact, I think part of his secret of staying fresh in the most demanding job I can imagine is being creative about every aspect of his work.

See if the ways this minister is creative could apply to any of your own work.

ASKING THE RIGHT QUESTIONS

Several factors influence my ability to produce, to be creative. One is being attentive and rightly responsive in conversation. Yesterday I met with two people who had lived together for more than thirty years. One has cancer, and doesn't want to think about dying, and the other already has him buried. I was trying to stay in tune with the feelings of each and help each one hook up with the other. I had to ask the right questions and not feel anxious; yet, I was anxious. It was one of those days when everything was happening at once. So that's one kind of creativity, in counseling people.

Another kind is meeting with people and developing solutions to problems in the parish. It's easy to think up a whole batch of solutions, but they may not really have relevance. It's hard to think up viable solutions.

A third kind of creative work I have to do is writing—sermons, reports for Vestry and committees that are very important, that not only must have information but clearly lay out the choices that must be made.

In writing sermons, there has to be a connection between Bible verses and experience. Maybe there's a story I listen to and say, "That's something people would respond to—maybe it's something I can tell to others to help them understand their lives."

You have to develop an ability to see what works and what doesn't. It's easy just to churn out repetitions of what you've said before. There has to be constant reflection on whether it works—does it wash?

I think there has to be pleasure in the work. Maybe there are people who hate their work and yet produce wonderful things, but I find it hard to imagine. I think there has to be pleasure, in the music of words in writing, for instance. That's not a denial of the pain and pure laboriousness of it, that's the price you pay for doing good work, it's paying our dues.

NO SHORTCUTS

There are times I'll weep at the thought of having to write a sermon. Yet, when people come out of church the next day, and if I feel I've touched something significant in the lives of six of them, I'm rewarded. There has to be a willingness to pay the dues of hard work—there's no shortcut, no way around doing it. I've heard ministers preach who had insight but didn't want to do the work necessary to take it beyond the first quick insight. When I hear that, I get irritated or indifferent.

I think rest is very important to doing good creative work. The longer I'm in this church—and I think this is true of all institutions—the more demands that are made on you and the less energy you have. Getting rest is the hardest discipline. I'm lazy, so I often just go on working.

There's the discipline of attention—attentiveness; the discipline of work; and the discipline of recreation—"re-creation." They're all hard, but for me recreation is the hardest. When I went on my sabbatical a few years ago for six months—and it was the first time since I got out of college—that time was terrific. I had all kinds of ideas, insights, and it wasn't just pie in the sky, they were important ideas and insights. The key to it was, I was rested—I didn't have the continual pressure, pressure, pressure.

Finally, I think there has to be love for the recipient of the work. I mean that specifically—an affection, a sense of identity, a realization that you have been granted a piece of the universal that's theirs as well as yours. You were chosen to hold it up to them so they can look at it. It may be a seemingly trivial thing—but that little chip is a reflection of an infinite sun, even if only a momentary glimpse, that tells them there's something significant

*and beautiful here—the act of connection, to the audience, the congrega-
tion, the people in church.*

GIVING BACK TO THE ONE

I love preaching to a small congregation. I love the Sunday after Easter. Not
that I don't enjoy preaching to a full house at Easter—but the people who
have come on days like the Sunday after Easter, they've come very specifically for something. I feel a real sense of responsibility to them. And I realize I'm not just giving something to them. Ultimately I'm giving back to that
One who gave it to me. So it doesn't matter how many people heard the sermon, whether it was on the radio or in church or something they read—they
are a screen through which I return it to the Source, to the Giver. It's in-
credibly important as I get older to see how little public impact I have. Yet
despite that, I sense that whatever I gave, I was "giving it back"—at least
the best of it, and I don't blame myself for what I did that was just trundling
out the obvious.

The sense of giving it back is really important. With the kind of sermon
that satisfies, it's as if I could say to God, "I gave you back some of what
you gave me." I hope someone heard that and caught it—it's a gift that's given
you, like a boomerang—it comes to you and you put a little spin on it for
people as it goes by you.

I came back here one night after the Easter Vigil, the Saturday night
before Easter morning, and I was tired, and I hadn't even begun the sermon
for Easter. I knew there would be four or five hundred people expecting
something, and I had no sermon. I knew I didn't want to go to the barrel and
get something I'd done before, it's so unpleasant to do that, so obvious. So
what I did was, I remembered an incident, and I started writing it—typing it
up. I had been to Jerusalem at the church of the Holy Sepulchre, and walked
down these steps, out of the way, and found myself in a chapel. There was a
crucifix, and incense, and candles, and I started to pray, when a voice behind me called out, and I saw a man in a black robe and tall black hat. He
was Orthodox, and he said something and pointed at my feet. I realized he'd
said "shoes," so I took my shoes off and said a prayer and then we talked,
and I told him I was a minister. He asked me to come back, and he'd take
me to his house and have tea. I left the church and I never went back. In a
curious way it became hooked up with the resurrection. I regretted not going
back, I felt he was waiting for me, that maybe I would meet him later, I'd

find him somewhere. I began the Easter sermon with this story of a failure. It was as if the resurrection took my story and elevated it to the level of meaning. I was struck by the response, I've never had such a response to an Easter sermon. It was not due to my ideas, it was a pure gift; yet, I felt very creative about it. It was very nice work, imaginative work, trying to sense the depth of meaning of the experience.

Earlier in my career I worked hard on my sermons, and some were clever, like an exercise, but that's all they were, an exercise. I think back now on the cleverest sermon I ever wrote—oh, it was a real showpiece!—I gave it all over the place, and now I wouldn't even want to read it again.

GOD AS THE GIVER

I don't use prayer for creativity. I used to do that, but I found my prayers for inspiration became very labored—a sort of sullen "I've prayed to you, now will you please come through!" It's much more important in my daily prayer, asking God to help me receive what God wants to give me—to see God as the Giver. I try to live a life of openness to what God wishes to show me—not to be sullen about what God gives someone else. I sometimes read a sermon or column and it will be lovely and well done and I'll have a feeling of jealousy—ah, I wish I'd said that! That makes me less attentive to what is being shown to me.

I often pray just before the sermon, "God, you know what a patch job I brought to the pulpit today—let them hear what they need to hear." I'm asking God to speak to them while I am speaking.

When I write I operate in a set way—my books close enough to reach—some sort of nearby symbol, and I like to have a firm chair. I need to be cocked, set to go, like a runner on the blocks.

I used to write with a pre-dinner drink. It was only one drink but it got in the way, it dulled the edge, and I stopped trying to do it that way.

If I don't walk or run every day I feel badly. Now I'm doing tai chi and that's another way of being attentive and focused—movement is a way of focusing. I run every two or three days. I alternate it with cycling, or using the rowing machine. Walking is still wonderful to me—it's a blessing to be able to walk.

Hiking I love, but it's very rare I get a chance—maybe three to five times a year. I've had good religious experiences hiking—I do it as much for my soul as for my body. I had a wonderful hike last weekend with several *parishioners, but I'd rather hike alone. For me, hiking is a time of prayer and meditation. With people, I get irritated because they want to talk. I enjoy the people immensely whom I went hiking with last weekend, but I felt they couldn't stop talking. I thought, Why do we have to talk—we're here!*

GISH JEN

Novelist, author of Typical American *and* Mona in the Promised Land

The publisher of my novels, the late Seymour Lawrence, created a community of his writers, introducing them to one another's work, and then to the fellow authors themselves. He was excited one day as he told me with pride and enthusiasm about a new author whose first novel he was going to publish. The book was *Typical American*; the author, Gish Jen. I was hooked on the novel from the first page; this saga of a Chinese American family was not only insightful but wonderfully funny, disarming in its humor as it limned the pains and pleasures of the Chinese American experience.

I met Gish Jen a few years later, in the spring of '93, when Sam Lawrence brought all his authors to Oxford, Mississippi, for the dedication of a special room at the university library containing manuscripts, correspondence, and memorabilia of his publishing imprint and its authors, ranging from Kurt Vonnegut and Katherine Anne Porter to Jayne Ann Phillips and Susan Minot. The dedication event was flanked by celebration—parties, dances, book signings, and dinner at a local catfish restaurant. I got to know Gish a little bit during these happy festivities, and a month or so later when I was in Boston, I went over to the Cambridge apartment where she lives with her husband and young son to talk about her creativity.

AN ACCIDENTAL POET

One of the myths I believed about creativity was that you had to be in an altered state—I thought it was an irrational process over which you had no control. With fiction writing, it's surprising how analytical a lot of it is. You control it a lot more than I thought—though when you're waiting for it to be there, it's not there.

I didn't grow up in a climate of caring for things because of being artistic. I fell into it—so the romantic ideas about it were never there for me. My first writing was by accident. I signed up for a class in prosody at Harvard with Robert Fitzgerald. I wanted to know why poetry was written in those funny lines. I wanted to understand the nuts-and-bolts level of literature. We had a weekly assignment, which I thought would be a paper of some kind, like a critical study—I didn't know the assignment would be to write a poem! I thought, Oh my God. But I found I loved it. It was completely absorbing in a way nothing I'd ever done had ever been.

Gertrude Stein said a writer's work is "locating the world in himself." I look for a nerve, then I back away from the nerve and ask if it has any relation to the world. Then I go back to the personal. I try to write on the nerve, see what it has to do with the larger world.

There is a large self-healing aspect to the way I write. Once you work a nerve, it's never as sensitive as it was before.

I hit a point in the writing where I don't know what happens next, maybe at the end of a scene. I take a "creative nap," having the problem in mind, and after the nap I discover I've found the answer. I associate my ability to create with my ability to take deep naps. When I nap I drop off really fast—I can still do that like a child, and come out of it very quickly.

Another myth: I always thought there were certain gifted people who did creative work, and I thought I was not one of them.

I didn't grow up thinking creativity was valued. Quite the contrary, it was regarded as something frivolous. The concept of creativity is very American. I don't think my parents used the word creativity until I was thirty, and even then, when they used it, it had quotes around it. Even today there's part of me that's a little cynical about the word creative. Everybody's trying to be creative—it seems self-indulgent sometimes. In America anything creative is thought to be good, but that's not always true. Creativity can be valuable because it offers a solution to something—but the creative solution may not necessarily be a good solution. I don't worship at the altar of creativity.

In China the role of the artist is not valued as it is here. The whole premise of the artist as one who stands outside society is not at all supported in China. People should not just know the rules of society, but should live by the rules. And part of me doesn't condemn that, though I'd have had a hard time there in China. In America it's easy to say, "Oh, it's so conformist," but that culture is adaptive for that place, with its huge population and scarce resources. People are not encouraged to stand outside society and make Spy magazine–type comments.

My father is so creative we take it for granted. He was a consultant for the army, navy, and air force. They'd have some multimillion-dollar machine that didn't work, and he'd stick a tongue depressor into some part and it would work—we didn't call it creative, we didn't have a name for it. The way my father has lived his whole life is creative. To start as a Chinese man and end up as an American man is maybe the most creative thing of all!

He was a civil engineer who became a plasma physicist, then a real estate mogul. He went into real estate quite late in life and everyone said he couldn't do it, he didn't know enough about American business—but he'd already done what people said he couldn't do.

Now he says, "My daughter's very creative," but he learned to say that. My parents didn't encourage creativity in me as it's thought of today—when I was five, they encouraged me to keep my mouth shut and get good grades.

Sometimes people in the arts are the most conformist in their lifestyle—like all painters wear black—there they all are in uniform. You're supposed to shop in thrift shops, and know a certain kind of trivia.

I'll probably bring up my son in the great American way and support his creativity—but not blindly. It's important to be tempered with another ability.

What's really important in a work of art is that it emanates from your entire being. With my father it emanates from who he is. A lot of what passes for creativity in America is gratuitous inventiveness—not authentic quality but applied.

THE CAPACITY TO WONDER

My parents were latecomers to Catholicism—I was a religious Catholic when I was younger, and it had an influence on who I became. I don't know if feelings of awe came because I went to church or if I was drawn to religion because of feelings of awe. I'm very drawn to spiritual experiences. I think it's a necessary characteristic of most writers. If they don't have the capacity to wonder, I don't know how they can really be writers. I'm very proud that the favorite thing my son says when he's imitating me is "wow!"

I'm fascinated with the mystery of things—the mystery of what's right in front of you.

Writing is a spiritual experience. There's a sense of transport. A lot of *the moments I think I've been visited by the muse, what comes out is funny—the big moments with me in my work are laughter, utter delight.*

I'm in a writers' group of women writers. We mostly talk about being moms—things like preschools, discipline. There's moral support for being a mother and a writer at the same time. That overrides artistic issues.

We read each other's work, but not in the group. It's good as a reality check—is this something that belongs out in the world? Is it working?

I used to write letters to myself. I'd try to understand what I'd written, I'd look at it myself and try to understand, and at parts I would say, I'm off the nerve, I've left the work.

THE THOUGHT POLICE

I'm writing in a highly charged context because I'm Asian American. It's like trying to work in a room with a wind blowing through it. I have to be more careful—my book will be scrutinized. I write about race and it's hot, hot, hot. It's part of my natural subject matter—but I have to ask myself, Is everybody going to jump on me or not? A lot of my energy goes into that.

I'm read in a lot of courses—so far so good. But there are thought police everywhere. I think a lot has to be examined today, but to be writing in this context right now is tiring. I sit down and rip it out and then think, think, think. Jayne Ann [Phillips] helps me, she says, "I think you're okay here."

Since the advent of multiculturalism, though, I've had better response to my writing. Ten years ago, Asian American writers were never even in a major publication—it was a given that we weren't a significant enough part of America. Editors would send back my stories set in America and say, "We prefer your more exotic work"—meaning stories set in China. They assumed I had nothing to say about America.

There's a gang of guys who've made their careers attacking Maxine Hong Kingston and Amy Tan. They feel Asian men are always portrayed as weak—why not show a strong Asian male? I haven't heard from them— I don't know if I'll pass muster in the end. But this reaction is a good thing in part. It's like when minimalism was in fashion, Bharati Makherjee wrote an essay calling for "maximalism." Her idea was that minimalism involved a kind of code, a kind of winking to insiders, that in a large heterogeneous society more should be spelled out.

This is a large, diverse country—we should be writing in a way that includes everybody. It's a lot more work for a writer, but it's good—it will help

us all in the end to get beyond ourselves. The trouble with American litera-
ture is, it's so self-indulgent. In the great first-person novel we sing of our-
selves and to ourselves—the autobiographical impulse is a potent vein, but
let's make it matter. My own influences? Jane Austen, F. Scott Fitzgerald.
I've always loved the Jewish writers—Malamud, Roth, Singer.

MARCIE HERSHMAN

Novelist and teacher, author of Tales of the Master Race
and Safe in America

In 1974 I was asked to judge the undergraduate fiction writing contest at Boston University. The stories I liked best were by a student
named Marcie Hershman, whom I met to congratulate on her prize.
We became good friends and supporters of one another's work—and
life. Marcie published some stories, excellent book reviews, and journalistic interviews (a memorable one in Ms. magazine with May Sarton), but her hard work on three novels came to naught. They were
admired by editors, but didn't get enough support to be published.
Then, in 1990, she went with her brother to Germany for an assignment he had as a TV producer. Some of her own family had been
killed in the Holocaust, and she wasn't anxious to go to Germany,
but while she was there something creative happened that led to her
first published novel, the widely praised *Tales of the Master Race.*
Marcie has since received a Bunting Fellowship at Radcliffe and continues to teach English and writing at Tufts University. She recently
published a second novel, *Safe in America,* which has also been
highly acclaimed.

THE MORAL COMMUNITY

I have to be isolated and separate to write, but when I'm writing I'm almost
communal—I'm connected—my subject matter takes me to different eras
through different eyes. I have to see the world in a way that's egoless. Spiri-
tuality is a moving beyond ego to something that transcends personal needs
and desires and problems to something that touches and can be inside others.
It means I can't be Marcie looking at my character Felix Breslauer—I have
to be inside Felix as Felix, doing things that make him who he is. I can't slap

him upside the head and say, "Don't do that, it's a terrible thing." I have to let go and in my letting go I learn, even though I may not like the lesson.

The springboard for Tales of the Master Race *came out of a spiritual anguish. Who would do this to people connected to me? Who would make individuals anonymous and dispose of them? Who saw my great-grandmother taken out of her house, put on a cart, and taken to Auschwitz? That can only be seen by seeing inside her neighbors—the word* neighbors *implies community.* Tales *is about the moral community or lack of one—the word* we. *When you forget the word or misuse it, you have what* Tales *is about.*

The idea came when I returned from a trip to Germany with my brother Rob, who was making a documentary there for the CBS news program "West 57th Street." I didn't want to go to Germany, I just wanted to travel with my brother. When I got there it was like a great door opening for me— a door I had needed to keep shut. In Germany I saw I had already walked through—on the other side of the door was all I'd repressed. There was a new willingness to listen openly.

Writing for me is about listening openly and deeply—to voices underneath our voices, the little growl or laugh or yelp of pain or surprise we cover up.

I was in Passaw and Munich for seven days. The editor who bought the book thought the author was a German woman in her sixties and the book a translation.

There are different ways to get quiet before writing. Sometimes, on my Sierra Club calendar, I record the events of the day before. This helps to clear my mind, to empty it. I say I had dinner with so-and-so, wrote in the afternoon, got upsetting call from someone. There's only about an inch across the page to write these things in. But it helps me get rid of them, stop thinking about them.

Sometimes I sit on the floor in the middle of the room and meditate. It doesn't feel like emptying out so much as opening up. My need is, Let me open. I run before breakfast so I can sit still and not notice my body. I can sit all day, but my real writing doesn't come till around four in the afternoon. I can't get there till this long time. I sit there—starting at ten—I have lunch at my desk, the real writing is from four to six.

During the years of my novels getting rejected, a belief sustained me— that what I'd learn to say would have value. I was angry a lot, I'd cry. But I believed I was knowing something—that I had an obligation to keep doing it—if I didn't write I felt lousy, as if I was lying, somehow.

My first novel was autobiographical and I'm grateful it didn't get taken by a publisher. I put it under my bed.

BEING A LESBIAN AND A WRITER

I haven't written directly about being a lesbian, but I think it's behind all my works—the person who's somewhat outside society trying to make choices to be outside. It doesn't matter what the difference is, society tries to obliterate individuality. In economic terms there's now a market that's legitimate for writing about gay life. But now I'm forty-two and the issues of twenty-two are not enough for me—I'm not interested just in coming out stories.

I'm interested in philosophical, larger issues of how that's played out. My new book is set in the '30s and '40s and also now in the AIDS crisis. Is the crisis of the Holocaust related to trying to save relatives from AIDS? Is that a gay book? What drives it for me is not simply that question—I want to hold the unity. I'm writing love scenes that are heterosexual—also moments of tenderness between two men, and I'm a woman. Can I do that and have it be legitimate? You bet! I don't stop where the label stops—if the reader can see me behind it, I haven't done the job. It's like saying, What's behind the curtain? I don't want to have characters who are two-dimensional and me behind the curtain. I want the reader to be in people's lives, inside the characters.

It's the issue of spirituality—getting beyond the self and connecting. If people in Tales *acted like middle-class Americans there'd be no book. It comes down to my serving the book and the characters, not them serving me!*

I try to hear the voices of the characters. I make little stabs at it on the computer.

When I'm stuck or feel blocked, I just walk around outside, and tell myself I have to do it. You have to want it, have to be determined. Hard times come when there's silence, or learning to sit still—but I know it needs to happen. In other occupations, sitting still is rest time—for us it's still work! It's like trying to empty yourself.

Sometimes when I'm stuck I do this little exercise where I try to write the thing as bad as I can—your aim is to make it bad—but you have to really psyche yourself into that, you can't pretend, and after writing it that way, as bad as you can, it sometimes leads into the right way of doing it. Also, sometimes I write an essay or review of something else, someone else's work, and it gives me some perspective.

Sometimes I use the kitchen stove timer. On days when I don't want to write, I go set the timer on the stove to go for sixty minutes. I say to myself, You only have to write till the buzzer goes off, and then I work this hour, and I set it again. My mother used to set a timer for me when I practiced the piano, I think that was the source of this thing. It didn't help me be a good piano player but it helped me have discipline, and that's good for all the arts.

I also had a talisman, or token, when I was writing Tales—my grandmother's certificate of U.S. citizenship—and on the dining table, a circle of lace my great-grandmother made—I had to pass it on the way to the timer. My great-grandmother was killed at Auschwitz. I'd look at my grandmother's citizenship papers, and pass the circle of lace her mother made so intricately in the house that she was dragged out of and taken away. I'd want to honor that—so I'd sit there until I was able to do what I needed to do.

When I started the new book I'm working on now, the mood of Germany still lingered, but I was drawn to the situation today of my brother with AIDS and his friend of ten years. How do I do that? How do I respond to human trials and joys during this time of great struggle? When I'm writing I don't know if I'm happy—but I'm connected, and it's a great satisfaction.

This new book deals with two eras, centered in one family. What does it mean to be safe when others you care for are not? That question is the hinge for me, the anchor of Safe in America.

DOING IT DECAF

I entered college in '69 in Boston. Once I tried writing when I was stoned on marijuana. I looked at it the next morning and knew it was lousy. I never used marijuana to write again. I do drink coffee and decaf mixed when I write—if I can't get going on that, forget it.

There are people who are into being perceived as writers and artists— they put on booze or drugs like the clothes of being an artist—a writer is someone who writes, not someone who does a certain drug.

Our mythology of creativity at BU twenty years ago was about the music. Listening to records, the popular music, was the predominant way of talking to our generation. Supposedly everyone was stoned doing that music, but I learned that wasn't always true, either.

I heard that a writer was someone looking for his father. Well, I didn't need to look for my father, I knew where my father was—he was in Cleveland.

I didn't have a terrible childhood, either. I had a happy life, I grew up in middle-class suburbs. So how could I be a writer? I wasn't a man, I wasn't looking for my father, and I didn't have an unhappy childhood.

The contemporary women writers I admired at that time were Sylvia Plath and Flannery O'Connor—one had committed suicide, and the other had a degenerative disease and was living near a chicken coop or something. Then Joan Didion came along and I memorized Play It As It Lays *because she had a voice of her own but she wasn't destroyed.*

The lives of women writers when I started out—before Didion—were perceived differently. Whereas Hemingway's madness couldn't be more bronzed or adorned, Plath's madness was perceived as small—and anyway I wasn't after madness, I was after connection. Jean Rhys said that what's important is to "feed the lake"—the lake is literature—we all have our ways of doing it. I remember it's important to feed the lake—this is one of my cheerleading mantras!

I first got published under the name M. F. Hershman. Some of the same poems that were turned down when they were sent in under the name Marcie Hershman were accepted as M. F. Hershman. As soon as I became M. F. my acceptance quotient went way up! I started writing back letters to editors who addressed me as "Mr. Hershman," saying, "Thanks, and by the way, I'm not 'Mr.,' my name is Marcie. I'm so glad you like the poem. Thank you!"

I thought about starting a George Club—where, like George Sand and George Eliot, I and all the women writers I knew would send our work to editors under the first name George. In the end I didn't do it, but the point wasn't to deceive—the point was to be taken seriously for writing about big things. Poems that were turned down when they were by Marcie because they were thought to be only about love, were now seen to be about big philosophical issues, when written by M. F.

JILL NELSON
Journalist and author, Volunteer Slavery

At the Boston convention of the National Writers Union I heard an author read the first chapter of a new book that was so funny and compelling that I wanted to read it at once. Copies weren't available yet, so I asked *The Nation* magazine if I could review this new book, called *Volunteer Slavery,* Jill Nelson's account of being an African American woman reporter at the *Washington Post*—and in the world. It reminded me of a journalistic version of Julia Phillips's hilarious and withering inside look at Hollywood, *You'll Never Eat Lunch in This Town Again*. I loved the book, and called my review "She'll Never Eat Lunch at *The Post* Again."

A few months later I went up to Jill's neighborhood in Morningside Heights and we drank coffee and talked about creativity.

TO DULL THE PAIN

When I was growing up, I got the feeling that creativity was tied up with pain. Then the next lopsided step from that was to find ways to dull the pain, and that's where alcohol and drugs came in. I saw writers as larger-than-life, tragic figures—women writers even more so. Emily Dickinson, Phillis Wheatley. There was no crystal staircase to writing, creating, so whatever it took to get there was okay.

I read anything, but I was particularly attuned to stories about women, no matter who wrote them. If they were also written by women, all the better. I didn't care which women—Toni Morrison to Jane Austen. This was before Toni Morrison, though, so the African American women I was reading then were Gwendolyn Brooks and Phillis Wheatley.

In high school the major writer for me was James Baldwin. For a year I did nothing but read his stuff. That's when I thought, I really want to do this.

I didn't separate the process of writing from being a writer—and that meant hard living, drinking, smoking—angst that seemed crucial to my writing. I thought, If I'm not in pain, will I have anything to say?

I think a lot of that has to do with the Judeo-Christian ethic—that there has to be pain in doing anything worthwhile. That's complete BS. It's better when you're not in pain.

In the '60s, altering your consciousness with drugs or alcohol was standard operating procedure.

If you smoked reefer when you were writing, it seemed like all your ideas were brilliant. But when I read what I'd written with that, it's so bad—even the typing is bad. It's like when you're on a trip with acid—you get the facade of brilliance—but if you're doing it a lot, you don't even remember the brilliance was only a facade.

I had already stopped drinking and drugs when I was writing Volunteer Slavery. *I can't imagine doing it now any other way.*

There's a romanticization of self-destruction—I'm trying to create a life as an artist that's self-affirming. As writers we deserve to live a decent life. Poverty or drunkenness are no longer badges of honor.

Things are opening up for more models for African American women. I didn't see myself in the writers I read—I saw around them—I didn't think I had the luxury of too much drinking. The group, the society, wasn't supporting me at all. So I had to be more serious about it.

People are still fascinated by the intersection between drugs and creativity. I think it's because it's really attractive to think you can put on a persona—if you take on that persona, of the doomed artist, you can abuse alcohol and drugs with impunity, you can go around and be sort of a moody shit—and justify it by saying you have creative urges! It's attractive to step into a whole persona like that just because you like to write.

I was twenty when my daughter was born. I was the only person I knew from a black, middle-class background who had a child. Raising her was a constant struggle to figure ways to write, and spend time with her, and earn a living. The old models of society weren't even possible—the model mom, the nuclear family model, or the model of the welfare mother who spews out babies. I had to figure out how I wanted to live, and how I wanted her to live.

I had to figure out how to sit on the floor with a typewriter on top of a box with a toddler crawling around, or a two-year-old running around. I was creating what to do with that situation.

I spend a lot of time staring off into space. When I sit down to write I know where the story begins and ends, and that jump-starts me. My ritual is a lot of thinking, which people who aren't writers don't understand. They think, How can you just lie on the sofa? So much of the process is internal.

As a writer it's easy to OD on words. My head is backed up with words. I spend twenty or twenty-five minutes a day exercising, on the exercise bike, with no words, and that's cleansing. Recently I've started being much more structural on meditation—otherwise my mind becomes white noise. I do a daily meditation, and at some point every day I go to the gym.

I don't write sequentially, so if I'm having a hard time writing, I just go on to something else. I don't have the luxury of being stuck. If you don't produce, you don't eat. Journalism is good training, especially freelance, because that's how it is. This is the first time I've had the luxury of being able to work on a book and turn down other offers. I used to have to take on everything because I needed the money.

DAN LICARDO
Short-story writer

Through my friend Mary Beth Coudal, the stand-up comic, I met a writer whom she worked with at their "day jobs" at an office. Later I went to celebrate the publication of his first short story in *The New Yorker*. "A Riverine Tale" is a satiric, funny, wise improvisation, reminding me of a mix of Donald Barthelme, Kurt Vonnegut, and Ring Lardner. If Lardner were alive I might think it was he who had written another of Licardo's stories, "Men Who Love Women Who Fly," published in the *Columbia Review*.

I enjoy and admire Dan's work, and I was interested in what a fellow Columbia graduate of his generation (he just turned thirty) thought about creativity. I went up to the historic West End bar and grill near Columbia where Kerouac and the Beats used to hang out, to talk with Dan about creativity. Upsetting tradition, we drank coffee, and Dan told me his current thinking on the old mythology.

INEBRIATION AND INSPIRATION

With rock 'n' roll and people like Jimi Hendrix, I assumed drugs and creative activity went together. In college, I began to associate drugs and alcohol with writing when I became interested in writers' lives, especially Hemingway and Fitzgerald and the whole Paris group. While I admired their work, I didn't want my own life to turn out like theirs did. I didn't feel a kinship with them as I did with other writers who were not alcoholics—Mark Twain, T. S. Eliot. They weren't alcoholics—were they?

I read The Portable Dorothy Parker *and I really liked her. Then a friend told me she was alcoholic, and that she died alone. I thought of her life differently. It's very tragic, the disparity between what people produce and the life they lead. You'd think they'd be happy doing what they love and being paid for it. I had wanted to idealize my favorite writers and hoped they led pretty good lives. After that, hearing about Parker, it didn't matter so much. I learned to separate the artist from the art.*

My friends and I in college didn't drink, mainly for health reasons—I had asthma as a child. But we had other forms of escape. We immersed ourselves in entertainment, especially movies and television. That was a form of abuse, really! Pop culture! I'm sure it had a negative effect on us, mainly on our attention span. I guess we've been entertainment addicts since we were kids. All our lives we abused entertainment.

I'm serious about that. It's still a limiting thing for me. I can't sit down for more than an hour to write. Since I work during the day, I can only spend so many hours a week on writing. I wish I could spend more. When I have a whole day to myself, I do write more. I think my friends are the same way.

For the first eighteen years I watched a lot of TV, but when I went away to college I didn't have a TV at all. During my twenties I basically ignored TV, and when people got into discussions about their favorite shows, I'd be left out. Last summer, though, I broke down and bought a TV and a VCR. I thought it was going to be a lonely winter, so I gave in to this urge. I was afraid that having a TV would make me write less, but my output hasn't changed. I still get fidgety after about an hour of writing, but I don't feel too bad about it because E. B. White said he was a fidgeting writer, and he couldn't sit down for very long either. That's probably how he wrote all those brilliant short pieces for "The Talk of the Town" in The New Yorker.

I was born in the Philippines and moved here when I was seven. I approach most familiar things as a foreigner, and I keep a distance from things to get a certain level of irony. I'm not attuned to ethnic themes, I don't feel a need to explore them. Mostly because ethnic themes aren't funny, and right now I like to write funny stories. I think what I'd have to say about being an immigrant would mostly be sad.

There's a tourist brochure that calls the Philippines the "Land of Friends." So it was sad coming here and meeting with prejudice. I don't feel a need to explain it. I don't really deal with it in real life either, I brush it off. As a kid I felt special because I was different. I got called on a lot. I was the "affirmative action kid," I actually felt good about it.

Most Philippine poets and novelists are very political—there's always a big message in what they write. I get kind of wary of that.

The writers I admire are Vonnegut and Barthelme. I like funny writers. In my own work, I'm always torn. Do I want to be a real artist, or do I just want to entertain? Do I want to go for developing a story psychologically, or just get a really good laugh out of the reader? I hope I end up doing both.

DR. LOUISE EMMONS
Biologist, author of Neo-Tropical Rain Forest
Mammals: A Field Guide

I first read about Dr. Emmons in the *New York Times* science-page article by William K. Stevens about the Rapid Assessment Program she works on. The *Times* described it as "an ecological SWAT team . . . in the forefront of an emerging new strategy for exploring the world's threatened store of living things under the pressure of habitat destruction."

Two of the scientists on the team had been killed in the tragic crash of a small plane where they were working in the jungles of Ecuador. Dr. Emmons, a mammalogist who "signed on [to the team] from the Smithsonian" was described as a daring researcher:

"A favorite modus operandi of hers is to go out into the forest at night with a miner's lamp on her head, prospecting for animals. Once, colleagues say, she was stalked through the Peruvian rain forest by a jaguar wearing a radio collar, its presence clearly signalled by Dr. Emmons's clicking tracking receiver. 'She's crazy,' says Dr. Mittermeier admiringly." (Dr. Russell Mittermeier is president of Conservation International, the Washington-based nonprofit organization that put the Rapid Assessment Team together.) I spoke to Dr. Emmons on the phone from her home outside Washington, D.C.

ART AND SCIENCE ARE VERY CLOSE

A high school biology teacher got me interested in science when I was fourteen, and I decided that was what I was going to do. I never once even toyed with the idea of anything else. She encouraged me, got me a summer job at Woods Hole on Cape Cod. I went to college at Sarah Lawrence, hardly took any science courses, mostly English. I was interested in poetry, and I would have liked to write poetry, but I didn't have it to do. It didn't matter that I took mostly English courses at college, you do most of your science in graduate school. I went to Cornell for my doctorate.

I think art and science are very close in a funny way—anyway, the kind of science I do. I go out in the world with nothing but a notebook and a pencil—I extract something. What I decide to extract and what it is—that's a creative process. The whole world is out there and you've got to decide which piece is of interest, then assemble it into a structure, a set of ideas that all fit together—and then convince someone of the story you're making of this! Writing it is crucial—some of the best writing is scientific writing because you have to say exactly what you mean. You want to write it perfectly, to convince others—it's like pulling a piece out of nature and building a paradigm around it.

A lot of scientists wouldn't agree with me about the creative aspect of science. They think it's a lot of facts—but Einstein felt it was mostly intuition. It is—you're faced with so many bits of information, and you have to decide which is important. You have to extract out of the data, and it takes intuition to see what's in it. After you get the answer then you work on proving it. You create in your mind—I believe these things exist and I have to make an order out of it. Create an order.

On my thesis I was working on squirrels in Africa—they make a lot of calls. I couldn't figure out what the calls were about. One day I watched and watched and it suddenly clicked—I understood the context of it—I had spent enough time. I watched for a year and a half—all different species have a variety of different calls. They have a set of simple calls—one call they make when they want to signal another animal that they have a friendly intention. Some scientists had said it was a mating call, it only wants to say it's friendly. But mothers make it approaching their children, so it's not mating. Eventually, I watched them for four years, and wrote a long paper on vocalization.

You won't find out the answer just by listening—you have to be anthropomorphic, and some people don't want to be anthropomorphic. I consider us animals, like the others.

There's a point at which you understand it, and it all makes sense. Before that it doesn't make sense. You know you've found it when it makes sense.

Now I'm studying tree shrews in Borneo. I got interested because they have a strange way of raising their young. The mother puts them in the nest and then only goes to feed them every other day, and only spends a minute and a half, then leaves. They've never been studied except in captivity, never in the wild, so I wanted to find out why they did that.

It's more dangerous to walk around the streets of New York than to do what I do. There are some dangers, though. There's tropical disease, of course; and two of my colleagues were killed in a plane crash. I just got back from New Guinea, and we landed in a helicopter on an underwater raft—it was the hairiest helicopter landing I've ever had.

There are quite a few women field biologists, but not many mammologists. In New Guinea, there were twenty men and me. It wasn't a problem, not for me, I just went ahead and did what I wanted to do. I didn't know the culture of New Guinea, and I later found out I wasn't supposed to bathe upstream from any men. I guess they think in Melanesian culture that women are unclean. In some places women are not allowed to step over anything owned by a man. I'm not too fond of that culture. In most places it's not a problem.

Part Five

Living the Creative Process

Chapter 11

DOING IT
DAY BY DAY

If we can create stories, pictures, and songs; transform raw food into gourmet meals, steel and cement into soaring buildings, why can't we use our creative powers to enhance our own daily lives? If we can learn through exercises and conscious use of our senses to gain access to our creativity for making books, paintings, and buildings, why can't we call upon this spirit within us to enhance our moment-by-moment experiences in order to live them more fully—more creatively?

Here is a rough blueprint for doing that, created from one person's own idiosyncratic experience and outlook. Try it, and see if any of the ideas or suggestions could be applied to your own life. Then, with this as a model outline, create a blueprint of your own.

A BLUEPRINT FOR CREATING A DAY
1. WAKING

For many of us, this is not as easy as it sounds, and in fact, may be the most challenging part of the day.

I am not a morning person. I have never in my life jumped out of bed immediately upon waking, pointed eagerly toward the window, and exclaimed, "Look, the sun!" My natural tendency is to pull the covers up over my head and hide.

Ever since I can remember, clear back into childhood, my process on waking has felt more like some interior ancient re-enactment of the whole human drama, going back to protozoic times, rising through the slime, struggling up from the sea to reach land, crawling inch by inch over the dry terrain, and then, millions of eons later, by performing a miracle of will and coordination, rising to stand and then move forward on only two legs! That's the part where I actually manage to get my feet off the bed and onto the floor, stand up, and propel myself, step by step, to the bathroom, where, in the mirror, I confront some strange, sleep-ridden hallucination that reminds me of the theory that God formed his creatures from clay.

My mood was shifted—uplifted—for the morning challenge a decade ago when I came back to Boston from Hollywood and discovered a radio program that began at seven o'clock in the morning with bird calls (repeating them again for later risers at eight o'clock, and every hour on the hour till noon). I bought a clock with a radio alarm and set it for the station with the bird calls—a program called "Morning Pro Musica" hosted by the sonorous, deep-voiced Robert J. Lurtsema, a cultural hero of New England. Following the bird calls, one was not jolted by some harsh, staccato, speeded-up standard announcer's rap, but soothed by the amazingly slow, low, dulcet tones of Robert J. He played mostly classical music, music that rolls into your consciousness with the richness of spirit of the masters, Beethoven, Brahms, Bach, Vivaldi, Telemann, Albinoni, Pachelbel . . .

BIRDS, NOT BUZZERS

Such music brings a noble mood, a sense of the variety and possibilities of life, the power of beauty, and the capacity of humans to create it, with horns, drums, harpsichords, pianos, strings, woodwinds, each of these instruments conceived, invented, created by some mere creature or combination of creatures as mere as myself, then mastered and imagined in intricate combinations by some composer (think of the intricacy of such composition), then performed and led and produced in concert, pouring over us and into us (if we allow it) with the whole force of creation.

Wake to bird calls. The sound is gentle, sweet, melodious, relaxing yet interesting, a nonshock way to lure you into the day, as opposed to the rude shove of an alarm or the hard bump of a buzzer, both of which begin your day with a nasty jolt. If you live in the country, or some quiet place where birds outside your window provide your wake-up call naturally, all the better. If you don't have that advantage, buy a bird-call record. If you can do it, or know someone who can, rig your record player or CD so it goes off at the time you want to wake by playing the birds' music, followed by other music you find uplifting, whether it's the classical style or not, whatever stirs you, gives you a sense of the spirit—the animating or vital principal.

INSCRIBING THE DAY

One day Robert J. announced after the bird calls that he was going to play a piece by Bach called "Christians, Inscribe the Day!" The idea struck me, and I could feel a tingle of anticipation at what it suggested. To be stirred by it you don't have to be a Christian (if you're not, substitute Buddhists, Jews, Muslims, or just People—or simply say your own name with it, as in "Dan—inscribe the day!" or "Alice—inscribe the day!") What moves me is the concept that we stand at the beginning of a new day, and instead of just letting that day happen to us, roll over us (sometimes it seems like an oncoming freight train), it's actually possible for us to *inscribe* the day—to make our mark on it, cause something we want to happen in it, take some action that will affect it. That's not a bad thought to have on waking.

Inscribe the day.

How?

Write down something you'd like to make happen in the day that you hadn't thought of before.

Get up a half hour early and write in your journal—thoughts, observations, ideas, descriptions, names, places. Read a writer's journal or notebook to see how he or she organizes and categorizes subjects and lists and ideas. Some of my own favorites are the notebooks of F. Scott Fitzgerald, published at the end of his unfinished novel *The Last Tycoon*, in the edition with an introduction by Edmund Wilson.

Fitzgerald loved to keep lists, ideas, overheard snatches of dialogue he might use later in a story.

As well as being a record of our daily journey, a journal can be like a creative warehouse of parts that can later be assembled to make a story, play, script, or novel, or a place where the creator of a fiction can rummage to find just the right missing part for a work he or she's constructing at the moment (a line overheard in a coffeehouse, a description of dawn at the beach, an experienced emotion of anger or love that may fit one of your characters.) Or one of those stored parts may serve as the spark for a new creation.

If you have a meditation practice, and are accustomed to doing it in the morning, that is obviously part of a powerful beginning of the day. If you don't have such a practice, or you like to meditate later in the day, at least take five moments to be still. Breathe in and out, become aware of your breathing. Settle. Be still, before becoming active. Center yourself before moving out into the whirlwind of work and the world that will push and pull you in different directions.

2. EATING BREAKFAST

Sit down before you eat.

It's not only more relaxing, it's more civilized. Rabbi Harold Kushner explains in his book *To Life!* that, though it is little known, "there is a Jewish law forbidding us to eat standing up. Animals eat standing up. Human beings turn the act of ingestion into a much more dignified one. They sit, they offer a prayer of thanks, they eat their food in a leisurely manner rather than gulp it as animals do."

This is part of the larger purpose of the Jewish laws, Rabbi Kushner explains, "to teach us how to take the ordinary and make it holy."

If you eat at home, listen to music you enjoy.

Light a candle. Eating dinner by candlelight makes it special, an occasion. It never occurred to me to eat breakfast by candlelight, until my friend and favorite photographer, Theresa Mackin, invited me for breakfast once and lit two candles at the table before serving bowls of oatmeal with raisins. (Theresa has taken most of my book jacket photos since 1985, and always creates a way to make me smile and not look goofy. She is one of the most creative people I know.) It was lovely. Why shouldn't breakfast be special sometimes? What's the occasion? It's a new day, a day that never existed before in the entire course of history, and you are alive in it.

Why not celebrate? Why not honor the day, and the meal, and your partner or family or roommates—or yourself alone—with this glow.

A PAUSE THAT REFRESHES

Before you begin to eat, take a moment to stop, breathe, and think about what you're about to eat. Some years ago I began to silently offer a prayer of thanks for my food, my health, and my life before eating breakfast in the morning. If not a prayer, then a meditation of thanks is appropriate and empowering, a quiet acknowledgment of the life force, the abundance of the world that provides this sustenance, the fuel or power that keeps you going.

When you eat, notice how it tastes. Food isn't just fuel that we ingest because we need it to operate, it also provides enjoyment. If you don't enjoy what you're eating, think about what you might have for breakfast the next day that you would like better. Don't just use food as background you take for granted, but take the pleasure as well as the sustenance from it.

Read cookbooks, or books about food and cooking, for other people's ideas, new ways of doing things. A whole new world of appreciation opened up to me back in 1971 when a friend pressed on me some books by M. F. K. Fisher. The books had intriguing, witty titles like *How to Cook a Wolf*, *With Bold Knife and Fork*, and *Consider the Oyster*. "You must read these books," my artist and writer friend Eve Babitz told me. "They're like Proust—but with recipes!"

Ms. Fisher was a great storyteller, and she wove her tales around food and cooking and eating, making me freshly aware of the wonders of taste and the joy of eating—not just gourmet meals but homemade dishes like meatloaf with catsup. Fisher continued writing marvelous books until her death at age eight-four in 1992, and she heightened my awareness of the *fun* of eating, the downright pleasure.

Before rushing out the door, stop for a moment, go back and sit down on your bed or in a comfortable chair. It only takes a minute to do this, but just taking a deep breath, centering, bringing yourself into focus, is relaxing and reassuring before moving out into the world.

3. GOING TO WORK

If there is any way to walk or ride a bicycle to work, by all means, do it. If you have to drive, or take taxis or buses or subways, notice the people you see. Imagine their stories. See how they dress, what they read, what their body language tells you. Listen to what they say.

People evoke ideas. Look at them. Listen to them.

"You've written fourteen books and hundreds of articles and stories—where do you get your ideas?" someone once asked me.

"Walking down Charles Street," I said. That's "Main Street" in the neighborhood where I lived in Boston.

It's even all right to smile at people you see on the street.

I know you'll say that's dangerous today, especially in the city, but you can make a pretty good guess at a person who isn't going to get hysterical if you smile at them. Trust your own instinct. It's especially all right to smile at a waiter or clerk in a store, the place where you buy a newspaper.

WHEN I CHANGE, YOU CHANGE

Here's a way to test a philosophic principle. Vivekananda says, *"When I change, you change."* The simple-sounding phrase has the deepest and most far-reaching implications. It means you don't have to wait for the troublesome people in your life to mend their ways, or get out of their rut, or alter their attitude toward you. Change yourself, and they cannot remain unaffected by it.

Test this principle in the smallest way—smile at someone and see what happens. Does their expression remain the same? See if in this minuscule way you can demonstrate one of the powerful truths of human behavior: *When I change, you change.* It may enable you to see how the principle works in much larger ways, with people much closer to you, people important in all aspects of your life—boss, employee, wife, husband, friend.

Take with you on the bus or subway a book you have already read whose ideas inspire you, whose thoughts make you look at things in a deeper (or "higher") way, give you an angle of vision you usually don't get when you're going to or from work. I've carried around a book with many underlinings, called *Abandonment to Divine Providence*, written by Jean-Pierre de Caussade, a seventeenth-century French Jesuit whose letters to nuns of that era seem to speak to my current condition in America in the '90s! I'll never forget standing on the subway platform of the Red Line stop at Charles Street in Boston at a time of particular distress in my life, waiting for a subway I thought would never come. I pulled Caussade's book from my briefcase and opened it, by chance, to this underlined passage: "All things conduct you and support you. Your way is lined with banners as you advance along it in your carriage. All is in the hand of God."

A smile broke across my face as I imagined a big, flapping banner unfurling out from the subway platform, and a carriage rushing up from out of the tunnel underground. I went to Cambridge feeling royal. When I got off at the Harvard Square stop, the full, deep tones of a cello playing a lovely, plaintive melody greeted me, and I stopped to listen to a young man with long hair making music there in the subway cavern. Before moving on I emptied the coins from my pocket into his open cello case, and went on my way, feeling lighter.

Carry a seashell with you. Take a small shell from a beach, and keep it in your pocket. Throughout the day, when you take something out of your pocket, touch the shell and remember the beach, and the sun, and the water. Let the warmth and refreshment come back to you. Think of the ocean, and how immense it is compared to whatever problem you are dealing with at the moment.

4. WORKING

Whether your work is physical, mental, social, or solitary, before starting it, take a moment to think about what you want to accomplish. If the work you have to do that day seems overwhelming, play a "witness" game with yourself. In meditation, the "witness" part of our mind is the part that observes our thoughts and feelings, which separates us from them, gives us some distance from them and control over them. Imagine for a moment that you are an outside observer, watching you do your work. Visualizing yourself doing it brings a distance and a kind of relief, lifting the weight or burden of the task. From time to time during the day play the witness, observing yourself doing the work and standing aside from it, as if you were watching it in a play or a movie.

In a sense you are the director of your own movie—the movie of your life. You do the casting by choosing your friends and associates, you scout the locations when you decide what apartment or house to rent or buy in what city or landscape or neighborhood; you're also the musical director (what radio station do you listen to, what CDs or records do you play?) and the art director (you choose the clothes you buy and what you wear on a given day). As such you not only guide it, you can give it whatever interpretation you want.

PLAY A NEW ROLE

You can see your role in any particular situation—work, marriage, relationship—as hero or heroine or victim, and when you view it this way you have an opportunity to alter it, whether in interpretation or in action. How? Remember, you write your own lines; nobody hands you a script to memorize at the beginning of the day. You are free to "change your character," speak in a different way, express different thoughts and opinions, challenge others or accept them. The freedom of this becomes evident when you are aware of it, conscious of your opportunity.

A few years ago I heard Arlo Guthrie interviewed by Robert J. Lurtsema (now retired from Boston radio, unhappily for his fans). Arlo is the folksinger son of Woody Guthrie, and the author and singer of the '60s hit song "Alice's Restaurant," which became a popular movie about the life and times of him and his friends. Arlo was living again in the old church that was featured in the movie, writing new songs, gathering new friends in good projects of peace and music. Robert J. asked Arlo if there was going to be a movie about his new life and times.

"Oh, there's another movie, all right," Arlo said quite matter-of-factly. "I'm just waiting to see how it turns out."

All of us have movies of our lives ongoing; I had a new one begin a few years ago when I moved to New York without any definite return date, deciding to take it one year at a time. Look at the turning points in your own life, and the new ones you know are coming—see how you are living your own movie. See how you can direct it in a creative way—include a scene or a person who wasn't otherwise going to be in the movie of your day, and see how the whole thing changes.

MAKING DIALOGUE SING

You can change the whole meaning of your movie, and affect your relationship to all the other characters in the "cast" not only by what lines you say—but how you say them. I am not speaking theoretically, I am thinking of Karen Monti Lindo at *New Age Journal*. People called expecting the usual rote—often rude—boring and bored announcement. Instead they got music, as well as information.

Something like that alters your mood, it makes you think of other possibilities, it surprises you out of apathy. It reminds you that someone out there is alive, and likes it, and wants to make it more likable for you, too. I can think of no better example of creating with the spirit than the way Karen Monti Lindo answers the telephone at her office.

EVERYTHING COUNTS

When I lead workshops in Spiritual Autobiography, I am struck by the small but significant incidents people remember and write about that involve some phrase or deed of kindness someone did for them, or they did for someone else, and how it changed a mood, a day, a life, created a turning point. One woman wrote of going to a restaurant for a Christmas-season lunch when she was ten years old, with a girlfriend, and the harried waitress was nice to them even though they were kids and the place was crowded, so they pooled all their change to leave her a tip, and knowing it wasn't enough, they wrote a note of thanks on a napkin as well.

Looking back through the window, the kids saw the waitress smile as she picked up the change and read the note. A small thing. Yet it brought a moment of pleasure to people's lives—not just the waitress, but the two girls, one of whom remembered it years later, when it brought new pleasure to a roomful of other people who heard the story. The thought comes to me over and over when I hear such stories, that the smallest gesture we make to someone has a meaning, a resonance: *Everything counts*. Lives may later turn on a smile, a frown, a hand stretched out in friendship or support.

F. Scott Fitzgerald once observed, "It isn't given to us to know those rare moments when people are wide open and the lightest touch can wither or heal. A moment too late and we can never reach them any more in this world. They will not be cured by our most efficacious drugs or slain with our sharpest swords."

Bear that in mind when you go out the door. Remember it when you open the next door. Look around you and see the people. They aren't just background and decoration for your movie set. Pay attention to them. Honor them. Remember, each one is the star of his or her own movie, just as you are of yours.

"By being kind to others—if it's done properly, with proper understanding—we benefit as well," writes the American Buddhist nun Pema Chödrön in Start Where You Are. "We are completely interrelated. What you do to others, you do to yourself. What you do to yourself, you do to others."

Chicago Bulls coach Phil Jackson believes that leadership "means treating everyone with the same care and respect you give yourself—and trying to understand their reality without judgment." When we begin to be aware of our relatedness, Jackson says, "we begin to understand, directly, remarkably, that we're part of something larger than ourselves."

5. TAKING A BREAK

The Writers Room, where I went to work most every day when I lived in Boston (I like to go to the office, too, like everyone else!) is a series of cubicles with desks and word processors or typewriters, in office spaces located in the Transportation Building, a state agency. It's an atrium-style building, and outside the offices is a wide walkway with tables and chairs. During the course of the day many of the office workers come out for a break, and drink coffee and smoke cigarettes. The smoke is tangible and smelly and I walk through as if it were a gauntlet.

It saddens me to see the faces wreathed in smoke. I know—as a formerly continuous smoker—that smoking not only makes the throat and gums sore, it numbs and lulls and dulls rather than wakens or alerts the mind (not to mention its causing disease and death).

A ONE-LUNG SHOCK

I know this is an addiction and is not easy to stop—some say it's harder to end than alcohol. My own was ended by an unexpected shock. A friend came to visit me who had just had an operation to have a lung removed. I thought, with such a drastic result of his chain smoking he would have stopped. Though I still smoked a pipe at the time, and it was making my gums sore and my teeth yellow, I was putting off the time I would give it up. When my friend Paul came to visit, I was shocked to see that he was still smoking. He would take a puff of his cigarette, then he would break out into terrible deep, hacking coughs, and then he would squirt some kind of medicinal spray down his throat.

This went on all during the evening, and when I woke the next morning my living room was filled with that fog and stench of continuous smoke. I wanted to get out of the house and I went for a walk in the Boston Public Garden, taking in deep breaths of fresh air. I was clenching my own pipe in my teeth in anger at Paul, who seemed bent on destroying the one lung he had left. Suddenly, in anger, I took my pipe from my mouth and threw it into a trash bin. That was it. I have never smoked it since. Now when I write, instead of fiddling with pipe and tobacco, I chew on those wooden toothpicks called Stimudents, which serve me just as well. I think the shock of my friend's self-destruction, before my very eyes, shocked me out of my own addiction to tobacco.

BEING A TREE

My favorite work break is doing a yoga balance posture called the Tree. You simply stand, balanced, then shift the weight of your body to your right leg—fix your eye on an object on the wall in front of you—and lift your left leg with your right hand, bracing the left foot against the right leg, letting the left knee bend to the side. If you can stand that way, slowly lift your arms in the air, straight up, and hold the posture. Now you're the tree. Hold the posture for a minute or so, or as long as you can, and then switch to the other side. It gives both centering and balance and leaves you refreshed.

If you don't feel you can stand up and "be a tree" in your office without getting kicked out or jeered out, you can always breathe at your desk. I mean consciously taking deep breaths, counting slowly on the inhalation and exhalation, getting long steady breaths that calm and center you. This, too, helps you think more clearly, and create.

6. LUNCHTIME

Instead of going to lunch one day, go to a museum, art gallery, or exhibit of sculpture, drawings, or photography. Look at the artwork on an empty stomach.

Often necessity is the mother of invention in creative thinking. Hardship sometimes forces us to new ways of perceiving things. Hemingway had some great ideas, when he was writing about his art, rather than alcohol or violence or his idea of man-woman relationships. (We can lose valuable insights if we throw away all of Hemingway because of the booze in his books.) When "Papa" was a young writer in Paris, he sometimes skipped lunch to save what little money he had, and to take his mind off his hunger he went sometimes to the Luxembourg Museum.

He says in his memoir of that time, *A Moveable Feast*, that hunger increased his appreciation of the artwork he saw: "All the paintings were sharpened and clearer and more beautiful if you were belly-empty, hollow hungry. I learned to understand Cézanne much better and to see truly how he made landscapes when I was hungry."

Hemingway found that all his perceptions were heightened in those days when he was hungry, and when he went in that condition to visit Sylvia Beach's bookstore on the rue l'Odeon, "The photographs looked different and you saw books that you had never seen before."

EATING LESS AND SEEING MORE

To see what we have never seen before exercises and flexes the creative muscle, making it more powerful to use in our own artistic creation. I don't recommend going hungry all the time, which saps the strength and makes us ill, but try at least occasionally to heighten your perception on purpose. Instead of going to lunch one day, go to a museum and notice what more you see and experience. Afterward, write what happened in your journal, describe what you saw, what you felt, and what you understood as a result of the heightened perception brought on by the temporary hunger.

"Hunger is healthy and the pictures do look better when you are hungry," Hemingway said, and immediately added, "Eating is wonderful too and do you know where you are going to eat right now?"

Hemingway can hardly wait to tell us where *he* is going to eat— the hunger increases his appetite as he goes to a restaurant called Lipps, and reports, "Every place I passed that my stomach noticed as quickly as my eyes made the walk an added pleasure." He takes pleasure in the food as well as the art, ordering potato salad and reporting with obvious delight, "The *pommes a l'huile* were firm and marinated and the olive oil delicious. I ground black pepper over the potatoes and moistened the bread in the olive oil. . . . When the *pommes a l'huile* were gone I ordered another serving and a *cervelas*. This was a sausage like a heavy, wide frankfurter split in two and covered with a special mustard sauce."

You don't have to starve to be an artist!

On the other hand, you don't have to gorge yourself, either. Michael Jordan, an artist on the basketball court, whose ability to jump and "hang" in midair has earned him the nickname "Air Jordan," was kidded by his teammates for "eating like a bird." Jordan's reply: "Birds can fly."

LOOK THROUGH ARTISTS' EYES

Another way to go to a museum and see more than you ordinarily would see—without even being hungry!—is to invite an artist you know, or a teacher of art, and ask them to take you on a personal tour, show you some of their own favorite paintings, and tell you what it is they admire in them and what their own understanding is of the painting and the artist who painted it. Artists and art teachers often enjoy doing this, and can show you things—ways of seeing the artwork— that to the untrained, unschooled eye are a mystery.

If you don't know any such artist or art teacher, get a small group of friends together who would also like to learn to see more, and ask everyone to contribute a sum of money so you can offer payment to a painter or art teacher in your community to take you on such a tour. I know how much fun and how literally "eye-opening" this experience can be, because I've done it.

Every year the Beacon Hill Civic Association in Boston holds an auction to raise money for its work, and neighbors donate their services to be bid on—someone might offer to come to your house and cook a French dinner for twelve guests, another might play the piano at your party, someone else could take you sailing in Boston harbor. One year a local psychiatrist offered six hours of family therapy! Paul Taylor, who is an art professor at the University of Massachusetts at Boston and a distinguished art critic and author, offered to take a group of people on a tour of the Boston Museum of Fine Arts, showing them his favorite paintings and talking about why he appreciated them. My novelist neighbors, husband and wife James Carroll and Alexandra Marshall, won the bidding for that service, and invited me and nine other friends to go on the tour.

I never took art appreciation in college, and I feel embarrassingly uneducated about art, mumbling with every other philistine in the world only that I know what I like—but I don't even know why. The tour with Paul Taylor made me see every painting he talked about in a new way, and made me realize how much I was missing.

I also saw that as a writer I was losing out on what I could learn creatively from painting that would apply to my own craft and art with words. Reading of Hemingway's days in Paris, I realized he was not just creating his innovative style by learning from other writers—literary mentors like Gertrude Stein and Ezra Pound. He was also learning about literary style from looking at the artwork of the great French painters. He wrote that he "was learning something from the painting of Cezanne that made writing simple true sentences far from enough to make the stories have the dimensions that I was trying to put in them. I was learning very much from him but I was not articulate enough to explain it to anyone. Besides it was a secret."

In the same manner of opening up to unfamiliar arts through a professional practitioner, ask a musician friend to prep you before going to a concert with you, explaining the kind of things to notice and listen for—no matter what instrument or music they play. Afterwards tell what you heard, and listen to what your friend heard that you weren't even aware was going on (the next time you will be.) A friend who did this said, "A jazz guitarist once taught me wonderful things about Mozart's string quartets."

What do the other arts have to teach you about your own? The poet Baudelaire immersed himself in art and found in paintings, sculpture, music, and poetry "the concordant parts of all the arts and the similarities in their methods." What are the similarities in the methods of the other arts to your own? How could you apply them to your own art, your own work, your own relationships—your own life?

Another discipline to exercise on a lunch break is simply "noticing." Being aware—noticing—is a crucial part of our creative power. Noticing is also a kind of meditation, for when we are paying attention to who and what's around us we are taken out of the ego-trap of our tiring self-absorption. Anthropologist John Murra, who taught at Vassar and Cornell, used to tell his students to "notice the different way people from other countries and cultures open doors, light cigarettes, greet you, say good-bye. It gives you clues about their culture and its suppositions."

Architect Evans Woollen learned from his mother as a child to notice buildings; the architect who designed the Skydome in Toronto got his idea for the concept from looking at a lobster shell; biologist Louise Emmons discovered the meaning of the calls of African squirrels by watching them closely for a year and a half; chef Odette Bery notices how people approach their food. Hemingway noticed people and places for his use as a writer, saying of his days in Paris, "I would be listening to other people and noticing everything, I hoped; learning, I hoped."

Listening, noticing, and learning also make everything more interesting. It is boring to walk around the block at lunch break if you just remain inside your own head and let the interminable chatter of automatic nonthought carry you along with it—the past regrets and future worries, the should-haves and would-haves and mights and never-will-bes that clog and clutter our mind and numb us. We can interrupt that boring tape by looking, listening, noticing, learning from people, places, faces, all around us.

Baudelaire loved to walk the streets of Paris, and he urged artists to paint urban landscapes, reminding them, "The life of our city is rich in poetic and marvelous subjects. We are enveloped and steeped as

though in an atmosphere of the marvelous, but we do not notice it."
(There's the tip to *notice* again.) We complain so much about cities
now that we hurry through them without paying attention, averting
our eyes, keeping our heads down, longing for some pastoral vista and
losing the richness of what's around us.

Woods and fields and lakes are not the only places of inspiration.
Reverend Cecil Williams, the magnetic minister of San Francisco's
Glide Memorial Church, which welcomes people of all faiths, backgrounds, races, and nationalities, preaches that God is in the sidewalks, the crowds, the nitty-gritty of the city. On Easter he leads the
children on an urban Easter Egg Hunt to show that it is even more
miraculous to find such prizes on the pavement instead of in the grass.

Take another look at the streets and sidewalks you see every day
on the way to and from work. Hunt for your own miracles. See if you
can find, as Baudelaire did, "the religious intoxication of great cities."

RETURNING TO THE FORM

Some people do a class in aerobics on their lunch hour. Some are
lucky enough to have a yoga or tai chi class near where they work. If
you don't have such a class available to you at lunch hour, be sure to
do one after work, at least one evening a week. It can transform many
aspects of your life. The benefits go far beyond the hour or so you are
actually in the class.

The segments of our lives should flow together, rather than remain
compartmentalized. Yoga and tai chi have the power to flow into your
behavior in all areas of your life and work, giving you ways to move,
and be, and even create, in the form and rhythm of these powerful
disciplines.

After work, if you don't have a class in aerobics, tai chi, or yoga,
try a half hour of exercise on a stationary bike or rowing machine, or
just go jogging, walking, or bicycling for that length of time, and then
take a long shower. Doing this is not tiring, but enlivening, and gets
to be a habit that you miss if you do without it. This purpose can be
served in many ways—dance classes, or the varieties of body awareness
methods, like Feldenkrais or the Alexander Technique.

ADDICTED TO HEALTH

Just as there are destructive habits like smoking and drinking on a regular basis, there are also healthy habits, routines that refresh us. I have seen a new kind of criticism lately, people putting down Twelve Step programs because they are "addictive," that they only replace one habit with another, and that physical exercise does the same thing, creating addictions to running, jogging, or bicycling. This criticism is made as if there is no difference between getting drunk or riding a bicycle. What madness! I am grateful for my healthy habits. I am happy and proud to be so addicted to riding my stationary bike every day for a half hour that if I don't do it I feel stale, grubby, and cranky. I am trying now to get addicted to doing a yoga routine every day, too, instead of just during the once-a-week class I attend. Bring on such addictions! They are the way of discipline, the way of the creative warrior seeking the fullness of life.

Pay attention to the senses. When we're not numbing them with tobacco and alcohol we are free to use them for our enjoyment and to expand our own creativity.

7. THE EVENING MEAL

Don't forget the sense of taste. At least one night a week take the time to create your own meal from natural food instead of the frozen or canned stuff. At a hardware store, for a dollar or so you can get a metal steamer to put at the bottom of a pan. Put in an inch or so of water, put the collapsible metal steamer over it, put raw vegetables on it, and steam them. If you're like me, you may have never known the real taste of vegetables until you've steamed them. You can steam carrots, beets, corn on the cob, broccoli, and bring out the true flavor. Don't drown them in sauce, just experience the natural taste. It may be a revelation!

Another way to increase your sense of taste and appreciation of food is to participate in a Silent Meal. Invite a friend or friends. Play music in the background, but agree not to talk during the meal. You will have an opportunity to concentrate on the food, to really taste it, perhaps for the first time. I have taken part in Silent Meals that are held once a week at the Rancho La Puerta health spa. Each time is a relaxing, restoring experience, a time of fellowship with the other people gathered in silence at such a meal, a whole other dimension of community and communion.

TASTE, TOUCH, SMELL

Taste for inspiration and ideas. We think of playing music for inspiration, but often forget that Proust got the inspiration for his great work, *Remembrance of Things Past*, by eating a "madeleine"—a cookie—that brought back to him the memories of childhood, the very taste of what it was like. (Bring back your own childhood sometime by tasting tapioca!)

Use your nose, your sense of smell. Different scents evoke entire eras, scenes, events, people in our lives. See what memories the following smells evoke for you: wood smoke, bacon frying, Vicks salve, coffee boiling, patchouli perfume, lemons, wet grass, motor oil, the sea. There are stories in the memory of each aroma.

Try using scents for inspiration. Here's how a woman who took my workshop in Austin, Texas, used scent to evoke a childhood taste that evoked creativity. Patricia Speier wrote that

> Being in my grandmother Speier's kitchen was a spiritual experience. I say spiritual because I felt safe and connected in that place, and I also felt the glow of anticipation and the hope of magic there. Magic sometimes came in the form of cupcakes, iced with vanilla butter cream frosting. About a year ago I casually picked up a vanilla-scented votive candle while shopping. Immediately I was transported back to my grandmother's kitchen; I could absolutely taste those cupcakes. Now I buy those candles by the dozen. I have one in my bathroom that I light first thing in the morning. Lighting that candle each morning is a prayer. I bask in its delicious aroma while I shower and dress. I keep another candle in my study next to the computer. I don't light it every time I turn the computer on, but only when the work I am doing calls for communion with the muse. Lighting a vanilla votive ensures the presence of the creative spirit, even if it does not ensure a quality product.

Burning incense when you meditate provides a refreshment. A writer I heard about brings in a pot of fresh soil from her garden every day and puts it by her desk to inhale the scent while she works, making her mind feel awakened and inspired. Balzac used to keep a rotting orange by his desk to smell for freeing his imagination.

See what the thought of touching these things brings to mind: a wool blanket, a cashmere sweater, tree bark, silk, autumn leaves, a baseball glove, corduroy, leather, a shell, a stone. Keep a stone by your desk for a while and when you're stuck pick it up and rub it. Maybe an idea will come out.

"Texture can be very evocative," Judy Collins said in an interview with Bonnie Allen for *Ms.* magazine. "It's like the madeleines that Proust speaks of—you taste something and it sets off a whole series of images. Color, fabric, scent, texture, the sight of something . . . they each can set up a whole series of creative thoughts for me. So they're part of the way I'm stimulated to write my music. They're all very much connected."

As well as using your senses, use your heart. Connect with other people. At least one night a week do something that makes you part of a community. It's part of being human. It's part of being creative. What communities can you become a part of and be expanded and enlivened by? How can you make a contribution to other people, to your own community?

Remember the wisdom Albert Schweitzer passed on to a graduating class of medical students: "I don't know what your destiny will be, but one thing I know, the only ones among you who will be really happy are those who have sought and found how to serve."

8. A TIME TO CREATE

In the busy schedule that most of us must keep, one of the most difficult disciplines is to find time for our creative work. Some brave souls get up early in the morning to write, paint, draw, compose, or play music for an hour. When I was writing articles for *Esquire* back in the early '60s, I wondered how Gay Talese was able to turn out so many superb pieces for the magazine while he held a full-time job at the *New York Times*. I was a full-time freelancer, able to use my time as I chose, but he had to report for work every day at 9:00 AM. When I asked him what his secret was, he said, "I get up at 4:30 in the morning."

I want to make clear that I never got up at 4:30 in the morning to go to work, but I know it's humanly possible because Talese did it— until he had his first bestseller and was able to leave his reporting job at the *Times*. If we want to do something badly enough, we can always find a way.

Richard Blanco, a poet in the graduate writing program at Florida University, goes off by himself on his lunch hour from his full-time city engineering job and works on his poetry. His fellow workers know and respect what he's doing, and support his efforts and his need to be by himself at that time.

During the time of my first job after college as a reporter for a weekly newspaper, I would go back to my room at a local rooming house and work at night, and on weekends, hammering away at the fiction it would take nearly another decade to publish, but which gave me experience, practice, and the knowledge I was writing, and thus, a writer.

The way to become a knight is to act like a knight, the legendary professor Mark Van Doren told his students at Columbia when he lectured on Cervantes's *Don Quixote*. By the same token, the way to be a writer is to write; to be a painter you must paint. And the biggest problem for many people is to find the time.

The standard wisdom is that you have to do your artistic work every day. Certainly that is ideal. Getting into a rhythm, a routine, by doing the same creative process every day is tremendously powerful, and works for many kinds of disciplines. Explaining his process for creating the nightly monologue on "The Tonight Show," Jay Leno told an interviewer for *Entertainment Weekly*, "It's a 24 hour thing. If I think of something, I'll make a note. And then when I go home I put them on cards. It's like lifting weights. You've got to do it every day."

Not everyone has the freedom to work in his or her chosen creative field every day, however; but that doesn't have to stop anyone. If you can't do it every day, do it when you can. Do it on weekends, do it on vacations, do it on "sick days," on slow days at work, and holidays. Stay up all night to do it, or get up before dawn to do it. Fight for the time, and take what you can make.

Many people find a way to produce their art and hold down a full-time job, and/or raise children at the same time. The late Kay Boyle was a distinguished and highly productive novelist, short-story writer, and journalist who raised five children and, during the time I knew her in the 1950s, taught school full-time. One of Kay's daughters, the painter Clover Vail, works by day in a legal office, and paints at night and on weekends. (It's not a matter of genes, but of commitment.) The flamboyant novelist Harry Crews taught himself to write by churning out "practice" novels while he served in the Marine Corps. Malcolm X and Eldridge Cleaver wrote in prison. Today at Sing Sing Prison I know men who are creating fine art, in painting and writing, in circumstances and atmosphere hardly conducive to creativity. Yet they create. They not only survive, they create.

You can, too.

Commitment is the key. If you're not clear about what that is, or what it means to be committed, here is the best explanation I know, written by W. H. Murray, author of *The Scottish Himalayan Expedition*:

> Until one is committed there is hesitancy, the chance to draw back, always ineffectiveness. Concerning all acts of initiative (and creation), there is one elementary truth, the ignorance of which kills countless ideas and splendid plans; that the moment one definitely commits oneself, then Providence moves too. All sorts of things occur to help one that would never otherwise have occurred. A whole stream of events issues from the decision, raising in one's favor all manner of unforeseen incidents and meetings and material assistance, which no man could have dreamt would have come his way.
>
> I have learned a deep respect for one of Goethe's couplets: "Whatever you can do, or dream you can, begin it./ Boldness has genius, power, and magic in it."

FIND YOUR PRACTICE

Try to find a meditation practice that suits you, and make it a part of your routine. There are courses and books on all different kinds of simple techniques, from breathing or using a mantra to meditating "on" natural objects. Bring this kind of centering and silence in to your life. It is restorative and calming, and deepens your capacity to appreciate and to create.

Go to the woods. Take a day to go out to the nearest wooded area near where you live. Walk through and look and listen. Find a place to sit and meditate. Think about the natural world.

Think about what Einstein meant when he wrote:

> My religion consists of a humble admiration of the illimitable superior spirit who reveals himself in the slightest details we are able to perceive with our frail and feeble minds. That deeply emotional conviction of the presence of a superior reasoning power which is revealed in the incomprehensible universe forms my idea of God.

Meditate after reading this passage from the Book of Job (Job 12:7–10):

> But ask the beasts, and they will teach you;
>   the birds of the air, and they will tell you;
> or the plants of the earth, and they will teach you;
>   and the fish of the sea will declare to you.
> Who among all these does not know
>   that the hand of the Lord has done this?
> In his hand is the life of every living thing
>   and the breath of all humankind.

9. GOING TO BED

Before you go to bed, put a notebook and pencil beside you in case you wake with dreams or thoughts you want to write down. Read Edmund Wilson's book *Night Thoughts* to see how creative he was with these middle-of-the-night ideas. Read some books on dreams and dream work to enable you to remember your dreams and use them creatively, in your life and art. (Notice in the interviews with creators how many people use dreams, and how they incorporate them into their creative work.) Remember a line from Baudelaire: "Sleep is full of miracles."

He noted in his journal that "one must desire to dream and know how to dream. The evocation of inspiration. A magic art."

Give thanks for being part of creation, for being blessed with the animating or vital spirit that enables you to create. Read something you find empowering, affirming, and wise. Remind yourself you belong here, on this planet, and that your own role here is as important to the people you touch in your own daily life as is the president's, or any Nobel Prize winner's. It's especially important to remind ourselves of our worth when things are not going smoothly, when our plans seem to run up against brick walls, when our messages don't seem to penetrate.

When Cardinal Newman left the Anglican Church at the height of his influence to become a Roman Catholic, he was subjected to scorn and rejection. He lost old friends and was thrown in with strangers who suspected his motives. In this dark time he wrote to himself a message that I find strength in myself. Most of us, at some time or other, need and can find comfort in this powerful affirmation:

"God has created me, to do Him some definite service; he has committed some work to me which He has not committed to another. I have my mission—I may never know it in this life, but I shall be told it in the next. I am a link in a chain, a bond of connection between persons. He has not created me for nothing. I shall do good. I shall do His work. Therefore I will trust Him. Whatever, wherever I am. I cannot be thrown away."

Chapter 12

NEW MODELS: CREATORS OF THE SPIRIT

I was into my third Bloody Mary when the writer hosting that Sunday afternoon soiree said I was mistaken, Dostoyevsky was not an alcoholic—in fact, hadn't even been a big drinker. The shock and disillusionment must have showed on my face, for everyone burst out laughing. One of my other writer friends pointed at me and said through his cackling laugh, "You're mad that Dostoyevsky wasn't a rummy!"

It was probably twenty-five years ago, but I can see that room now, as I can taste the thickish film of tomato juice on my tongue and feel the vodka at the roof of my head. It seemed like a silvery substance up there, like mercury, coating the very inside top of my cranium and causing a slight ringing sound that would grow more piercing as the day wore on. It would combine with the white bright light of the winter afternoon to create a headache of killer intensity, but still I drank on, even though I didn't even like Bloody Marys. I took whatever alcohol was offered in whatever form or concoction, and once I started, would no more imagine stopping than ripping off my clothes and jumping into a snowbank. Are you kidding? Don't even offer me coffee, it cuts the high, stops the iron-locomotive progress of the booze fueling me along like a runaway train until I crash into bed and oblivion.

I was lucky to survive. Too many writers, some of them friends of mine, crashed right into their graves while riding the booze train. Instead of burying any more artists and writers, let's bury the myth that booze is a muse, that alcohol and drugs are a spur to creativity. The path to creativity begins with clarity, which means clearing the mind and body of substances that numb the senses and cloud perception.

The old model of creativity was booze, drugs, and deterioration of the work as well as the physical and mental condition of the creator, leading to early death, like Dylan Thomas (thirty-nine), and F. Scott Fitzgerald (forty-four), or somewhat extended life with self-inflicted injuries and abuse of the body leading to hospitalizations, like Faulkner, or ending in mental aberration and suicide, like Hemingway. The myth was propagated that illness and early death was not only glamorous, exciting, and noble, but necessary for the act of creation itself, like a sacrifice to the Gods, trading health and sanity for art and literature.

The new model of creating from the spirit replaces numbing with enlivening, by replacing drugs and alcohol with clarity, by using all the techniques that bring us into that state. A process of emptying, filling, and creating enables us to tap into our spiritual resources, our deepest selves, for inspiration and sustenance. The clarity prized by recent creators who recover from drugs and alcohol and wrote about it, like Raymond Carver, and those who never bought into the old model, like Toni Morrison, America's newest Nobel Laureate for Literature, supports and validates the new model of creativity.

As I explored the subject for this book, and became aware of the myth that creativity was restricted to the arts, I saw that I could learn from teachers and practitioners in many different fields. The old idea that people in the arts are the only creators is a good example of a restrictive myth, one that limits possibilities. Getting rid of such myths gives a liberating feeling, opening doors and entire vistas that weren't visible before. That's been part of the fun of "living into" the new model of creativity based on clarity. (By "living into" I mean aspiring toward, having your actions be consistent with your goal—a concept and term I learned from Landmark Education courses.)

BEING TAI CHI

Some of the new mentors I found inspiring in the way they create their lives and work were in the new fields I was starting to explore, like tai chi.

I was lucky to have as a teacher David Zucker, who really embodies tai chi. In the way he moves and holds himself, in the clear,
low-key manner in which he speaks, David seems to exemplify the
concept of centeredness. There's a feeling that if you pushed him
down, he would simply bounce back up to his original position without any effort, by means of some internal balance. As well as teaching
tai chi, David is a creator in theater, an actor, mime, and director, and
his centeredness is integrated in his work.

I asked him once to tell me how a man who grew up a Catholic in
Chester, Massachusetts, became a teacher of tai chi as well as a sixth-
degree black belt master of the Zen martial art of swordsmanship
called Shim Gum Do.

"In the late '60s and early '70s," he said, "I got interested in spirituality through Zen and Taoism. I used to haunt the bookstores for
books on those subjects. I saw this book on something called tai chi,
which I'd never heard of before. It said it was 'meditation in motion,'
and since I was a very active person—I began doing mime and acting
in college at U Mass/Amherst, then got an MFA in theater at Bran-
deis—it seemed right up my alley."

He bought the book on tai chi, found a Chinese master of the art
in Cambridge, studied for several years, and began to teach it to his
friends, then to classes at the Boston Center for Adult Education.

"Before I got into tai chi," David told me, "I did a lot of drugs, a lot
of marijuana. I'm totally anti-drug now. There's a very big difference
in my lifestyle since I started tai chi, but it was a gradual change. I
don't know how much to attribute directly to tai chi, to Zen, or to
Christianity. It was all a kind of a turn to God."

Tai chi has been called a form of self-defense, yet in studying it
I never had the sense I was learning anything that might fend off a
mugger. There are no kicks or yells or punches involved in the graceful movements of the form. I asked David how it could be used in
self-defense.

"In tai chi, you learn to confront in a positive way," he explained.
"You dance with the other person, you turn it into a dance. Since I
started doing tai chi, I've never been in a fight in which I've had to
physically defend myself, but I've been in plenty of situations where I
could have been killed if I hadn't reacted spontaneously and immedi-

ately—like car accidents that were avoided when I saw headlights coming at me down the other side of the street and reacted instinctively. Tai chi becomes an art you use daily, rather than waiting for the one moment of your life when you use it in self-defense. I tell people it's a waste of their money if they're learning it for self-defense because they'll maybe use it once in their life or maybe never use it—but in fact that's the highest form of self-defense, if you never have to use it."

David tries to do his tai chi at least a half hour every day, but he says, "In a sense I'm always practicing, because even when I'm not doing the actual choreographed form itself, any movement I do can be tai chi. If I'm in the kitchen and I reach for the cupboard, I try to open the cupboard with my whole body. In tai chi, you unify your body from the soles of your feet to the top of your head, you try to move as one unit. I can do that walking down the street—I still slip on the ice but I don't fall down anymore, because I've learned to keep my weight low. Anything I do all day is a dance of a sort because my body is moving around."

I recommended tai chi to my minister, Carl Scovel, and he took a class at a time when David didn't teach, and was not altogether satisfied with the experience. I urged him to take it with David, he would see the real thing, and the next year he did, and thanked me. Some time after that Carl gave a sermon in which he talked about the distinction between teaching and being. To illustrate his point he used the difference in taking a tai chi class with his first teacher, and then with David Zucker. The first teacher, Carl said, was a good man, completely competent, who taught tai chi in a clear, able manner. The difference in the class with him and the class with David, Carl explained, was that "The first man *teaches* tai chi; David *is* tai chi."

A WRITER'S "PALPABLE GOD"

In a similar way I came to admire the novelist Reynolds Price, who not only writes precisely and eloquently about his faith as a Christian, in essays as well as fiction, he *is* that faith. I first knew Price's work as a talented writer of fiction from his first novel *A Long and Happy Life*, a kind of tour de force that was printed in its entirety in *Harpers Magazine* when it came out in 1962. I admired it, but hadn't followed Price's later work, so I was surprised and intrigued when Carl Scovel (my minister pointing yet again to the right clue) loaned me a book by Price he thought I'd enjoy, called A *Palpable God.*

The book begins with a long essay, "The Bible as Narrative," which tells how Price came to a crisis in his faith and his work. To address it, he wrote literal translations from the Greek of Old and New Testament stories of the Hebrew-Christian Bible. These comprise the rest of the book. I had not known Price was a practicing Christian and I was impressed with the passion and strength of his faith, its central place in his life and work. I began to read the rest of his novels. I found in them an underlying theme of humans engaged in the quest for meaning and understanding, grappling with God and the Christian faith they were born into in the American South. These are not overtly religious novels; yet, religion is a part of them, as it is a natural part of the daily lives of the characters, even though they may not even be churchgoing people—even though they may feel, as character Kate Vaiden does, that faith is not easy, that sometimes in trying to pray and be in touch with God she feels "like Helen Keller in a barrel."

I was shocked and dismayed to learn from a newspaper story that Price was stricken in 1984 with "an astrocytoma in his spinal cord" that resulted in paraplegia, and that he was confined to a wheelchair for the rest of his life. The disease struck him while he was in the middle of writing the novel *Kate Vaiden,* one of his most ambitious and accomplished works (it would win the National Book Critics Circle Award for fiction). He not only finished the book, he made the occasion of what others (like me) would have taken as a tragedy to be a blessing. The publisher's description of his career for his 1987 book of essays A *Common Room* reports that as a result of his physical incapacity, "The new access of time and energy has enabled him to complete two novels [*Kate Vaiden,* followed by *Good Hearts*], a collection of essays, and a trilogy of plays called New Music. He continues teaching at Duke."

I wanted to meet such a man. I had given my workshop in Spiritual Autobiography to the Cowley Fathers in Cambridge, and I offered to give it at their retreat house in Durham, North Carolina, where Reynolds Price was living, in hopes of getting to meet and talk with him. I had that privilege in October of 1989.

I wrote to Price and asked to meet him for dinner. He suggested a

local Mexican restaurant where he was driven by an assistant, a graduate student, in his specially equipped van with a ramp for his wheelchair. Price had written that he was born in Macon, North Carolina,
"a village edged by cotton and tobacco fields but split down the middle
by the Seaboard Railway," in 1933. That was the year after I was born;
yet, he seemed not only much wiser in understanding and intellect,
but at the same time, as youthful in spirit (evidenced by a genuine enthusiasm for life and work) as any person I know, of any age. His main
preoccupation and enthusiasm that evening was that his trilogy of
plays was going to be put on the following week at a theater in Cleveland, and he was looking forward to going there to see the production.
It was clear that his physical limitations would not prevent him from
carrying out any aspect of his work.

He continues to use what others would call his handicap as an opportunity to create. To try to relieve some of the pain produced by his
condition so he could sit and write for longer periods, Price went to a
hypnotist. During the sessions he not only eased the pain in his back,
but found that the hypnotic trances brought memories of early childhood that had never been accessible to him before. When the hypnotic therapy was successfully completed, Price asked the hypnotist if
he could work with him using the same technique to bring back other
early memories. The hypnotist agreed, and out of those trance-induced
memories he recovered from his past the material for a brilliant autobiographical memoir, *Clear Pictures*. Since then, Price has completed
two more highly praised novels, *The Tongues of Angels* and *Blue Calhoun*, as well as a uniquely powerful personal account of his experience
with cancer, *A Whole New Life: An Illness and a Healing*. He continues
to work and produce at the highest level, at the peak of his artistic
powers. Reynolds Price is a heroic example of one whose bodyspirit,
even in crisis and physical restriction, has led to creative fulfillment
and triumph. Price embodies his religious faith, acts it in his life and
work, and when he writes about it, as he does in his essay "At the
Heart," his words carry the weight and ring of earned authority:

> The most difficult and constant of our struggles is with our-
> selves, with our predictable but always surprising tendency to
> choose the wasteful course, our busy devastation of other crea-
> tures and of the planet itself, a succession of error that blinds

us to the rare glimpses God permits of his moving hand. When those choices have led us into harrowing dark nights of the soul, and he and our fellows seem absent or unwilling to help, then the next likely cry—parched and blameful—is "Abandonment! No just God could treat me thus."

But as the mystics of many creeds assert, God does not entirely abandon us. He does however take us seriously; even more terrifying, he loves us and craves our love. A great part of what we call evil is not the result of divine sadism or fickle disappearance but of the reverse.

We steadily flee a creator who can tend both the slow wheel of the galaxies and our own feverish escape while he awaits our return. For his own purpose as he waits, he may hide behind all but impenetrable screens—holocausts, individual agonized lifetimes—but the merciful intent of his hand is eventually discernible by any patient witness.

And the tale he is choosing to tell himself and all creation will not finish but will amend and augment itself, blossoming ever more grandly like the radiant choruses of Mozart's *Magic Flute*, swelling to transform a world of farce, trial, pain— unfolding with unimaginable and individually appropriate rewards for each worthy creature (perhaps for all human creatures if each—as seems increasingly possible—was bought by the sacrifice of his only son), a goal of unbroken justice and joy for all creatures known to God by name.

TONI MORRISON'S MONUMENT

Whether his theology is yours, all people of spirit can find in Reynolds Price's life and work a nobility of faith as well as achievement, a large and courageous vision of a quality and scope I have witnessed in other writers working now as well. I heard it in the voice and message of Toni Morrison when she came to receive the Melcher Book Award, given annually by the Unitarian Universalist Association for the book that "most advances the cause of liberal religion." I served on that committee when, for the first time in the history of the award, it was given for a work of fiction, Morrison's novel *Beloved*. I had until the judging avoided reading the book, thinking I already knew about slavery, or knew enough, and didn't see the point in being further depressed by hearing another dramatization of its evils. But when I read the novel—with increasing fascination and compulsion to finish—I realized I had essentially known nothing at all of slavery, certainly never had plumbed the depths of its dehumanizing horrors and blasphemy of soul until I was *compelled* to do so by the genius and compassion of the novelist.

After our committee announced its award in the spring of 1988, we learned that *Beloved* had won the Pulitzer Prize. We worried that the growing and well-deserved success of the book and increasing fame of its author would make it unlikely that she would come to Cambridge that fall to receive our own less-prestigious award.

Toni Morrison did come, though, explaining at a reception in her honor that she wanted to acknowledge the Melcher Award in person because it was especially important to her that the novel was recognized for its *religious* value. She spoke to an overflow crowd at the Unitarian Church in Harvard Square (two hundred others were turned away), telling with brief, sure, eloquent delivery that it wasn't until she had finished a book that she really knew the reason she had written it. When she finished *Beloved* she realized she had written it as a "monument" to the slaves. There are many monuments in this country, she said; monuments to generals, to soldiers and sailors, to presidents and captains of industry. There are monuments to people who *freed* the slaves, but there are no monuments to the slaves. "Not even a bench," she said, "on the Mississippi River."

And so she dedicated her book to the sixty million people who died as a direct result of slavery.

Now there is a monument to their memory, a monument that may finally be more lasting and memorable than the monument to the presidents carved out of Mount Rushmore.

Ms. Morrison took questions from the eager, admiring audience, answered them succinctly and gracefully and with the dignity and command of moral as well as literary vision. Yes, it was hard to write the book, she said; it was sometimes very painful, and sometimes she wanted to stop. At those times she heard the voices of her ancestors saying, "You think what *you* are doing is hard? Putting words on paper? Think what *we* did!"

And she would take up her work again, and continue. She explained that she had to set for herself the highest standards because she was writing this for her ancestors. Knowing that, she said, she could not write "junk." "They are not interested in *junk*," she said, with withering contempt for the shabby, the sloppy, the less than first-rate.

Hearing Toni Morrison that night was one of those experiences that made me proud of being a writer. I called my friend Marcie Hershman, who was struggling to write her own "monument" to ancestors who had died in the Holocaust, to tell her about the evening. Marcie had returned from the trip to Germany with her brother Rob, which had wakened something in her, stories of people who lived their daily lives during the Holocaust. Marcie had completed one of the stories and it was published in the magazine *Tikkun*, and she had continued to write other stories set in the same fictional town of that era; and yet it was a struggle. It was difficult and painful to re-create in her imagination that time of destruction to people of her own family. She had even been tempted to stop, to put the whole project away, give it up. I told her what Toni Morrison said about how hard it was to write *Beloved*, and how she heard the voices of her own ancestors saying to go on, to remember how much harder it had been for them, and that her book was a monument to them. Marcie said she knew exactly what was meant, and it was helpful to hear Morrison's experience. Marcie did continue on and finished her powerful novel *Tales of the Master Race*.

Passing on Morrison's words to Marcie was not the one crucial factor that enabled her to complete her own monument, forge her own moral vision in fiction; but it helped, it was one of the many messages of meaning and encouragement and courage, and I felt honored to serve as the conduit. I was reminded of the idea of spirit moving from one place to another, through the work of writers like Morrison, who are its purveyors, who reach beyond what seems possible and bring it, a kind of moral lightning, down to us.

FROM DEATH TO HEALING

Another book born out of personal pain transformed into a moral vision of meaning to people of all faiths, or no religious belief at all, is *When Bad Things Happen to Good People*. I first read the book when I was part of a small prayer group that met once a week at King's Chapel. We took turns sharing with one another poems or psalms or passages from the Bible or books we were reading that we found insightful and helpful in our lives. A young man whose father and brother had both died in the same year read to us from this book and spoke about how its understanding of personal tragedy had helped him in dealing with his loss. It was shortly after that I met the author, Rabbi Kushner.

In his book *To Life!* Harold Kushner again writes out of his personal struggle to understand and live by a religious vision. He explains, "When my wife and I learned that our three-year-old son had an incurable illness that would cause him to die young, I could not accept the notion that God wanted this bright, innocent child to suffer and die. But I could believe that, in the face of genetic misfortune, God could give us the strength to cope, to survive and ultimately transcend the tragedy. Unable to keep my son from dying, God showed me how to redeem his death from being a statistic and forge it into a book that would bring healing to millions."

As often happens, creation was forged out of pain, the pain was transformed, and transforms others. It was not the creation that caused the pain, but rather, that turned it into something else, as in a process of alchemy—for creation *is* a kind of alchemy, not by heating and mixing of ores and metals, but using the even more precious lodes of spirit and imagination.

I started writing this about new models of creation without an outline, without knowing who or what I would use to make a point I had not yet articulated even to myself. I decided to just plunge in. I didn't know I'd be writing about my old tai chi teacher, followed by two Christians and a Jew, or two novelists and a rabbi, or three writers with religious themes. I only went for whom and what I admired and had moved me personally. Now I see something else these people have in common as well as their creativity and spiritual attunement—their moral vision of the universe. The writers, like the tai chi teacher, are all people who strike you at once as deeply centered; people whose bodyspirit conveys a confidence, not of egotism but of vision, and whose voices also convey a power, a strength, not of volume but of clarity. In their person as well as their work they portray conviction, balance, wholeness, awareness, and a sense that their life and art and spirit are fully integrated, are one.

All have known their own dark night of the soul and easily could have remained in darkness or emerged broken or resentful or both, but all have come back from it bearing meaning and story, not only for themselves but for others. That is the work of the spirit and how it moves, guiding us—in the Navajo phrase—"on the gleaming way." That is the way of creation.

LET A JOY KEEP YOU

We needn't search for suffering to inspire us, or seek pain to prod us into poetry. As M. Scott Peck said in the opening sentence of *The Road Less Traveled*, which struck a chord of recognition in millions, "Life is difficult." Our measure of suffering and pain will find us; we needn't glorify it, wallow in it, or sink beneath it; rather, we have the choice of creating ways to deal with it, to transform it.

Creation not only can transform pain and bring joy, it also is born of joy, like the story I wrote in New Hampshire that autumn afternoon from a feeling of fullness and gratitude, of delight in being alive in that time and place and all the times and places before, the splendor of all that life pouring through me. Joy is the essence of John Cheever's last novel, written while he was finally living and writing sober, just as Raymond Carver celebrated the joy in his decade of living and writing sober in his poem "gravy."

We can't all transform our pain into works of art, but we can find joy in our own expressions—writing, painting, sculpture, dance, music—and more. Beyond the traditional creative arts are millions of different creative possibilities every day: in the work people talk about in these pages, from cooking a meal to designing a building, answering an office telephone to giving a massage; in sports, sales, teaching, and science, any field offers a chance for creation. So do the materials around us, the stuff of daily life.

I remember a King's Chapel church retreat called Zen and the Art of Bread Baking, led by Sue Spenser, who left lawyering to become a minister and served for several years as our seminarian. She had the idea for this retreat, and got us all to participate in pounding the dough that we would bake into rolls and bread for breakfast. There was joy in sinking my fingers into that dough, kneading it and shaping it, "being with" the feel of the stuff, the raw material I knew would rise and transform to bread. I reveled in the wonderful gooey play of it, the fun of whapping it around as others were laughing and doing the same with their own dough, a general joyousness in the big camp dining hall, bringing back memories to all of us. Scenes returned to me of long-forgotten taffy pulling, followed by other delights of home cre-ation; my mother canning tomatoes for winter in the steam of our kitchen, my father and mother and I as we made our own root beer, which we proudly poured into bottles we capped ourselves, which later exploded in the basement, making us think for a moment we were un-der attack, and then exploding with our own laughter.

The sudden joy of that laughter dispelling the sometimes sadness of our small white green-roofed house with all the passions contained within evokes a line of Carl Sandburg I loved as a boy; words accom-panied in memory with the goose-bump wonder and mystery of the *New World Symphony* that called up a love of the land I was born in and love of friends and family past and present, an exhortation and blessing, all summoned by the memory of making bread, that simple act of creation: "Let a joy keep you."

BEING PART OF THE FLOW

The whole earth lies around us and a universe spins in our heads, all available to use for our own creation, moment by moment, day by day. Whether it is lighting a candle over oatmeal at breakfast or staying up all night to write a story or a song, creating transforms our lives and the lives of others. We ignore its power and accessibility at the price of joy, of life itself.

Living free of the myths of creativity does not answer all questions or solve all problems, nor does the clarity that is part of creating from the spirit ease all pain. In fact, clarity sometimes makes us *feel* pain that we once numbed with quick fixes of booze and drugs, but that pain is usually a warning, a message whose disregard may lead to more serious, deeper trouble. With clarity we feel more of everything, in-cluding the natural joy to which we are also heirs.

In shedding the myths of creativity, in "living into" creating from the spirit, I, of course, still blunder and stumble, experience the doubts and self-delusions of the human condition. But I never have felt more free. I feel part of a larger flow that is not just of my own creating, but I've helped create my opportunity to be in it. This feeling comes through my workshops, which feed and inspire me, and passes on into my writing, as in this book. The chance to be of use, to share my experience in community with people through speaking and writing words, is not only privilege but deep pleasure. I feel and enjoy it more fully now than I ever have in my life.

Not long ago I had a dream, in which I was standing by the ocean, talking with people wiser than I—they were some kind of sages—who asked me what I wanted, how I wanted the rest of my life to be.

"I want to be a wave," I said.

When I woke, I knew what I had meant—that I wanted to be part of something larger than my petty self, something of service to others, to all. It meant not to simply create for my own ends, my own ego, but to do so in a way that was part of creation itself, as a genuine "co-creator" with the spirit—the life force, God, whatever name one uses. George Bernard Shaw expressed this sentiment in a way that I'd endorse as the highest goal of creating from the spirit:

This is the true joy of life, the being used for a purpose recognized by yourself as a mighty one; the being a force of nature instead of a feverish selfish little clod of ailment and grievance complaining that the world will not devote itself to making you happy. I am of the opinion that my life belongs to the whole community and as long as I live it is my privilege to do for it what I can. I want to be used up when I die, for the harder I work the more I live, and I rejoice in life for its own sake. Life is no "brief candle" to me. It is a sort of splendid torch which I have got hold of for the moment, and I want to make it burn as brightly as possible before passing it on to future generations.

I add my own "Amen."

Grateful acknowledgment is made to the following for permission to reprint previously published material:

Addison-Wesley Publishing Company, Inc.: Excerpts from *Minding the Body, Mending the Mind* by Joan Borysenko. Copyright © 1987 by Joan Borysenko, Ph.D.

The Boston Globe: Excerpt from "Jordan Stepped Into Another Dimension—The Highlight Zone" by Michael Madden.

Cornell University Press: Excerpts from *Louis Agassiz as Teacher* by Lane Cooper.

Cowley Publications: Excerpts from *A New Christian Yoga* by Nancy Roth. Reprinted by permission of Cowley Publications, 28 Temple Place, Boston, MA 02111.

Constance H. Gemson: Excerpt from "On a Swim to Find Serenity" by Constance H. Gemson, *New York Newsday*.

Donadio & Ashworth, Inc.: Excerpt from "Tomatoes" by Laurie Colwin, *Gourmet Magazine*, August 1992. Copyright © 1992 by Laurie Colwin.

Grove/Atlantic, Inc.: "Gravy" from *A New Path to the Waterfall* by Raymond Carver. Copyright © 1989 by The Estate of Raymond Carver.

Little, Brown and Company: Excerpts from *A Drinking Life* by Pete Hamill. Copyright © 1994 by Deidre Enterprises, Inc. Published by Little, Brown and Company.

The New York Times: Excerpt from "Recycling a 60's Issue . . ." by Walter Goodman, January 6, 1993. Copyright © 1993 by The New York Times Company. Excerpt from "Class Acts: Drinking It All In" by Vicki Matthews-Burwell, February 12, 1994, Op-Ed. Copyright © 1994 by The New York Times Company. Excerpts from "The Pop Desk" by Sheila Rule, March 24, 1994. Copyright © 1994 by The New York Times Company.

Random House, Inc.: "September 1, 1939" from *W. H. Auden: Collected Poems* by W. H. Auden. Copyright © 1940 by W. H. Auden.

Scribner, a Division of Simon & Schuster, and Harriet Wasserman Literary Agency: Excerpts from "At the Heart" from *A Common Room: Essays 1954–1987* by Reynolds Price. Copyright © 1987 by Reynolds Price.

Patricia Speier: Excerpts copyright © 1995 by Patricia Speier.

St. Martins's Press, Inc., New York, NY: Excerpts from *Ascension: John Coltrane and His Quest* by Eric Nisenson. Copyright © 1993 by Eric Nisenson.

Index

Baziotes, William, 90
Before and After (Brown), 38
"Be here now" approach, 129–30
Bell, Madison Smartt, 90
Bellow, Saul, 49
Beloved (Morrison), 302–4
Belushi, John, 83
Benson, Herbert, 126–27, 133
Berlin Stories, The (Isherwood),
     169
Bernays, Edward L., 57
Berryman, John, 65, 74
Bery, Odette, 10, 190, 193, 197,
     201, 232–37
Bhakti yoga, 136
Bias, Len, 85
Blake, William, 83–84
Blanco, Richard, 292
Blown Sideways Through Life
     (Shear), 19
Blue Calhoun (Price), 301
Blunk, Rebecca, 48
Body and Soul (Roddick), 23
Body Shop, The, 23, 40
Bodyspirit, 132–34, 136, 137,
     139, 143, 144
Boone, Daniel, 30
Borysenko, Joan, 128–30
Boslough, John, 142
Bowen, Elizabeth, 101
Boyd, Jenny, 17, 83
Boyle, Kay, 51, 293
Braverman, Kate, 78
Brown, Christy, 143
Brown, Rosellen, 38–39

Carroll, E. Jean, 32
Carroll, James, 286

Carver, Raymond, 54, 73, 77–80,
     297, 306
Castenada, Carlos, 144, 168
Catcher in the Rye, The
     (Salinger), 193
Cather, Willa, 151, 168, 176, 180
Caussade, Jean-Pierre de, 279
Cedar Bar, New York, 64–65
Centering prayer, 126, 128
Centering Prayer (Pennington),
     126
Chagall, Marc, 56, 58
Cheever, John, 65, 76–77, 306
Chekov, Anton, 71
Child, Julia, 200–1
Chödrön, Pema, 282
Churchill, Winston, 39
Ciardi, John, 105–6
Citara, Bill, 40
Clarity, 12–13, 95–110
Clear Pictures (Price), 301
Cleaver, Eldridge, 293
Clinton, Bill, 39
Clinton, Hillary Rodham, 39
Cobain, Kurt, 11, 83
Cocaine, 5, 85–87, 90
Cohen, Elizabeth, 24
Coleridge, Samuel Taylor, 82
Collins, Judy, 6, 10, 130, 145,
     150, 196, 197, 203–8, 291
Collins, Martha, 15
Coltrane, John, 8, 16–17, 21, 89
Colwin, Laurie, 103
Common Room, A (Price), 300
Concentration camps, 144
Conroy, Frank, 49
Cooper, Lane, 177
Coudal, Mary Beth, 125, 214–17

ABOUT THE AUTHOR

DAN WAKEFIELD is a novelist, journalist, and screenwriter who grew up in Indianapolis and graduated from Columbia College in New York City. His most recent book was *Expect a Miracle: The Miraculous Things That Happen to Ordinary People*, which was number two on the *Library Journal*'s 1995 national bestseller list for religious and spiritual books. His book *Returning: A Spiritual Journey* originated with an article in the *New York Times Magazine* called "Returning to Church" and became a selection of the Quality Paperback Book Club in its Penguin edition. His book *The Story of Your Life: Writing a Spiritual Autobiography* won a Silver Gryphon Award from *Publishers Weekly* as one of the ten outstanding religious books of 1990. The book evolved from workshops he gives in Spiritual Autobiography in churches, adult education centers, and prisons, throughout this country, as well as in Northern Ireland and Mexico. He also gives workshops in Creating From the Spirit and Expecting Miracles.

His novels *Going All the Way* and *Starting Over* were national bestsellers and Literary Guild selections, and the latter was adapted for a movie starring Burt Reynolds and Candace Bergen. Wakefield created the NBC-TV series "James at 15," and wrote and coproduced the CBS movie *The Seduction of Miss Leona*, starring Lynn Redgrave, and a ninety-minute PBS dramatization of Mark Twain's *The Innocents Abroad*.

He has won a Rockefeller grant for creative writing, a National Endowment for the Arts Award for the short story, and a Bernard DeVoto Fellowship to the Bread Loaf Writers Conference. He was writer in residence at Emerson College in Boston, and currently holds the position of Distinguished Visiting Writer at Florida International University in Miami. He is a member of the Authors Guild and the National Writers Union.

Inquiries about his workshops may be addressed to Dan Wakefield Workshops, P.O. Box 1190, Burlington, MA 01803-6190.